WILD
guide

Scotland

Hidden Places, Great Adventures
and the Good Life

Kimberley Grant, David Cooper & Richard Gaston

WILD
THINGS
PUBLISHING

WILD
guide

Contents

Regional Overview

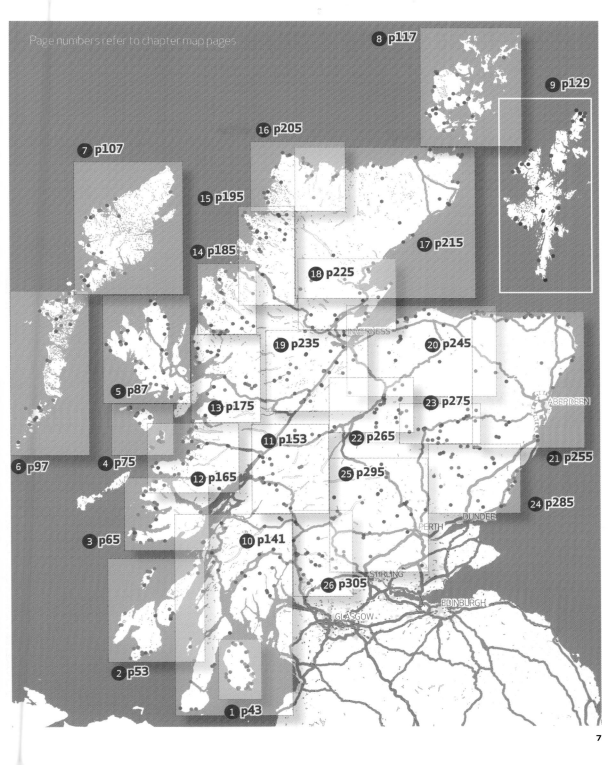

8 p117

9 p129

16 p205

7 p107

15 p195

14 p185

17 p215

18 p225

19 p235

20 p245

INVERNESS

5 p87

13 p175

23 p275

ABERDEEN

11 p153

22 p265

21 p255

6 p97

4 p75

12 p165

25 p295

24 p285

3 p65

10 p141

DUNDEE

PERTH

STIRLING

26 p305

EDINBURGH

GLASGOW

2 p53

1 p43

Introduction

Dip in sparkling lochans nestled below towering corries, their crooked gullies still white with snow left over from last winter. Snuggle up in your sleeping bag and peek out your tent door, watch the shifting mists swirl around the sharp peaks. Wander alone through fragrant Scots pine, spying deer shifting silently through the ancient undergrowth. Drink smoky whisky distilled from the local waters with friends in cliff-top bothies, a fire flickering in the hearth. Canoe around turquoise-blue inlets and bays, pulling up for a picnic on a pristine white beach without another person in sight. Listen to the owls hooting in the moonlight as you lie next to the glowing embers of a campfire, the evocative smell of wood smoke lingering on your clothes the next day.

A sense of adventure

The most beautiful and memorable experiences are those that are fleeting, unique and impossible to recreate – the 'you had to be there' moments. The beauty of Scotland lies in the nuanced and ephemeral nature of the relationship between its unique and varied landscape and the constantly changing weather systems. Scotland is an ancient landscape where everything happens slowly but in constant interaction with fast-moving and unpredictable weather. So the best adventures in Scotland are often the ones in which the stars align perfectly and your free time matches up with a period of decent weather. This produces an insatiable questioning in the mind-set of the explorer – what will it be like this weekend? The unpredictability of adventure in Scotland is addictive – after all, if it was all completely predictable, where would the sense of adventure be?

That adventure is in the melancholy feeling you get driving home with the sun setting perfectly over the brooding peaks of Glen Coe, knowing you had the most unforgettable weekend because of the people you spent it with, the atmospheric weather conditions and the amazing spots you didn't even

know existed until curiosity got the better of you. The moment you realise that the terrible weather forecast has actually produced a gloriously dramatic scene of mist, mountain and low-lying light. The adventure is bound up in the subtleties of these experiences, in shunning the obvious in favour of the obscure.

Wild places

Scotland is alluring and inspiring, but is it truly wild? Look it up and you will find synonyms like uninhabited, uncultivated, and desolate. Though it appears to be a wilderness, the vast and rugged landscape of Scotland has been shaped by thousands of years of human intervention. Even the emptiness is as much a result of historical events, such as the Highland Clearances and the use of huge estates for sporting pursuits, as it is of genuine environmental desolation. Scotland is not wholly uninhabited or uncultivated, although the landscape can be desolate. However, wildness is also relative, and if the term applies anywhere in the United Kingdom, it most certainly applies to large parts of Scotland, which offer plenty of places to find freedom and reconnect with nature:

Rivers & lochs The lifeblood of so many communities in Scotland, rivers have shaped the land and provided sustenance and transport. To the traveller they offer places to swim, canoe, or just sit and watch the wildlife and waterfalls.
Mountains & glens The rugged backdrop that gives the area its character and personality, with peaks to scale for exhilarating views and sheltered spots to camp in glens that change with every passing cloud.
Cliffs & shoreline Scotland has perhaps the most dramatic coastline of the whole island, host to vast and important seabird colonies and visited by a wide array of marine wildlife.
Forests & wildlife The ancient forest habitat supports the wide variety of flora and fauna to be found in the Highlands, a perfect place to lose yourself and find tranquility.
Ancient remains & ruins The landscape is dotted with often mysterious and sometimes melancholy symbols of our fascinating past. Let them carry your imagination back to more turbulent times, or ancient ceremonies and ways of life that can only be guessed at.

The good life

As with travel to anywhere remote, exploring much of Scotland requires common sense and an awareness of the risks an area entails. Further information on specific dangers will be included in subsequent chapters, but it is the ethos of the Wild Guide series that, though often risky, interaction with the wilder environments of the natural world is increasingly beneficial in a digital age that prioritises a tethered existence, subservient to calendars and social media updates and slaves to our email inboxes. The Highlands and Islands of Scotland are the perfect antidote to this existence – phone signal is patchy, the internet can be slow, and post takes a bit longer to arrive. Shops are often shut on Sundays, and ferry services can be intermittent and confusing. But Scottish culture is known the world over for its friendliness and traditional good humour. The key is to take the change in pace on board, cast aside any cosmopolitan conceptions or prejudices and just let the landscape lead you on. Exploring this wilder world makes us healthier, happier and more opened minded about our connection to the landscapes we inhabit – a connection that is often disregarded and ignored. It is more imperative now than ever.

It became apparent during the course of writing this book that the Highlands and Islands of Scotland have always been a constant in our lives, and we realised that we have spent countless hours journeying through them in a never-ending adventure that frees us from the stresses and strains of city life. Scotland is the perfect country for 'getting away', and is by far the wildest area that the urban populations of Britain can easily reach. We hope in the course of reading and using this book that you find your own sense of wild. Perhaps in the future we will run into some of you in the hills.

Stay safe, stay curious and let us know how you get on.

Kim, Richard and David
adventure@wildthingspublishing.com

Finding your way

Each wild place can be located using the overview map provided at the end of each chapter, along with the detailed directions, but to be sure of finding your way you'll need to use the latitude and longitude provided. This is given in decimal degrees (WGS84) and can be entered straight into any web-based mapping program, such as Google, Bing or Streetmap. The latter two of these will also provide Ordnance Survey mapping if you select that option. Print out the map before you go, or save a 'screen grab' and email it to yourself. You can also enter the co-ordinates into your GPS, car satnav (enable 'decimal degrees') or your smartphone, if it has GPS. All maps apps will take decimal degrees, and the ViewRanger app will even give you turn-by-turn instructions to guide you to your point. In this edition we've included more postcodes too, as these are often quicker to enter into a device and have a specific point location. If you have paper maps, look up the equivalent national grid reference in the conversion table at the back of the book. Approximate walk-in times are given, for one way only (we allow about 15 mins per km), and abbreviations in the directions refer to left and right (L, R) and north, east, south and west (N, E, S, W).

Wild & responsible

1. Fasten all gates and if you must climb them, use the hinged side.

2. Keep your dogs under close control, especially around livestock and in nature reserves.

3. Keep to public paths unless you are on Access Land.

4. Take your litter home, and gain good karma by collecting other people's.

5. If you wash in streams or rivers, only use biodegradable soap, or none at all.

6. Take special care on country roads and park considerately.

7. Take map, compass, whistle and waterproof clothing when venturing into remote or high areas.

8. Always tell someone where you are going, and do not rely on your mobile phone.

Best for
Beaches

Scotland has a good selection of the most uniquely beautiful and unspoilt beaches in the world. In the Outer Hebrides, some of these stretch on for miles, with pristine white sands rinsed by the North Atlantic and high undulating dunes backed by colourful flowering machair. Others are hidden within sheltered rocky coves where the sea is azure-green and crystal-clear, perfect for a peaceful and refreshing swim!

Even on dull or stormy days, there is a brightness along the shimmering silver sands on the west coast. At beaches in the north, you can wrap up warm and watch powerful waves roll in and crash along the coastline, creating pools of sea foam on the sand. The most accessible beaches are still largely quiet places, while those which are more hidden and remote, often requiring a long walk in, are often completely deserted – just you, the sea and views out over the Scottish islands.

Check tide times before heading out, as some beaches are best accessed, or even only reachable, during low tide. Also take sensible care when swimming; the sands may look Caribbean, but the weather here can be extremely unpredictable, and some beaches are prone to rapidly changing currents.

West Beach, Berneray, p93

Best for
Wild swimming

Water is literally the most immersive landscape in Scotland as it's the only one you can truly get inside – you will never know a mountain top the way you know the loch you swam in at its foot . The water quality is often exceptional, but temperatures are very low. That said, after the initial shock of plunging in, wild swimming in Scotland provides an incredibly invigorating and often therapeutic experience.

Plunge into a deep highland river pool, bathe in limpid water at a peaceful sandy beach, paddle underneath a cascading waterfall or slowly swim across a still, wild loch fringed with ancient Scots pine. All the rain that falls on Scotland endows it with many cool freshwater lochs, clear, clean rivers and rushing falls. These are often situated within beautiful glens or wild mountain scenery, and many have rocky cliffs to jump from and deep, long gorges to float through.

Often there is no one else around so do take great care whenever entering the water. With our unpredictable weather, rivers can be highly dangerous when in full spate, and water can rush quickly down from higher ground to lower pools. Always try to take someone with you, and never underestimate how your body might react to the cold, because the effects can be surprising. Bring something warm and wrap up well after your swim.

River Etive, p145

Be safe

1 Never swim alone, and always keep a constant watch on weak swimmers.

2 Know your limits and stay close to the shoreline. Cold water will decrease your swimming range and can lead to cold cramps. People with a heart condition should avoid rapid entry into cold water.

3 Never jump into water you have not thoroughly checked for depth and obstructions.

4 Avoid strong currents, such as those found under large waterfalls, rapids or weirs: they can drag you under.

5 Always make sure you know how you will get out before you get in.

6 Wear footwear if you can.

7 Watch out for boats on any navigable river. Wear a coloured swim hat so you can be seen.

8 Avoid direct contact with blue-green algae and be wary of water quality in lowland areas during droughts and heavy rain. Cover cuts with plasters if worried, and if you develop flu-like symptoms tell your doctor you have been wild swimming.

Best for
Glens & mountain scenery

Scotland is a country largely made up of mountains and glens, so picking the best of these is a particularly difficult task. In geological ages past, the Highlands of Scotland were Himalayan in stature, and have been slowly eroded and sculpted by complex forces into the gnarled and weathered landscape that so inspires us today. The Highland Boundary Fault is a tectonic fault line that traverses the country and provides the clear Highland/Lowland divide that in turn informs Scottish identities.

This geological activity has produced the long, narrow glens that are woven through Scottish history and culture, and shape its economy and ecosystems. Beautiful and varied examples are to be found in this book, but the list is by no means exhaustive; there are as many examples as there are glens, and there are a lot of glens in Scotland.

Scottish mountains may be small in stature compared with other ranges in the world, but never forget that the influences of the weather here mean they are as harsh and dangerous as any in the world, especially in winter. Countless lives have been needlessly lost by not understanding this truth. If you are heading into the hills, proper clothing and equipment are absolutely essential – and with the vagaries of the British weather, that means at any time of year.

Best for
Ancient remains & ruins

Even today Scotland has an atmosphere of mystery. This is partly due to the particular relationship between humans and the landscape here, which has been heavily influenced by the rugged inaccessibility of the mountains and glens. Historically Scotland has been largely impregnable, its lofty peaks and deep valleys a natural barrier to invading armies and conquering forces throughout the ages. This has allowed it to retain local culture and customs and forge a strong sense of Scottish identity. Many of the physical remains of history testify to this fierce independence, and many of the structures that evoke the past most vividly are defensive in nature, from ancient forts and brochs through medieval castles and keeps to Second World War sea defences.

The Highlands feel wild in part due to the low population density. Even the farthest corners of the country were inhabited from ancient times, as Pictish brochs and stone circles testify, and much evidence of Viking settlement has also been uncovered. But this was always a sparse population, a situation exacerbated by events such as the Highland Clearances of the 18th and 19th centuries, when people were moved from the land to make way for sheep farming. Many sad and lonely village ruins remain to this day, a reminder that 'wild' is a complicated and confusing term.

Always exercise caution when entering or approaching old ruins: by definition they are falling down and may be unstable, and some of the most picturesque are perched on the edges of eroding cliffs.

St Kilda, p103

Best for
Caves, caverns & sea stacks

Scotland's coast has a complex geology and its exposure to rough battering seas has left it with many spectacular formations, including the UK's highest cliffs and most spectacular sea stacks, as well as many legendary dark caves and caverns.

Undoubtedly the most famous cavern demands a sea journey to the Isle of Staffa to see the magical basalt columns that form the cathedral-like Fingal's Cave. A swim to the back, listening to the haunting music of the waves, is an experience you will never forget. Likewise some of the highest and most spectacular sea stacks are scattered around the extremely remote archipelago of St Kilda, steeped in incredible history and home to one of the largest colonies of gannets in the world,

But there is plenty to see without such voyages. The closer islands and mainland boast caves used by everyone from kings to chapel congregations, and every kind of arch and sea stack including extraordinary ones resembling elephants or even musical instruments to a charitable eye.

Duncansby Stacks, p211

Be safe ▼

1 Always carry back-up torches if you're entering a dark cave.

2 Never enter a wet cave – one that contains a stream or water flow – if rain is likely or if there are reservoirs upstream. Caves can flood violently and quickly, trapping you or sweeping you over underground waterfalls.

3 Never enter more than a few metres into any mine tunnels (adits) without an experienced guide. It's safer to peer in from the outside.

4 Remember that mine tunnels can have false floors over deep voids, which may be rotten and could give way at any moment. Partially flooded tunnels with water underfoot are somewhat safer in this respect, as the void is already filled.

5 Wear a helmet in any wild or narrow cave, in case of possible rock falls and to avoid banging your head.

Best for
Forests & wildlife

The landscape of Scotland starts from three basic environments: mountain, water and forest, each providing the ecosystems needed to sustain and develop the unique forms of flora and fauna that make Scotland such a fascinating place to visit. After the last Ice Age almost a fifth of Scotland was covered in the Great Caledonian Forest, which was at its mightiest some 7,000 years ago. First the warming climate diminished it, and then humans brought grazing livestock and a need for wood, and reduced it to barely a twentieth of the land area. Beautiful examples still exist in Glen Affric and Balmoral, and many estates are working hard to increase tree cover.

At the other end of the wildlife scale are the flowers of the vast coastal machair. This is a fertile, grassy dune landscape unique to the crushed-shell sands of north-western Scotland and Ireland. In spring and summer stretches of the islands and mainland coast erupt with colour when thousands of wildflowers bloom, including rare orchids.

Seabirds and marine mammals are common along the shores around Scotland, with thousands of birds flocking to the steep cliffs every year and ample opportunities for sighting seals, dolphins and even whales, especially in the Moray Firth. Deer are a huge part of life in Scotland - vital to the economy and a cultural symbol of the Highlands, although rigorous management is necessary to protect the forests from their grazing. The sight of a stag silhouetted against a mountain backdrop is about as quintessentially Scottish as it gets.

Best for
Slow food & accommodation

With the sea on three of its four sides, fertile land, a wealth of game and famously pure water, Scotland is a rich natural larder. Virtually free of food miles, local produce can be a highlight of any trip, giving delicious and fascinating insights into each area's cultural and natural history.

From fresh west-coast shellfish, Shetland salmon, highland venison, Aberdeen Angus beef and haggis to our famous whisky and a healthy scattering of local breweries, there are many culinary delights to sample. There are a growing number of artisanal food producers, bakeries and farm shops to visit, and welcoming traditional inns to relax in and enjoy a dram after long day outside.

There are friendly hostels and beautifully situated campsites to stay in. You can sleep in a bunkhouse within a charming old blackhouse at Gearrannan, Lewis, or watch the sunset from your tent at Invercaimbe campsite near Arisaig. Those looking for a place to themselves can choose from a cosy highland cottage to a designer island shed or an eco-friendly yurt hidden away in the forest.

Gearrannan Blackhouse Village, p105

Best for
Wild camping & bothies

The Scottish elemental experience wouldn't be complete without the rewarding feeling of arriving at a bothy after a long hike, or the humbling experience sitting by the campfire. Bond with a fellow hiker in a remote bothy, sharing stories by the fire with a dram of whisky, or have your highland experience in solitude as you pitch your tent and listen to nature's repertoire: flowing rivers, ocean sounds or wildlife going about their day.

As you awake early, ready to continue your hike through the mountains, witness the first light peer over the hillside evaporating the morning dew. Spot an early glimpse of deer running through the valley or eagles soaring overheard.

Given Scotland's 'right to roam' act, you have permission to access and camp on most of the land – mountains, forests or coastal areas to name a few – providing you do so responsibly.

Ensure you bring appropriate sleeping apparatus. A sleeping bag, insulated ground mat and tent / bivvy bag will ensure you enjoy Scotland's Highlands at their finest. For all Bothies, refer to the listings marked **B** and for recommended wild camping spots, look out for the ◪ symbol.

Be responsible

1 Camp well away from towns and villages.

2 Leave no litter, remove other people's, and don't bury litter.

3 Take extra care when lighting any fires, ensure nothing will be damaged, bring your own wood and never cut from trees.

4 Stay for only one night.

5 Keep groups very small – only one or two tents.

6 Camp as unobtrusively as possible, with inconspicuous tents that blend into the landscape.

7 Take away tampons and sanitary towels; burying them doesn't work, as animals dig them up again.

8 Perform toilet duties at least 30m (100ft) from water, and bury the results with a trowel.

9 At all times, help protect the environment.

ISLE OF ARRAN

Our perfect weekend

→ **Abandon** your worries on the mainland and catch the ferry over the sea.

→ **Meditate** on the spiritual history of Holy Isle – or just admire the rare wildlife.

→ **Cycle** the coast road right around the island on a picturesque tour.

→ **Camp** at the atmospheric King's Cave, gazing out over the sea.

→ **Lunch** by an open fire at The Lagg Hotel, open for business since 1791.

→ **Bathe** in the fresh waters of lonely Coire Fhionn Lochan.

→ **Spy** eagles soaring over Lochranza, or herds of deer quietly strolling through the village.

→ **Bask** in awe of the rugged Goatfell range seen from Glen Sannox.

→ **Explore** the stone circles at Machrie Moor, a sacred landscape for thousands of years.

→ **Peer** over towering Eas Mor waterfall, set amidst dense woodland.

→ **Picnic** at peaceful Loch Garbad, soaking up the silence.

If you were to bring someone to Scotland and had only one day to show off the best of the entire country, you could do a lot worse than take a tour around the Isle of Arran. This kidney-shaped island in the Firth of Clyde, just 167 square miles in area, is often said to be 'Scotland in miniature'. A cliché perhaps, but a good one: the south of the island, like the south of the country as a whole, features squat rolling hills, good pasture and a well-ordered serenity, while the north of the island is the complete opposite, endowed with jagged granite peaks, deep glens and gushing rivers.

The Scotland-in-miniature accolade is relevant in more ways than one, with the famous 'sleeping warrior' profile of the peaks as seen from the Ayrshire coast resembling the country as a whole. The lofty slopes of those peaks relative to the neighbouring mainland point to an ancient significance. Arran lies at the extreme western end of the Highland Boundary Fault, which runs across Scotland to Stonehaven and marks the geographical dividing line between Highlands and Lowlands. Its position and history make these complex rock formations of interest to hill walkers, rock climbers and the amateur geologist. The dividing line of the Fault shaped Scotland not only geologically, but socially and culturally as well, and Arran packs a punch in terms of variety.

For a small island, 20 miles long and 10 miles wide, there are so many things to do and sights to see that you can leave with the impression that you've had several holidays in one. There are few places in the country with such diversity of flora, fauna and landscape on show in such a small area. Being within easy reach of Glasgow and relatively small, Arran is an excellent choice for a weekend break or as part of a wider touring trip. Straight off the ferry there are sights to behold, with Goatfell rising in the distance and beautiful Glen Sannox mere minutes away – don't miss out on a walk, swim and camp in this wonderful glen. A decent road rings the island, mostly hugging the coast, making a circumnavigation extremely satisfying, whether by car or bike. Cycling around the island with plenty of stops is perhaps the best way of seeing it, and a great opportunity to pack multiple experiences into a short trip.

The island is served by ferries from Ardrossan. Located on the west mainland coast, it is around an hour from Glasgow by train or car. The Calmac ferry crossing takes another hour, arriving in the main village of Brodick, nestled between the Goatfell mountain range and the sea on the east side of the island. In summer there is also a ferry from Lochranza in the north to the Kintyre Peninsula, for those looking to travel onwards.

BEACHES, COAST & ISLANDS

1 SANNOX BEACH

Backed by the rugged mountains of the Goatfell range, and looking out to sea, curved Sannox Beach is beautiful, and a great place to wake up in the morning.

→ From the car park at South Sannox (KA27 8JD) head N past the bus stop to the path at the N end of the gravel area, following it over the river via the concrete stepping stones and down to the sandy beach.

5 mins, 55.6631, -5.1527 🏖️

2 KILMORY BEACH

One of the best beaches on Arran, a long sweep of sand with views over to Ailsa Craig, a dramatic cone of granite out to sea. Easy access.

→ From the car park next to Kilmory village hall (W of KA27 8PQ) follow the path signed Torrylin Cairn downstream to the beach. The remains of a chambered cairn are in a field to the L of the path.

15 mins, 55.4376, -5.2304 🏖️

3 KILDONAN SHORE

This easy shoreline walk under rugged cliffs is a great way to view Arran's large seal

population. Just offshore lies the island of Pladda, with its lighthouse, and beyond that is Ailsa Craig. Beyond Struey Rocks at the W end the going gets much rougher.

→ From the car park at Porta Buidhe harbour, Kildonan (KA27 8SA) head W along the shoreline. Return by the same route.

30 mins, 55.4424, -5.1544 🏖️

4 HOLY ISLE

Holy Isle lies off the south-east coast of Arran, and is majestic seen from the ferry. It is home to rare Soay sheep, Saanen goats and Eriskay ponies, and the panoramic views over Arran and the Clyde estuary from the highest point of the island are not to be missed. A sacred place since ancient times, today it is home to a Buddhist community, which has established the Centre for World Peace in the north of the island. A summer ferry runs from Lamlash Pier, and visitors are met on arrival by a representative of the Buddhist retreat with information and advice on the island.

→ Ferry from Lamlash Pier (KA27 8LA) regularly in summer, less regular spring and autumn. Booking required for winter crossings. Arran Outdoor (01770 600 532) also run kayak trips to the island. Decent,

well signposted paths leave from the point of arrival to the highest point on the island, Mullach Mòr. Ferry 60 mins.

60 mins, 55.5335, -5.0881 🏖️

LOCHS

5 LOCH GARBAD

Favoured by fishermen seeking solitude (and trout), Garbad is a placid loch that makes a perfect lunch spot. It can be combined with Eas Mòr waterfall and library for a varied excursion.

→ Park in the car park off the A841, opposite the Kildonan turning (dir KA27 8RR) in the S of the island. Follow directions as for Eas Mòr Forest & Library (see 14), but where the path forks beyond the viewpoint, take the fork signposted 'Loch Garbad 1 mile'. Follow the good path to the loch, returning the same way.

35 mins, 55.4676, -5.1346 🏖️

6 COIRE FHIONN LOCHAN

This secluded and serene mountain loch features two beautiful white gravel beaches, one when you reach it, and a longer sweep at the far end. A refreshing place for wild swimming, in every sense.

→ Limited layby parking in the tiny village of

Thundergay (about 1½ miles N of KA27 8GD). Head E on a signposted and well-constructed path opp parking that winds through the houses and hills for about 1½ miles to the lochan.
45 mins, 55.6619, -5.3405

WATERFALLS

7 EAS MÒR WATERFALL

A free-falling waterfall some 30m high, gushing over a cliff amid lush and leafy scenery.

→ Park in the car park off the A841, opposite the Kildonan turning (dir KA27 8RR) in the S of the island. Follow directions as for Eas Mòr Forest & Library (see 14). The path reaches the Falls, with a decent viewpoint, before the library.
10 mins., 55.4547, -5.1316

8 GLENASHDALE FALLS

These spectacular waterfalls, also called Eas a' Chrannaig, are regarded as some of the best in Scotland, and with good reason; 42m of cascading water flows through two plunge pools. A viewing platform gives superb views of the falls.

→ By Ashdale Bridge, Whiting Bay (KA27 8QN)

park in one of the shoreside layby areas, and follow the signposted paths from the bridge up the river for about a mile to the falls.
30 mins, 55.4790, -5.1193

CAVES & CLIFFS

9 PREACHING CAVE

This cavernous grotto was used for religious ceremony for centuries – particularly when the congregation objected to the official minister appointed by the Duke of Hamilton in 1814 – and also as a schoolroom. Scratched markings adorn the smoke-blackened walls, the smoke an indication of its prolonged use.

→ Start at the small, walled parking area off the A841, 1 mile S from Blackwaterfoot (past KA27 8EY). Follow the track opp car park W towards the sea, and turn L along the coastal path to a succession of increasingly larger caves. Preaching Cave is the largest.
30 mins, 55.4879, -5.3255

10 KING'S CAVE

Airy and atmospheric caverns with incredible sea views, easily accessible from a high path that skirts the cliffs. There are many caves of various sizes along this fascinating

coastline, and according to legend, Robert the Bruce had his famous encounter with the spider whilst sheltering from the English in this one. More certainly, the 'aisles' of the cave bear ogham writing, cup-and-ring marks, a cross, horses, snakes and deer dating back at least to the Middle Ages, mixed up with the marks of more recent visitors. There are wild camping opportunities along the coast and in the caves themselves.

→ Head N from Blackwaterfoot on the A841. About ½ mile past KA27 8DX, park in the small, fenced parking area on L. Follow the path from this towards the sea and continue as it dips and enters a rocky gully leading to the shore. Continue S along the shore past a succession of caves to King's, the largest one. Return the same way or continue past the cave on the path, which shortly loops back up to the forest and back to the carpark.
45 mins, 55.5261, -5.3543

11 DRUMADOON POINT & THE DOON

Impressive lofty basalt cliffs defend one side of The Doon, a fort enclosed by the remains of an impressive wall to the E. Earlier visitors noted remnants of buildings, not discernible today, and it is thought this

may have been an ancient tribal centre. Can be visited as an extension of the King's Cave walk (see 10), or from the small town of Blackwaterfoot. There are numerous wild camping opportunities.

→ From the car park by the golf course, Blackwaterfoot (KA27 8HA) head NW along the beach and around Drumadoon Point to the cliffs of The Doon.
60 mins, 55.5067, -5.3553 🟡🔁➕🕸

GLENS, VIEWS & FORESTS

12 GLEN SANNOX

This atmospheric and quintessentially Scottish glen curves up from Sannox and into the heart of the rugged Goatfell range. Though it is close to the village, with the twin advantages of decent access and paths, it has a wonderfully remote feel. There are numerous opportunities for wild camping, and swimming in the Sannox Burn, which runs down the glen.

→ From the carpark in Sannox (near KA27 8JD) head W on well signposted paths, then follow the river up the glen.
60 mins, 55.6603, -5.1651 🟡🔁➕

13 GLEN ROSA

Like Glen Sannox, Glen Rosa is a typically beautiful Scottish glen that cuts into the Goatfell range, this time from the south. There are plenty of wild camping and swimming opportunities here too.

→ From Cladach car park N of Brodick (KA27 8DE) head W behind the brewery on well-signposted paths to pick up Glenrosa Water that flows down from the mountains beyond. Walk up as far as your time and legs allow (up to 3 hours).
90 mins, 55.6044, -5.2050 🟡🔁➕

14 EAS MÒR FOREST & LIBRARY

An eco-friendly library built from wind-blown timber with a turf roof, in the heart of a beautiful forest in the S of the island. Eas Mòr is an attempt to regenerate a once-overgrown glen and make it accessible for anyone seeking peace, solitude and a connection with nature.

→ From the carpark off the A841, opposite the turning to Kildonan (dir KA27 8RR) follow the good path N, turning R at the junction above the Eas Mòr waterfall (see 7). The library is just beyond the falls.
15 mins, 55.4540, -5.1323 🔵📖🔁

15 LOCHRANZA

Beautiful Lochranza in the north of the island is a peaceful and charming village that is well worth exploring. Almost any path from it is a starting point for an interesting walk. Graceful deer wander boldly through the streets, and with a ruined castle, a distillery where you can even lay down your own cask and an amazing sandwich bar (see 22), it has much to recommend it.

→ Head N from Brodick on A841 (KA27 8HL).
1 min 55.7044, -5.2934 🔶🔵🔁🔁

16 CLAUGHLAND VIEW POINT

A good first stop (and lunch spot) on a circuit of the island, this viewpoint has a magnificent vista extending over to the Goatfell range, and serves as a panoramic introduction to the beautiful landscape of Arran.

→ Leave Brodick heading S on the A841. About 1 mile past KA27 8BJ is a small car park R with a bench and view indicator identifying the peaks. 300m further is Cnoc na Dail car park and picnic area, set amid trees at a junction of signed forest trails.
2 mins, 55.5555, -5.1345 🏔🏕

17 LAGGAN COTTAGE

This remote and peaceful cottage is over the hills from Lochranza. The approach gives wonderful views over the Goatfell range and can be extended to a circuit that takes in the delights of the Fairy Dell gorge.

→ From the shorefront (KA27 8HL) follow the road to the Lochranza Field Studies Centre and take the dead-end road opp. This shortly bends sharp L, here take the path R signed Cock of Arran and Laggan. Head SE on the path uphill. After ½ mile take the L fork to the pass of Bearradh Tom a' Muidhe. The path then skirts the hill on the far side of the pass, heading down to Laggan with the sea on your L. Continue NW along the shoreline to Fairy Dell, and back around the bay to Lochranza.

3–4 hours, 55.7081, -5.2186 🌾🏔📷

BIKE HIRE

18 ARRAN BIKE HIRE

If you fancy a car-free tour of Arran, pick up a bike when you get off the ferry. They also have suggested routes on the island, with distances, climbs and estimated times.

→ The Shorehouse, Shore Road, Brodick, KA27 8AJ, 07825 160668

55.5768, -5.1458

19 LOCHRANZA BIKE HIRE

From the Sandwich Station (see 22).

→ Lochranza, KA27 8HL, 07810 796248.

55.7075, -5.3027

SACRED & ANCIENT

20 MACHRIE MOOR STONE CIRCLES

These six substantial and mystical stone circles are just some of the archeological wonders of this sacred landscape. Dating from the Neolithic period, Machrie Moor is home to a variety of ceremonial monuments, some towering almost 5m high, all with great views over to Goatfell and out to sea. There are information boards giving details of the many different stones and remains.

→ From the car park N of Blackwaterfoot on the A841 (see King's Cave) cross the road and head E on the farm track through the fields.

30 mins, 55.5403, -5.3152 ✝🚲🏔📷

21 GIANTS' GRAVES

Only the central chamber stones of these two Neolithic chambered tombs remain, but their location high on a ridge looking out to the sea can still have an eerie feel. Cremated remains, pottery and flint knives and arrowheads have been found here.

→ From Glenashdale Falls (see 8) follow the path to the upper falls and take a L signed for the Giants' Graves. Follow path around the hill to the graves, about a mile in all. Return to the falls, or take the path that descends to rejoin the river nearer Ashdale Bridge.

30 mins, 55.4766, -5.0980 ⛰🚶🚵

(see 8)

LOCAL FOOD

22 THE SANDWICH STATION

Cute little sandwich bar and delicatessen overlooking beautiful Lochranza harbour. Bike hire available. Closes over the winter.

→ Lochranza, KA27 8HL, 07810 796248. 55.7075, -5.3027 🍴

23 THE LAGG HOTEL

This family-run hotel is the oldest on Arran, in business since 1791. It has open fires and serves great food and drinks. Set in a peaceful wooded hollow on the A841 in the S of the island, it is well worth the stop on a trip round Arran.

→ Lagg, Kilmory, KA27 8PQ, 01770 870255. 55.4459, -5.2340 🍴🛏🚶

24 BRAMBLES SEAFOOD & GRILL

Wonderful local seafood, including amazing fishcakes, just a mile from the ferry.

→ Auchrannie Rd, Brodick, KA27 8BZ, 01770 302234.
55.5750, -5.1601

25 FIDDLERS MUSIC BAR & BISTRO

Owned and run by local musicians, this lively café near the ferry terminal combines music, food and drink in a friendly environment. The cullen skink soup is excellent.

→ Shore Road, Brodick, KA27 8AJ, 01770 302579.
55.5775, -5.1493 🍴🛏

CAMPING & BUNKHOUSES

26 SEAL SHORE CAMPSITE

Seaside camping at the SE tip of the island, with facilities for tents and campervans. Electricity, barbecue area, camping pods, a gypsy caravan and full facilities. Right by the shore, the sea breeze helps keeps the midges away.

→ Kildonan, KA27 8SE, 01770 820320.
55.4408, -5.1132 🚶🚩

27 LOCHRANZA YOUTH HOSTEL

Ranked as one of the greenest businesses in the UK, this hostel is right on the shore of the loch with its 13th-century castle. It makes an excellent and affordable base to explore Lochranza itself or the beautiful surrounding area.

→ Shore Road, Lochranza, KA27 8HL, 01770 830631.
55.7028, -5.2883 🚶

28 GLEN ROSA CAMPSITE

Near Brodick, described as 'almost wild camping'. Well situated in Glen Rosa.

→ Glen Rosa Farm, Brodick, KA27 8DF, 01770 302380/07985 566004. Visitarran.com/where-to-stay/glen-rosa-campsite
55.5907, -5.1723 ⛺

29 LOCHRANZA CARAVAN AND CAMPING

Good for wildlife – people have seen deer, squirrel, eagles while staying here. There are 3 pods. Closed for the winter.

→ Lochranza, Isle of Arran, KA27 8HL, 01770 830273.
55.6993, -5.2761 🚶

30 RUNACH ARAINN

Eco-friendly glamping in Scottish-made yurts, with wood burners and compost loos.

→ The Old Manse, Kilmory, KA27 8PH, 01770 870515.
55.4476, -5.2208 🚶

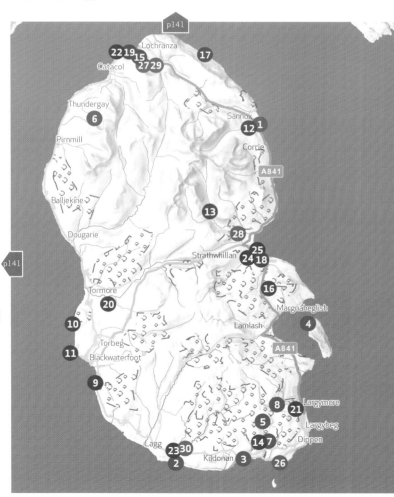

ISLAY, JURA & COLONSAY

Our perfect weekend

- → **Hike** through deserted settlements to Soldier's Rock on Islay.
- → **Explore** the Paps of Jura and take a refreshing dip in Loch an t-Sìob.
- → **Marvel** at the whirlpool in the Gulf of Corryvreckan, and see where George Orwell completed his masterwork at remote Barnhill on Jura.
- → **Wander** across some of Scotland's last great wilderness to Glengarrisdale Bothy on Jura.
- → **Swim** at the secluded beach of Tràigh Bàn on Colonsay.
- → **Bond** with the locals in the friendly bar at the Jura Hotel.
- → **Create** some amazing memories with family or friends in the expansive luxury of Kilchoman House on Islay.
- → **Breeze** along miles of golden sand at Kintra on Islay, and camp in the dunes when the sun goes down.

Uisge-beatha – 'water of life' in Gaelic – flows through the Inner Hebridean islands of Islay, Colonsay and Jura. Like all Scottish islands, water dominates here, from the sea that surrounds them to the peat-brown rivers and lochs that go into the famous single malts, with their evocative names – Caol Ila, Laphroaig and Lagavulin. Like many Scottish island groups, they are lumped together by virtue of geographical convenience, but in reality each island is uniquely interesting, and only the fundamentals are constant.

Islay, the 'Queen of the Hebrides', is the largest and most populous of the three, 239 square miles in size. Whisky dominates here: with eight working distilleries (and more planned), this is one of the five whisky distilling regions whose name is protected by law. East of Islay lies Jura, elongated and thin, and much wilder. There are few roads, more deer than people, and the scenery is much more rugged and the going rough – the prominent Paps give it a distinctive profile. Colonsay is the exception in that it has no distilleries, but it does feature an abundance of stunning coastal scenery, with quiet sandy beaches such as the one at Kiloran Bay. Time moves slower on Colonsay; it is a great choice for a weekend getaway.

As expected, whisky is a big draw for the islands, and many people make the journey simply to tour the distilleries and sample the single malts in their appropriate surroundings. It's not all about whisky though, as the islands are a paradise for anyone interesting in sea life, bird life, maritime history or dramatic coastal scenery. The compact size of the islands makes them easily navigated by bike, and in many ways this is preferable, as it avoids the need to take a car over on the ferry.

Calmac runs ferry services to the islands from Oban and Kennacraig direct to Islay and Colonsay. Jura is accessible from Islay, and therefore a bit more time consuming to visit, although crossings are frequent and quick. However, the close proximity of these islands to one another mean they are easily visited as a trio over the space of a week.

BEACHES & LOCHS

1 MACHIR BAY, ISLAY

Quite possibly Islay's finest beach, with marvellous unspoilt views and flower-filled machair in summer, ideal for sunset watching. There can be rip currents here.

→ From the A847 at the top of Loch Indaal, take exit heading NW on the B8018, signed Sanaigmore. When road turns R for Sanaigmore after 2 miles, instead continue straight ahead to Kilchoman for 3 miles (past PA49 7UX) to a car park at the end of the road. Park and head through the gate to the beach.

5 mins, 55.7809, -6.4574

2 KILORAN BAY, COLONSAY

Quite possibly Colonsay's most acclaimed beach, this is a lush bay of golden sand, backed by the highest hill on the island, Carnan Eoin (an optional climb adding 90 mins onto your time). Efforts are certainly rewarded, with spectacular views back over the bay.

→ Head NE towards Kiloran on the B8086 passing through Colonsay Estate. Shortly after taking a hard L you reach a car park on R (before PA61 7YT).

10 mins, 56.1036, -6.1829

3 LOCH AN T-SÌOB, JURA

A fine walk into the depths of wild Jura to Loch an t-Siob, a grand loch with perfect views of the Paps.

→ On the A846 on the E side of the island, park next to the turning for Knockrome (PA60 7XZ). Walk over the bridge, immediately turning R down a path towards the river. Follow the path NW about 2 miles to the loch.

90 mins, 55.8912, -5.9659

4 BALNAHARD BAY, COLONSAY

Secluded white beach at the most north-easterly point of the island. Often overshadowed by its neighbour Kiloran (see 2), this beach is favoured by others due to its remoteness. This route passes the highest hill on the island, Carnan Eoin, and the impressive cliff scenery of Meall na Suiridhe.

→ Follow directions as for Kiloran Bay and retrace your route back down the road to near the sharp corner, taking the path across the back of the bay NE to contour around the W flank of Carnan Eoin. Once the summit is behind you, make a quick detour L to visit Meall na Suiridhe headland. Retrace your steps and continue heading E on the path to the beach.

60 mins, 56.1237, -6.1403

5 GULF OF CORRYVRECKAN, JURA

Best seen with a strong south-westerly wind and flood tide, the raging currents often develop into a whirlpool – the third largest in the world – within the Gulf of Corryvreckan. In Scottish legend, the hag goddess of winter Cailleach Bheur uses the swirling gulf as a washtub, and then spreads her snow-white linens over the country. Several operators offer boat trips to see it (local knowledge is essential!), or view it from the tip of Jura.

→ At the most N end of the A846, continue NW on rough road past Ardlussa (PA60 7XW) until the end of the public road. Park and continue on foot along tracks past the signpost for Barnhill (4 miles) / Corryvreckan (7 miles). Pass through a gate slightly before the farmhouse at Kinuachdrachd and then onto a path signed Gulf of Corryvreckan. Follow path (sometimes indistinct and boggy) as it climbs and eventually reaches the N tip and viewpoint of the Gulf.

3.5 hrs, 56.1555, -5.7290

6 SANAIGMORE BAY, ISLAY

Tucked behind grassy dunes is Sanaigmore Bay, a tranquil sweep of pebbles and sand. Just NW of the bay is a hidden surprise, a yet-more secluded beach sheltered under the cliffs, named Port Ghille Greamhair. You may

well meet shy but curious Highland cattle.

→ From the A847 at the top of Loch Indaal take the B8018, signed Sanaigmore, and follow it to the end past PA44 7PT. Park at the small car park just after the monument at Sanaigmore and walk past the farm and through a small gap in the wall heading towards the bay. Continue NW along the coast over the grassy headland to reach Port Ghille Greamhair.

30 mins, 55.8522, -6.4150 🏖

7 KILNAUGHTON BAY, ISLAY

A long stretch of sandy beach backed by grassy hillside. A ruined chapel sits half buried by the rising ground in the graveyard above – look for the medieval knight's effigy, known as the Warrior's Grave, inside.

→ Follow the directions for Port Ellen lighthouse (see 14). Either walk back down the road from the large cemetery towards the woodland, where there is a gate entrance R that leads to the NE end of the bay, or walk onto the SW end of the sand from the old cemetery by the shore.

5 mins, 55.6293, -6.2176 🏖🌊🖼✝

8 SINGING SANDS OF TRÀIGH BHÀN, ISLAY

Beautiful secluded beach with scattered,

dramatic rocks and a peaty stream. The sands are reputed to 'sing' when boots are scuffed across the surface of the beach; you may not succeed musically, but have fun trying.

→ Follow the directions for Port Ellen lighthouse (see 14). Just before the last buildings approaching the lighthouse, take the signed path up the slope R. Follow it behind the buildings and over the ridge to the beach, taking care to shut the gates.

30 mins, 55.6177, -6.2170 🐚🌊

9 KINTRA SANDS, ISLAY

Also called the Big Strand, this enormous sandy beach stretches seven golden miles up Laggan Bay, and is the longest on the island. Greatly exposed to the Atlantic, it is perfect for kites, windsurfing, and watching huge, crashing waves come in from the ocean. Best viewed from the southern end; swim with care, rip currents can develop here.

→ Follow directions to car park for Soldier's Rock (see 12) and stroll down onto the beach.

5 mins, 55.6567, -6.2624 🏖🌊⛺🚶🚻

10 CORRAN SANDS, JURA

A fine stretch of shell sand spreading over beautiful Loch na Mile bay. Views of the Paps of Jura peeping over the hillside in one

direction, and the Small Isles across the bay in the other, with a stream halfway along.

→ Follow the A846 N from Craighouse until the road pulls away from the coast about 1½ miles after PA60 7XP. Turn R, then next R on a track that heads E towards beach. Parking.

5 mins, 55.8698, -5.9302 🏖🌊🔥⛺🏕

WILD COAST

11 DÙN URAGAIG, COLONSAY

The cliff-top promontory fort of Dùn Uragaig is defended by steep drops on three sides and a wall on the fourth. En route to the cliffs there are fine views of Kiloran Bay.

→ From Kiloran Bay (see 2) walk NW from the car park along the road towards Uragaig past turning to PA61 7YT. Follow the road as it takes a sharp R and heads downhill towards the beach. Pass L through a gate just before the white house and soon pass through another gate to make the short climb up towards Dùn Uragaig.

2.5 hrs, 56.1053, -6.2132 🏖🖼

12 SOLDIER'S ROCK, ISLAY

This rugged walk through an empty and beautiful part of Oa's coastline visits the deserted settlements of Kintra and a

14

13

spectacular sea stack – not named on the OS maps, but by Slochd Maol Doiridh. The coastal views are something to behold.

→ Leave the A846 at Port Ellen heading W for the Mull of Oa and where the road bends sharp L to the SW and Oa, continue straight signed for Kintra (past PA42 7AT) to park at car park near Kintra Farm. Walk W along private road, then through a gate. Head S on path parallel to the river, eventually crossing it, and turning a sharp R at a ruined house. Follow the path over the hill, broadly following the Sruthan Poll nan Gamhna river towards the sea stack.

2 hrs, 55.6479, -6.3036

13 MULL OF OA, ISLAY

Extremely dramatic coastline views considering the minimal distance on this incredible short walk to the American Monument. This commemorates two ships that were torpedoed during the First World War in 1918, losing 200 American and 60 British troops.

→ Follow the road from the A846 W to the Mull of Oa to the end, past the turning to PA42 7AU, following the next L bend to park at the car park. Walk SW through the RSPB reserve and a gate towards the monument.

30 mins, 55.5909, -6.3332

14 PORT ELLEN LIGHTHOUSE, ISLAY

Reached by crossing a rocky bridge, the distinctive square lighthouse is an iconic landmark on the island. It was built in memory of Lady Ellenor Campbell in 1832, but is also called Carraig Fhada lighthouse after the headland. Look out for otters in the bay.

→ Leave the A846 heading W to the Mull of Oa (dir PA42 7AX). Park directly after the large hillside cemetery, at the L signed Lighthouse, Singing Sands and Carraig Fhada Farm, or take that road down to a smaller, older cemetery and park immediately after it – limited space. Head along shoreline to the lighthouse; you can also walk to the Singing Sands (see 8).

20 mins, 55.6204, -6.2120

SACRED & ANCIENT

15 ORONSAY, COLONSAY

During low tides the magical island of Oronsay can be reached by walking over The Strand (often crossed wearing wellies). Visit the magnificent collection of carved gravestones, some of finest examples remaining in the country, at the preserved ruins of the Priory. This island is still populated by a small number of farmers who help to maintain the RSPB reserve. Check

tide times prior to setting off.

→ Head S on the B8085 towards Oronsay and park at the car park (PA61 7YS) at the end of the road. Walk SW over The Strand, and follow the track around the island.

3 hrs, 56.0251, -6.2353

16 BARNHILL, JURA

Not ancient, but still something of a place of pilgrimage, Barnhill was briefly the home to the famous writer, George Orwell, who completed *Nineteen Eighty-Four* while living there. Beautifully situated on the NE coast of Jura, it is remote, but has become a popular walk in recent years for Orwellians. Also available to rent weekly (01786 850274).

→ Drive and park as for the Gulf of Corryvreckan (see 5), walking along the tracks until the path for Barnhill breaks off R towards the house.

2 hrs, 56.1109, -5.6928

BIKE HIRE

17 BIKE HIRE ON THE ISLES

If you are visiting all of the isles, you may be best off hiring a bike on Islay and taking it with you, but bikes can also be hired on Jura and Colonsay: Bowmore Post Office,

Main St, Bowmore PA43 7JH, 01496 810 366; Nicol MacKinnon, Jura, 07768 450000; Isle of Colonsay Hotel, Scalasaig, Isle of Colonsay, PA61 7YP, 01951 200316

➜ Islay Cycles, 2 Corrsgeir Place, Port Ellen, PA42 7EJ, 07760 196592.
55.6279, -6.1812

LOCAL FOOD

18 ANTLERS BISTRO, JURA

Situated in the heart of Craighouse, this little terraced cafe is open for hot drinks, great cakes and lunch. Evening meal reservations essential, closed over winter.

➜ Craighouse, Isle of Jura, PA60 7XP, 01496 820496.
55.8337, -5.9512

19 PORT ASKAIG HOTEL, ISLAY

This family run hotel is located at the main ferry port in Islay, convenient for access to Jura and Colonsay. The Port Bar, which is the oldest continually licensed bar on the island, serves quality malts and beers from the very local brewery, while the Starboard Restaurant offers local Islay meat and seafood from the day's catch.

➜ Port Askaig, Isle of Islay, PA46 7RD, 01496 840245. Portaskaig.co.uk
55.8476, -6.1053

20 JURA HOTEL, JURA

The place to be on Jura, whether it be for food, drink, an overnight stay in the hotel or the campsite out front. The friendly staff, reasonably priced food and homely atmosphere makes this place a must for all passers-by.

➜ Craighouse, Isle of Jura, PA60 7XU, 01496 820243. Jurahotel.co.uk
55.8324, -5.9504

CAMP & STAY

21 KILCHOMAN HOUSE, ISLAY

Magnificent self-catering house for up to 10 people. A former manse full of history, furnished to give a taste of what life used to be like over a hundred years ago, but with modern comforts. Set amongst 37 acres of farmland, naturally sheltered by the surrounding rocky landscape.

➜ Kilchoman, Isle of Islay, PA49 7UY, 01496 850382. Islaycottages.com
55.7815, -6.4409

22 FEOLIN FARMHOUSE HOLIDAY COTTAGE, JURA

Former farmhouse converted into a self-catering holiday home in a secluded location with sweeping views over the eastern shores of Jura. A mile's easy walk S along the shore leads to the town of Craighouse.

➜ Craighouse, Isle of Jura PA60 7XG, 01285 720247. Juraholidaycottage.co.uk
55.8526, -5.9477

23 ISLE OF COLONSAY HOTEL, COLONSAY

Perched on the hillside, the hotel has commanding views across the sea to the island of Jura. Built in 1750, the exterior has since remained largely untouched, but the interior has been well modernised and has a restaurant, bar, conservatory and log room, with open fires and comfortable sofas. The hotel can arrange bike hire.

➜ Scalasaig, Isle of Colonsay, PA61 7YP, 01951 200316. Colonsayholidays.co.uk
56.0689, -6.1963

24 STORMPODS, ISLAY

These well-equipped cabins offer a warm and cosy alternative to camping all year around. The location, tucked into a hillside just yards from the sea (look out for a resident otter), ensures peace and privacy, and Lagavulin is also on the doorstep.

→ Lagavulin, Islay, PA42 7DX, 01496 300129. Islay-pods.co.uk

55.6344, -6.1297 🏄🐟🏊

25 GLENGARRISDALE BOTHY, JURA

The lonely bothy of Glengarrisdale, remotely situated on Jura's wild northwest coast, is a haven for those fond of the off-grid, off-mains wild. A walk across open moors leads to one of Scotland's last great wildernesses.

→ Park as for the Gulf of Corryvreckan (see 5) and begin on the same route. At a fork after about a mile, take the L which eventually leads NW, passing around the N end of Loch Doire na h-Achlaise and then the SW flank of Clachaig Mheadhoin, before dropping down Glen Garrisdale to the bay. 3 hour walk.

56.1068, -5.7901 🏄🅱🌳

26 KINTRA CAMPING, ISLAY

Pitch your tent in the dunes, make a campfire on the vast sands, and watch the sun go down. With no hook-ups, and right by an SSSI for choughs and Arctic terns. Summer months only, but B&B and self-catering available all year.

→ Kintra Farm, Port Ellen, Islay, PA42 7AT, 01496 302051.

55.6541, -6.2613 ⛺🥄🏄🐟

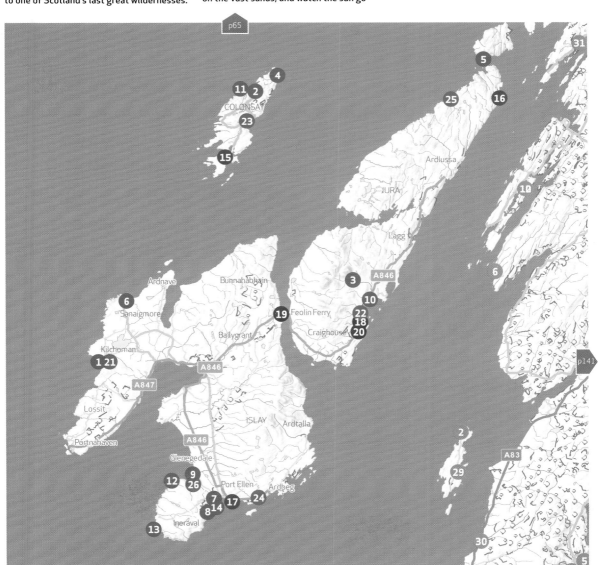

ISLE OF MULL

Our perfect weekend

→ **Take** a tranquil swim in the Dun Ara Bathing Pool before enjoying lunch at Glengorm Castle Tearoom.

→ **Sail** to the Isle of Staffa to see the puffins and explore the magical Fingal's Cave.

→ **Watch** the sunset and share stories around the fire when wild camping at Calgary Bay.

→ **Sample** local seafood and enjoy drinks outside at The Boathouse on Ulva.

→ **Enjoy** a picnic at the peaceful sandy beach at Tràig Bhàn before paying a visit to the famous Iona Abbey.

→ **Explore** the beautiful rough coastline to discover the atmospheric Mackinnon's Cave.

→ **Park** your camper or pitch your tent at Fidden Farm campsite and go kayaking in the beautifully clear sea.

→ **Travel** to remote Gometra and spend a couple of nights in one of the off-grid bothies.

→ **Swim** or stroll over to the tidal island Erraid and enjoy a picnic in a hidden cove.

The largest island in Argyll is a wild and beautiful one with something to please every preference. Board the ferry from Oban or Kilchoan and discover Mull's stunning sandy bays and beaches, deep forests, dramatic coastal scenery, high mountains and the magical islands scattered around its western seaboard.

The island's 300 miles of wild, rugged coastline are deeply cut by lochs and contain some of the most breathtaking cliff scenery and coastal features on the Scottish isles. Explore a series of spectacular natural arches at Carsaig or head deep inside the mythical Mackinnon's Cave.

Mull has earned a reputation for its exceptional wildlife, on- and offshore. Look out for eagles soaring in the beautiful Glen More, which lies next to the island's only Munro, or red deer hiding in the woods. In summer, journey to the Isle of Staffa and find hundreds of colourful puffins congregating on the cliffs. Confident swimmers can dive off the basalt columns and into the mouth of the legendary Fingal's Cave, allowing the tide to carry them inside on their back beneath the cavern's strikingly coloured roof.

In the south-west there are beautiful bays like Tràigh Gheal and Uisken, where soft sands are lapped by crystalline turquoise waters, and further west along the coastline kayakers glide between the rocky islets at Fidden Bay and families watch from the popular farm campsite. From here you can walk or swim across to the tidal island of Erraid and wild camp by the delightful cove hidden in its south side.

Colourful buildings wrap around the harbour in the lively main town of Tobermory, which is definitely worth visiting – but there are plenty of other places to eat and stay across the island. Devour incredible fresh shellfish at Creel Seafood Bar, close to the Iona ferry, and sample local dishes in The Boathouse on beautiful Ulva. Those looking for peace and quiet can head to Gometra and spend a few nights in a remote, off-grid bothy or wild camp by the waterfalls at Eas Fors.

BEACHES & WILD SWIMMING

1 TRÀIGH GHEAL, KNOCKVOLOGAN

Remote, beautiful white sand beach hidden amongst rocky outcrops and sheltered by the islet of Eilean Mòr. The cove is approached by a trail through a nature reserve, home to much wildlife, flowering plants and the ruined Tìr Fhearagain village.

→ Continue S down lane from Fidden (see 2) to Knockvologan to find small 'walks' sign at barns on L. Or bushwhack S across headland ¾ mile to tiny Tràigh a' Mhill.

60 mins, 56.2729, -6.2985 🚶‍♂️🍴🥾🐚🅿️

2 FIDDEN BEACH

On a sunny day the bay at Fidden could be easily mistaken for the Caribbean. The beautiful west-facing beach with its crystal-clear waters and pink granite outcrops is a perfect place for wild swimming, kayaking and watching sunsets over the islets lying in front of Iona.

→ Turn L in Fionnphort before the ferry, signed for Fidden and Knockvologan (PA66 6BL), and continue for 1¼ miles following signs for Fidden Farm until you reach small car park by the farm and campsite (see 25).

30 mins, 56.3085, -6.3670 🏖️🐚🅿️🏕️

3 UISKEN BAY, BUNESSAN

Sleepy, rock-encircled bay with a white sand beach, informal camping and fine views to Colonsay and the Paps of Jura.

→ Take L in Bunessan, signed Ardachy Hotel, and follow to Ardchiavaig (PA67 6DT) keeping L at two junctions. Bushwhack E for more coves.

5 mins, 56.2902, -6.2144 🐚🏖️🏕️

4 CALGARY BAY

Broad, white shell-sand beach, glorious machair and bright blue water stretch as far as the eye can see, all framed by low hills and craggy headlands. Calgary Bay is a true Scottish gem and one of Mull's most popular wilder camping spots. Make a day of it here and also take time to visit the nearby Calgary Art in Nature gallery and view some of the sculptures in the surrounding woodlands.

→ Head W from Dervaig on the B8073 about 4¾ miles until you reach the car park at the bay, just after PA75 6QQ. Wild camping with WCs at the S end of the beach (see 26).

5 mins, 56.5787, -6.2815 🐕🏖️🅿️🏕️💧

5 DÙN ARA BATHING POOL

Enjoy a peaceful swim in a lovely spot sheltered from the waves, which was constructed as a bathing pool. The pool,

revealed at low tide, is by the site of an old medieval fort and surrounded by striking land- and seascapes. There are other pleasant inlets around to the R, and this rugged coast is good for spotting seals and otters.

→ From Glengorm Castle coffee shop car park (PA75 6QE, but take R fork inside castle gate) cross bridge and follow the track through a gate and out onto grassy land to N of castle. Continue through a 2nd gate before swinging R on a fainter grassy path downhill, which soon reaches a T-junction. Turn R heading towards gate before crossing a stile and heading NW down the field, crossing a 2nd stile. Path goes through 3 more gates then curves L beside a crag where the ruin of Dùn Ara stands. The bathing pool (signposted) is further along path by the sea.

45 mins, 56.6405, -6.1989 ⬛🏕️🖼️🚶

6 EAS FORS, BALLYGOWN

Series of waterfalls with small plunge pools, the final fall plummeting 30m over a cliff into the sea. There are some great places for a picnic or take a dip by the middle and upper cascades, and a couple of wild camping spots for those who don't mind the midges.

→ 2 miles N of Ulva Ferry on the B8073 (past PL73 6LT) there is a small car park R shortly before a bridge by the waterfalls. Upper falls are just above the road, middle falls below, and the only way to view the lower falls safely is to walk half a mile back along road towards Ulva Ferry then onto the shore, following it back along to the falls (low tide only).

10–60 mins, 56.5030, -6.1524 🏞️🚶🔲

MAGICAL ISLANDS

7 STAFFA

The 'island of pillars' is home to summer colonies of puffins, wild flowers ungrazed by any mammals, and of course one of the most majestic places in Scotland, the remarkable Fingal's Cave. This sea cavern, over 20m high, is formed of fantastically beautiful hexagonal basalt columns and arches. During calm seas there is the opportunity to jump into the freezing cold sea and swim to the end of the cave. Listen closely to the eerie acoustics of the waves echoing at the back of 'the melodious cave', as the original Gaelic name of An Uaimh Bhinn describes it. Turus Mara from Ulva Ferry, 01688 400242. Turusmara.com

→ Staffa Tours from Oban or Fionnphort, 07831 885985. Staffatours.com

½ day, 56.4354, -6.3416 🔲🚤🔲🔲🔲

8 ULVA

This beautiful privately owned island, thickly wooded in parts and with striking basalt columns and cliffs, is home to native wildlife including red deer, seals and golden eagles. Around 16 people still live on the island and make a living from sheep, cattle, oyster- and fish-farming and tourism. The wonderful Boathouse restaurant (see 19) sits just above the pier.

→ S of Lagganulva (PA73 6LT), turn W off the B8073 to the Ulva Ferry (runs weekdays all year, plus Sundays in summer.) If weather is rough, call 01688 500226/07919 902407.

10 mins, 56.4743, -6.1528 🔲🔲🔲🔲🔲

9 TRÀIG BHÀN, IONA

The full name Tràigh Bàn nam Monach translates as 'White Strand of the Monk', fitting for this quiet sandy beach on the northern tip of Iona. Perfect for an early morning swim. On the way is Iona Abbey, a religious site since 586AD, with ancient high crosses, medieval cloisters and the burial ground for the Lords of the Isles.

→ Head N on road past abbey (dir PA76 6SW) to the field below the Iona Hostel.

30 mins, 56.3493, -6.3815 🔲🔲✝️

10

10 ERRAID

This small island featured in Robert Louis Stevenson's adventure story *Kidnapped*, in which the hero wrecked there did not realise that it is accessible at low tide by a sandy causeway. Privately owned, it is home to a small Findhorn community in the north, and has a beautiful cove on its south side.

➜ Walk past Knockvologan farm (Tràigh Gheal see 1) down track 500m and walk or swim across to Erraid. Walk SW across island to secluded cove Tràigh Gheal.

60 mins, 56.2902, -6.3744 🏊🐚🏕

11 GARBH EILEAN

At least ten isles and islets share this name, which translates as 'rough isle'. This one is a dome-shaped tidal island connected to the shore by a wonderful arced sandbar at Kilvickeon beach (not named on maps, but the accepted name).

➜ On the A489, ½ mile E of Bunessan turn dir Scoor House on road with 12t weight limit, becoming a stony track. Follow 2 miles, past PA67 6DW, bearing R at end of loch, to park on L just beyond ruined Kilvickeon church R. Track on R descends, sometimes muddily, to Garbh Eilean.

15 mins, 56.2902, -6.1862 🏖🏞

12 MACKINNON'S CAVE

Reputedly the deepest in the Hebrides at 150m, the dark and mysterious Mackinnon's Cave is a natural curiosity steeped in magic and myth. The most well-known tale is that of a piper who wanted to have a piping competition with the fairies in the cave. He entered the cave with his dog, but only the dog emerged, several hours later, terrified and without a hair on its body. Bring a torch.

➜ Only accessible below half tide, scrambling required on the shore. Turn W off B8035 onto unsigned tarmac road ½ mile S of Balnahard and park at signed car park just before Balmeanach Farm (PA68 6EH). Follow arrows to road end, past farm and through gate. Follow track as it winds steeply uphill to L, then follow fence leading onto turf of the cliff top. Go through 2nd gate and continue to L. When the waterfall is in sight, the path descends to the shore. Continue along the bay past waterfall, over boulders and slabby rocks to cave.

60 mins, 56.4132, -6.1516 🏖🌊🏞

13 CARSAIG ARCHES

Remarkable natural arches sitting at the foot of spectacular cliffs. The walk in is a long and rough 4 miles but takes in some of the island's most dramatic coastal scenery and an abundance of interesting wildlife.

➜ From the A849 W of Pennyghael, turn S signed Carsaig. Follow 4 miles, past PA70 6HD, to small car park N of the pier. Head W across pebble bay, cross the stream and pick up the path that emerges at the rear end of bay and goes through a gate. After a boggy section, a steep route emerges; ignore this and instead follow the rocky shore to where the path reappears. Continue along the coastal path past towering cliffs and waterfalls. Eventually after a slight climb over large boulders the first arch comes into view. The final section requires extreme care and dry weather; head up over the first arch to descend to the second arch. Return same way.

2–3 hrs, 56.2921, -6.0486 🏖🌊🏞🐾

14 FIONNPHORT QUARRY

Delightful pink granite quarry by the coast, with rusting machinery among the stones. After exploring the quarry itself, follow path down to sheltered sandy beach at Tormore.

➜ Free parking in village at Columbus Centre (56.3240, -6.3654). Walk E out of the village and turn N onto minor road signed for Ninth Wave Restaurant (see 23). Continue to

19

restaurant then follow the track leading uphill towards the old quarry workings. There is a clear path down towards Tormore pier and the small sandy bay.

1 hr, 56.3313, -6.3668 🚶🏊🐾

15 MACCULLOCH'S FOSSIL TREE

An impressive geological wonder reached by a long walk along the coast. This huge tree was once engulfed by lava flow 50 million years ago and now its trunk's impression remains embedded in a fantastical array of basalt columns by the shore. There are fan and circle basalt formations along the shore.

➜ Map needed. Turn W off B8035 at NTS sign for Burg, towards Tioran House Hotel (PA69 6ES). Follow road to small car park ½ mile beyond hotel. Go through gate and follow track which soon forks, take R and after 2 miles take L fork in path before Tavool House. Continue 1 mile to Burg Farm and when path splits, keep L, past Dùn Bhuirg and cairn. Track becomes narrow path and descends to beach then up along cliff and through boulder field, before descending a steel ladder to shore. Continue N past two waterfalls, fossil tree lies just beyond.

2½ hrs, 56.3719, -6.2078 🏊📷

16 TRESHNISH HEADLAND

Magnificent stretch of coastline sculpted into dramatic cliffs, sea caves, stacks and arches. Explore several deserted villages and the legendary Whisky Cave, hidden by an earth mound, thought to have been used as an illegal distillery – the round structure taken for the site of a still is used as a firepit by some visitors.

➜ Map needed. 275m S of turn off for Treshnish & Haunn cottages (PA75 6QX) park by B8073 in a disused quarry (56.5543, -6.2959). Head up turnoff past cottages and continue straight to coast, almost 2 miles. At track end head L along coastline. Whisky Cave is reached by carefully descending grassy slope to the beach, then turning immediately into the cleft. Follow the path S and inland up the next stream, through deserted Crackaig back to the road, turning L to arrive at the start.

90 mins–5hrs, 56.5327, -6.3262 🏕️⛺📷🚶↩️

BIKE TOURING

17 MULL ELECTRIC BIKES

Power assisted bikes to help you get around this very hilly island. Rental from half day to 1 week. Over 14s only. Open 9.30-11.30am.

➜ Arnabost, Dervaig, PA75 6QJ, 01688 400499. Mullelectrickbikes.co.uk

56.5899, -6.1873

LOCAL FOOD

18 CREEL SEAFOOD BAR

Fantastic family-run takeaway seafood bar by Fionnphort Pier. Take in the great views on one of the outside benches whilst enjoying wonderful fresh seafood from the surrounding waters of the island.

➜ Fionnphort Pier, PA66 6BL, 01681 700312. Thecreelisleofmull.co.uk

56.3253, -6.3695 🍴

19 THE BOATHOUSE, ULVA

Great stop for local food. Situated just by the landing pier on the Isle of Ulva. Serves own-grown oysters, home baking, teas, coffees, creel-caught shellfish and local Scottish meats and salmon.

➜ Visitors Centre, Ulva Ferry PA73 6LZ, 01688 500241. Isleofulva.com/the-boathouse

56.4808 -6.1533 🍴🚪

20 BALLYGOWN RESTAURANT

Quirky family-run restaurant with daily

changing menus, housed inside a charming traditional cottage.

→ Ballygown Cottage, Ulva Ferry, PA73 6LU, 01688 500113. Ballygownmull.co.uk
56.5139, -6.1810 🍴

21 THE GLASS BARN
Stunning plant-filled glass barn with a café and farm shop inside. Home to Isle of Mull Cheese, a small family-run dairy farm. Serves and sells delicious fresh farm produce, home baking, tasty lunches and of course some of the best Scottish cheese.

→ Sgriob-ruadh Farm, Tobermory, PA75 6QD, 01688 302627. Isleofmullcheese.co.uk
56.6197, -6.0885 🍴

22 GLENGORM COFFEE SHOP
Glengorm estate's renovated old stables now house a lovely café serving fresh baking, lunches, teas & coffees. Food is cooked on site using the estate's own produce from the farm and walled garden. A small deli sells more local Scottish produce. Closed winter.

→ Glengorm Castle, Tobermory, PA75 6QE, 01688 302321. Glengormcastle.co.uk
56.6364, -6.1747

23 NINTH WAVE
Small, award-winning restaurant, evenings only and booking ahead essential. Seafood, some caught by the owner, is key. One for the foodies, the table is yours for the whole evening, and no children!

→ Bruach Mhor, Fionnphort, PA66 6BL, 01681 700757. Ninthwaverestaurant.co.uk
56.3283, -6.3594 🍴

24 AM BIRLINN
Committed to serving quality local produce, Am Birlinn has gained a reputation as one of the best restaurants on Mull. The menu features primary local producers, from Kenny's crab & lobster half a mile away to Ony's pork 2 miles away.

→ Penmore, Dervaig, PA75 6QS, 01688 400619. Ambirlinn.com
56.5912, -6.2248 🍴

CAMP & SLEEP

25 FIDDEN FARM CAMPSITE
Wonderful large informal farm campsite located right by the beautiful Fidden Beach. Great base for kayaking and swimming.

→ Knockvologan Road, Nr Fionnphort, PA66 6BN, 01681 700427.
56.3071, -6.3657 ⛺🚿🐚🏊🚣

26 CALGARY BAY WILD CAMPING
Free wild camping by the beach with great views and basic toilet facilities. A very sociable camp spot and often busy during good weather. Large motorhomes and caravans not permitted, no drinking water.

→ S end of Calgary Bay just off B8073, S of PA75 6QQ.
56.5764, -6.2778 ⛺🚿🐚🏊🚣

27 SHIELING HOLIDAYS
Seaside campsite with pitches for tents, campers and caravans, large 'shielings' (permanent tent-like structures with basic furniture and electricity) and two charming cottages. Common room with stove and free wi-fi.

→ Craignure, PA65 6AY, 01680 812496. Shielingholidays.co.uk
56.4690, -5.6985 🚣⛺

28 GOMETRA BOTHIES
Remote off-grid cottages located a 7–8 mile walk away from Ulva ferry on the roadless Isle of Gometra, itself practically off any grid

there is. Very basic but charming interiors offering just a little more comfort than public mountain bothies. Enjoy the beautiful views and an abundance of wildlife on the island.

→ Gometra, Ulva Ferry, PA73 6NA, text 07525 751171. Gometra.org

56.4841, -6.2925 🖼🚶🅱🆈

29 LIP NA CLOICHE

Delightful B&B housed in a traditional style cottage and situated amid a beautiful densely planted garden and nursery. Great food at The Ballygown Restaurant is three houses along (see 20).

→ Ballygown, nr. Ulva Ferry, PA73 6LU, 01688 500257. Lipnacloiche.co.uk

56.5125, -6.1742 🖼♿

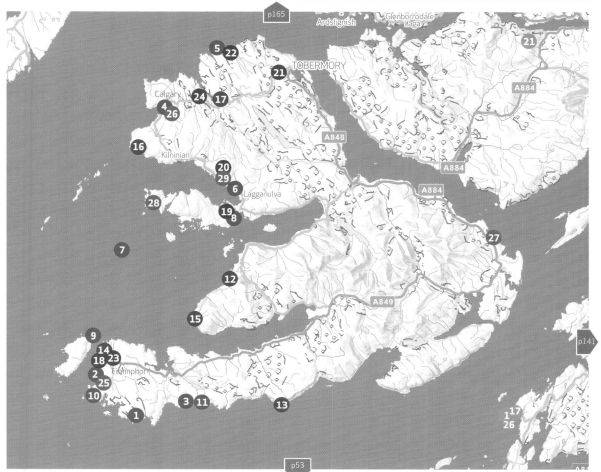

THE SMALL ISLES

Our perfect weekend

→ **Spy** deer roaming the beach against the distant backdrop of the Skye Cuillin at Kilmory Bay on Rùm.

→ **Climb** the iconic An Sgùrr, Eigg, and take in the amazing views from the summit.

→ **Watch** your compass needle lose its way around volcanic Compass Hill on Canna.

→ **Hunt** the beach for bloodstone before enjoying a dram by the fire inside Guirdil Bothy, Rùm.

→ **Find** great local food straight off the ferry to Eigg at Glamisdale Café, by the pier.

→ **Shuffle** your feet to hear the Singing Sands on Eigg and swim in the sea with incredible views of Rùm.

→ **Enjoy** the sunset before a good night's sleep in the cosy yurt at Cleadale Campsite, Eigg.

→ **Paddle** with views of the Rùm Cuillin or try and spot seals or island horses resting at Gallanach beach, Muck.

→ **Visit** the delightful Rùm ponies and take a tour inside the fascinating Kinloch Castle, Rùm.

The Small Isles are an archipelago of beautiful islands lying between the western mainland and the Outer Hebrides. The main islands – Rùm, Eigg, Muck and Canna – are close together but each is very different, offering its own distinctive charms.

Travelling to these islands is a pleasure in itself. The only way to get there is by passenger ferry (no cars!) from Mallaig at the end of the scenic 'Road to the Isles', the A830. As you cross the water there are views ahead of the Rùm Cuillin, a dark and forbidding mountain range that crowns the largest island of the group, the wildly beautiful Rùm. This sparsely populated land of volcanic peaks, rugged coastline and undulating moors is now run as a National Nature Reserve and home to sea eagles and thousands of red deer, which can be seen and heard in early autumn roaring on the hills or near the magnificent Kilmory Bay. They can also be found roaming Guirdil Bay, where you can spend the night in a charming bothy and in the morning scour the beach for fragments of bloodstone. The walks on Rùm are mostly long and often rough, but those who make the effort can find themselves amongst some of the most spectacular and unmapped wild scenery on the Scottish isles.

South-east of Rùm lies Eigg, the most populous island of the group. This vibrant isle is home to a thriving community, which gained ownership of the island in 1997. One of the world's greenest islands, it generates almost all of its own electricity from sun, wind, and water. Here you can visit beautiful beaches such as the Singing Sands and Laig Bay in the northwest, explore the dark Cathedral and Massacre Caves and the abandoned village of Grulin, or climb the highest point on the island – the striking volcanic plug of An Sgùrr.

Canna and Muck are beautiful, peaceful islands, and despite their small size there is plenty to discover. Muck, with its stunning small sandy beaches, is home to a group of creative and resourceful locals who use wool and other materials from the island for delightful hand-made crafts, rugs and garments, which can be purchased from the Craft Shop in Port Mor. On Canna you can visit the curious An Coroghon castle, enjoy wonderful views from the top of Compass Hill and then tuck into some delicious fresh seafood and home cooking at the very popular Café Canna.

WILD BEACHES & BAYS

1 KILMORY BAY, RÙM

Magnificent remote bay with a sandy beach, looking straight out over the staggering Skye Cuillins. Kilmory is the heart of the Red Deer Project, one of the longest and most complete studies of a wild animal population in the world. In late September and early October, it's sometimes possible to watch rutting stags near the bay. Good wild camping in calm weather.

→ From Kinloch Castle head N then turn L along S side of Kinloch River into Kinloch Glen. Continue past waterfalls, ignoring small path R after 500m, after another 1½ miles take R at fork. Follow track turning N another 2½ miles before heading down to the beach when it comes into view.

2–2½ hrs, 57.0499, -6.3545

2 HARRIS BAY, RÙM

Wild and remote bay on the southwest coast, with a raised beach, backed by the Rùm Cuillin. The bay is home to an old hunting lodge, the bizarre Bullough Mausoleum and the ruins of Harris, the island's largest settlement before the Clearances. The Rùm ponies are often here.

→ As for Kilmory Bay (see 1), but at the fork take the L track and continue on for about 4 miles before descending to the bay.

4 hrs, 56.9749, -6.3817

3 GALLANACH, MUCK

Beautiful white sand beach with good views of Rùm, bounded by two reefs and an old jetty. Many grey seals can be seen here, and you might also end up sharing the beach with the island's horses and cows.

→ From the pier head L through the village Port Mor on the island's only road, passing a school and craft centre. Continue to the N side of the island and beach at the end of the road.

30 mins, 56.8405, -6.2524

4 AM MIALAGAN, SANDAY

This perfect little white shell-sand beach on the tidal island of Sanday lies just west of the bridge linking it to Canna. It is backed by stupendous views of the mountains on Rùm.

→ From Canna pier walk past church to the junction, turn L and follow track round the coastline to cross the bridge. Once on Sanday, turn immediately R onto faint path on turf leading to beach.

30 mins, 57.0526, -6.5107

5 BAY OF LAIG, EIGG

This white shale beach, Tràigh Chlithe, has beautiful views of the Rùm Cuillin. A low tide reveals many delicate swirling patterns of light and dark sand.

→ From pier take R onto road N, dir Cleadale. After approx 3 miles, take 2nd L opposite post box in Cleadale, which leads down to the shore.

90 mins, 56.9167, -6.1573

6 SINGING SANDS, EIGG

Fine musical quartz beach in Camas Sgiotaig bay close to Cleadale, Eigg's main settlement. The beach, Tràigh na Bìgil in Gaelic, is named for the squeaking 'singing' sounds the dry sand makes if walked on or blown by the wind when it is dry. There are caves and a natural arch to the south, and good views of Rùm.

→ Follow directions as for Bay of Laig (see 5) but instead of turning L at post-box, continue to junction and keep slight R at fork in road. Pass through a gate and continue, following blue markers before bearing L to pass the R side of a sheep pen and towards the coast. Soon bear R to diagonally cross the farmland to a gap in the stone wall where you will pick up a path marked with blue paint leading to the bay.

40 mins, 56.9313, -6.1583

CASTLES, RUINS & CAVES

7 KINLOCH CASTLE, RÙM

Opulent and fascinating Victorian mansion built in 1897 by the former owner of Rùm, George Bullough. It is an almost untouched example of a purpose-built Scots Baronial shooting lodge, and is famous for its eccentric and lavish interiors and furnishings.

→ From the pier follow track around the edge of Loch Scresort, passing school on L and campsite on R. Signposted along the way.
20 mins, 57.0136, -6.2822

8 AN COROGHON CASTLE, CANNA

The remains of the small 'castle' tower are possibly medieval, more likely 17th century, and sit on a flat-topped stack between a pebbly beach to the north and a stretch of fine volcanic sand to the south. It was once used as a place of refuge and later a prison.

→ From Canna pier, walk past church to reach a junction, turn R here & follow track to the sandy beach. The castle sits to the N. Do not attempt to climb the stack.
20 mins, 57.0603, -6.4885 🅿️🔞

9 MASSACRE CAVE, EIGG

Uamh Fhraing in Gaelic, this secret cave has a bloody and disturbing past. Oral history has it that in 1577, during a feud with the Macleod clan from Skye, 395 MacDonalds were suffocated inside the cave when the Macleods built a huge fire in front of the small entrance. The numbers may be an exaggeration, but human bones were found here in the 19th century and many taken by collectors before the rest were removed for burial.

→ From the pier follow road uphill into woods, passing road to Cleadale on R. Continue for approx ½ mile then turn L onto track marked with purple waymarker. Just before the house veer L, following purple marks on faint path. When path forks, take R path and continue, passing through a kissing gate and across the field to gate at R end of second fence, leading to a narrow path down the cliff onto the shore. During low tide only, you can first visit Cathedral Cave (once used for Catholic masses); a short distance further along the coast is Massacre Cave.
40 mins, 56.8733, -6.1456 🅿️❓✝️

10 GRULIN UACHDRACH, EIGG

The lost village of Grulin, meaning 'stony place', was once a thriving township housing over 14 families, before all but one were evicted in 1853 during the Highland Clearances. Explore the many ruined blackhouses which lie under the south face of An Sgùrr – one remaining cottage, Carnan Ghrulin, is now a private holiday home.

→ As for An Sgùrr (see 12) but beyond Galmisdale House continue L along track ignoring path to An Sgùrr on R. Continue for 1 mile, passing a cairn on L, to restored cottage at Grulin. The upper and lower ruins can be visited via forks on the path before cottage.
90 mins, 56.8804, -6.1744 🅿️📶

NATURAL CURIOSITIES

11 BLOODSTONE HILL, RÙM

Steep rocky hill towering over Guirdil Bay, named after the semi-precious mineral which is found on its slopes and amongst the pebbles on the beach. The jade-green stone has flecks of red running through it, said to resemble drops of blood.

→ Bring a map. The safe route is as for Harris (see 2), but approx 1 mile after taking the L fork head R up the sometimes patchy path passing between Orval and Fionchra, then around the top of Glen Guirdil onto Bloodstone Hill. The hill can also be reached from Guirdil Bothy or the Subterranean tunnels (see 20 & 14), following the path from

Guirdil bothy and then bushwhacking up Glen Guirdil to join the path above. Combining these routes makes a spectacular two-day circuit.
Half day, 57.0176, -6.4255

12 AN SGÙRR, EIGG

Distinctive, prow-like black peak rising to nearly 400m in the south of Eigg, offering magnificent views of the surrounding islands. Great care is needed on the summit, as there are dangerous cliff edges on all sides.

→ From pier head uphill, passing road to Cleadale and turn off for lodge and community hall on R, then through gate across field to Galmisdale House, which sits before Sgùrr, and gate near R of house. Continue L for short distance behind house, then turn R onto rough footpath. Follow path as it climbs around N side of ridge then cuts L to the middle of the ridge and finally L again along ridge (marked by several cairns) to summit trig point.
2 hrs, 56.8841, -6.1660

13 COMPASS HILL, CANNA

This 140m peak on the east of the island is made of the volcanic rock tuff, which has such a high iron content that it distorts the compasses on nearby ships, making them point to the hill rather than north!

→ From the pier walk past church and turn R at junction onto track between 2 walls. Just before stone farm building, turn L through gate into field. Follow the faint quad track on R of field up through gate on corner and after, turn R to follow wall uphill and then follow track round to L before land begins to level out below cliffs. Continue L around the bottom of the escarpment and as it gets lower, head R to reach the summit. Take care near cliff edges.
55 mins, 57.0653, -6.4899

14 SUBTERRANEAN TUNNELS, RÙM

Remarkable section of coastline just north of where the Shellesder Burn falls into the sea. Majestic subterranean tunnels, red-hued caves and a huge natural arch to explore.

→ This route has many fords: do not attempt during or just after wet weather. Bring a map. From Kinloch Castle follow track for Kilmory Bay (see 1) but ½ mile after the R fork, turn L on the Glen Shellesder path as it heads gradually uphill and W between Minishal and Sgaorishal hills, past forestry plantation and old shielings. After approx 2½ miles the burn descends to the coast via a waterfall, and just N of waterfall are the subterranean tunnels and arch.
2½–3 hrs, 57.0321, -6.4073

BIKE & KAYAK HIRE

15 EIGG ADVENTURES, EIGG

Small family run adventure company offering mountain bike and kayak hire, bespoke sailing trips and archery.

→ An Laimhrig, PH42 4RL, 01687 347007. Eiggadventures.co.uk
1 min, 56.8773, -6.1309

LOCAL FOOD

16 CAFÉ CANNA

Canna's only café is a great licenced venue serving locally sourced produce and fresh daily specials that are so good, some people travel to the island just to eat here. Try the Canna landed lobster or famous Canna rabbit.

→ The Bothy, PH44 4RS, 01687 462251. Cafecanna.co.uk
57.0595, -6.4961

17 GALMISDALE BAY CAFÉ, EIGG

Bar and café serving wonderful home-cooked food using a range of fresh, locally sourced ingredients, including quality meat from the local butcher and fish from the merchant in Mallaig. A friendly island hub for both locals and visitors.

14

→ The Pier, Galmisdale Bay, PH42 4RL,
01687 482487. Glamisdale-bay.com
56.8772, -6.1305

18 ISLE OF MUCK SHOP & TEAROOM

Tasty, local home cooking and baking in a delightful tea shop, with a variety of lovely gifts and books for sale in the craft shop.

→ Port Mor, PH41 2RP, 01687 462990.
Isleofmuck.com
56.8354, -6.2279

19 RÙM VILLAGE SHOP & HALL

The village shop and post office sells groceries and picnic essentials, and in the summer the community often runs a small café in the village hall serving a selection of homemade soups, sandwiches and baking.

→ Village Hall, Kinloch, PH43 4RR,
01687 460328. Isleofrum.com
57.0156, -6.2801

STAY & SLEEP

20 GUIRDIL BOTHY, RÙM

Enchanting mountain bothy set amongst the ruins of a pre-clearance settlement in Guirdil Bay. The Guirdil River rushes down the glen and into the sea below Bloodstone Hill (see 11) on the south end. There are excellent views of Canna and if you're lucky you'll catch a beautiful sunset or see feral goats and deer roaming the bay. Bring fuel or gather driftwood on the shore.

→ Follow the route to the Subterranean tunnels (see 14). Carefully cross to S side of the burn via a ford 75m from the headland. Continue SW along the coast until the bothy is visible below, and carefully descend to the bay via one of the faint paths.
57.0253, -6.4183

21 EIGG TIME, EIGG

Three contemporary cosy hideaways, each in their own wonderful location. Sweeney's Bothy (56.9270, -6.1416) is a modern off-grid eco-cabin tucked into the cliffs above Cleadale, Laig Beach Bothy (56.9133, -6.1610) sits by the bay looking over to the magnificent mountains on Rùm and the cosy Shepherd's Hut (56.8785, -6.1328) is close to the pier and a great place for sunrises.

→ 01687 482414. Eiggtime.com
56.9270, -6.1416

CAMPSITES & HOSTELS

22 KINLOCH CAMPSITE & BUNKHOUSE, RÙM

Small, basic campsite on the shores of Loch Scresort with tent pitches, plus camping cabins and a BBQ bothy that each sleep up to four people and make a good escape from the midges in summer. There is also a wonderful modern bunkhouse with fire and huge windows overlooking the loch.

→ PH43 4RR, 01687 460318. Isleofrum.com
57.0109, -6.2775 ▲☂♨

23 CLEADALE CAMPSITE, EIGG

Tent pitches, Mongolian yurt and bothy located on a wonderful sustainable organic croft. There are fantastic views to Rùm and often beautiful sunsets. Buy free-range eggs and fresh seasonal veg grown on the farm.

→ Eigg Organics, Croft 13, Cleadale, PH42 4RL, 01687 482480. Eiggorganics.co.uk
56.9222, -6.1449 ▲☂♨⚑

24 EIGG CAMPING PODS

Cosy camping pods with views of the harbour. Owned by the community, with all profits from the pods put back into the facilities and infrastructure on the island.

→ An Laimhrig, PH42 4RL, 01687 347007. Eiggcampingpods.com
56.8780, -6.1318 ☂

25 GLEBE BARN, EIGG

Lovely hostel sleeping 22 and separate self-catering apartment for 2–4, situated beneath the ridge of An Sgùrr. In the middle of Eigg with a shop, café and restaurant less than a mile away.

→ The Glebe Barn, PH42 4RL, 01687 315099. Glebebarn.co.uk
56.9018, -6.1427 ☂

26 MUCK BUNKHOUSE

Delightful little hostel on the smallest isle, overlooking Port Mor. Sleeps up to eight and has all usual facilities. Close to Muck Tea Room.

→ Port Mor, PH41 2RP, 01687 462042. Isleofmuck.co.uk
56.8355, -6.2269 ☂

27 CANNA CAMPSITE

Excellent new camping and glamping site on lovely Canna. Sheltered tent pitches, pods, caravans, BBQ area. Campfires are allowed.

→ Canna Campsite, PH44 4RS, 01687 462477. Cannacampsite.com
57.0577, -6.5122 ▲☂♨⚑

p87

p165

p165

ISLE OF SKYE

Our perfect weekend

→ **Journey** to Loch Coruisk, Britain's wildest freshwater loch, and swim beneath the towering Cuillin mountains.

→ **Descend** into the beautiful Camasunary Bay and spend the night by the fire inside its open mountain bothy.

→ **Hike** uphill and around the famous 'Old Man' rock pinnacle below the imposing ramparts of The Storr.

→ **Swim** under the natural arch in the famous Fairy Pools at Glenbrittle.

→ **Sample** some delicious home baking at Jann's Cakes.

→ **Visit** the spectacularly situated lighthouse at Neist Point and watch the sun set.

→ **Wander** through the magical Fairy Glen and climb up the grassy hills to 'Castle Ewen'.

→ **Meander** along the winding single-track road to reach one of the most iconic landscapes in Scotland, the Quiraing.

Iconic Skye, the largest of the Inner Hebrides, contains some of the United Kingdom's most spectacular scenery and varied geology. The island is reached via the Skye Bridge from Kyle of Lochalsh, or by the Calmac ferry from Mallaig. Since the road bridge opened in the 1990s, Skye has become an even more popular holiday destination and has seen an influx of tourists and campers; you'll find many of them eating fish and chips beneath the rows of pastel-coloured houses that wrap around the bustling harbor, or sampling whisky in traditional local pubs. But there are still plenty of lesser-known and hidden wonders to explore across the island.

The irregular coastline is made up of a series of peninsulas radiating from a mountainous centre, crowned by the famous Cuillin mountains. Experienced climbers who make it to the summits are rewarded with otherworldly views of the surrounding land and seascapes. At the foot of the jagged peaks of the towering Black Cuillin, explore the wild and majestic Loch Coruisk, or further inland go swimming in the magical Fairy Pools in Glenbrittle. At the coast, climb up the natural flowstone staircase inside the otherworldly Spar Cave to bathe in its glittering Mermaid Pool, or spend the night in a former coastguard lookout perched on a cliff edge at the very northern tip of the island.

The Isle of Skye, or Eilean a' Cheò (island of the mist), is a photographer's dream, where the cloud, mist and sunlight work together to create dazzling spectacles upon mysterious landscapes shaped by fire and ice. On the Trotternish peninsula you can explore two of Britain's most extraordinary landslide features, The Storr – with its celebrated Old Man rock pinnacle – and The Quiraing. These are most impressive in the late afternoon, when the low sun throws dramatic shadows from their many fantastical features.

The relative accessibility of Skye among the Scottish isles makes it the island people are often drawn to visit first, and the dramatic scenery ensures they will keep coming back.

COAST & BEACHES

1 CORAL BEACHES, DUNVEGAN
Pretty beach made entirely of crushed white grains of coral-like maërl, resembling cake sprinkles. The best time is swim is at high tide, when it's possible go snorkelling and explore beautiful rocks at north end of the bay.

→ Leave Dunvegan on A850 N dir IV55 8WF. Pass Dunvegan Castle and after 3½ miles, at T-junction, park on L in Coral Beaches car park. Walk a mile down track and along coast, past one coral beach to larger second one. Behind hill at N end of beach find basalt column rocks on water's edge. Loch Bay restaurant (see 28) is well worth a visit while you're in the area.

40 mins, 57.5000, -6.6372 ⚲🚶🍴ℹ

2 LOCH NAN LEACHD, CORUISK
Tiny white beach encircled by Cuillin Hills. Reached by boat or long walk.

→ Walk or take boats for Loch Coruisk (see 7). Beach is 300m E of Stepping Stones crossing Scavaig River.

20 mins, 57.1958, -6.1514 🚲🚶

3 INVER TOTE WATERFALLS, LEALT
Descend to the pebble beach by this wonderful coastal waterfall and go for a swim in the sea, or under the waterfall itself. The ruins on the shore were a 19th-century kiln and processing works for the mineral diatomite.

→ Lealt (IV51 9JW) and Inver Tote are about 4 miles N of The Storr (see 12). From the large layby car park opp Lealt turning on A855 take the path to the waterfall viewpoint and then descend to the pebble beach for a swim in the sea, or under the waterfall itself.

15 mins, 57.5659, -6.1480 🏞🔲

4 LEAC TRESSIRNISH, THE STORR
Hook-shaped, natural harbour rock formation for snorkelling and jumps. Also try to reach the inlet 100m to the north, which leads to the foreshore rock plateau, from the end of which you can swim into several sea caves.

→ Head almost 2 miles S from Inver Tote (see 3) to find long layby parking/viewpoint signed Tobhta Uachdrach on L (set back from road) opp a gated track. Look down to see flat grass plateau with the Leac rock formation. Go through the narrow gate and bushwhack 300m R steeply down slope.

20 mins, 57.5417, -6.1402 🍴🏊🐦🏂🚲⛵

5 TALISKER BAY, CARBOST
Dramatic silver bay with waterfall and huge purple rock pools on far left. During strong south-westerly winds the waterfall often blows back up on itself!

→ As you enter Carbost from E on B8009, bear L up hill, signed Talisker, then first R dir IV47 8SF and cont 3 miles to parking and track 'to beach'. In Carbost visit the bay's namesake distillery and Carbost Old Inn (see 26).

30 mins, 57.2811, -6.4625 🔳ℹ

6 ORONSAY TIDAL ISLAND
Explore impressive high cliffs, small sandy beaches, a large cave, natural arch and deep ravine on this wonderful tidal island. Much of it is covered in short, springy turf, making it an excellent picnic or camping spot with spectacular views of the coast and Cuillin mountains.

→ Just N of Bracadale on A863 take minor road dir Ullinish Country Lodge (IV56 8FD). After 1 mile take L signed Oronsay Path. Park at end and follow clear paths from road along Ulinish Point and across the causeway. Check tide times before setting off.

20 mins, 57.3358, -6.4647 🔲🔳🔳

8

WILD LOCHS & POOLS

7 LOCH CORUISK

This magnificent, desolate loch is often described as the wildest in Britain. Surrounded by the towering, dark, craggy mountain walls of the Cuillins, it is truly one of the most majestic places on the islands. The walk involves the famous Bad Step, a scramble over sloping rock slabs not for the inexperienced, but there are half- and full-day boat trips.

→ From Elgol (IV49 9BJ) follow the coastal path 5 miles NW or take a trip on the Bella Jane (0800 7313089) or Misty Isle (01471 866288). One-way trips available if you prefer to walk back. Boat 30 mins. Walk 3-4 hrs.
3-4 hrs, 57.1993, -6.1579

8 THE FAIRY POOLS, GLENBRITTLE

One of Scotland's most enchanting wild swimming spots, the crystal clear pools lie at the foot of the dramatic Black Cuillin mountain range. Follow the stream towards the mountain and explore the numerous magical turquoise pools, small waterfalls and an underwater arch.

→ From B8009 just SE of Carbost take turn signed Glenbrittle 400m E of IV47 8ST. After 4 miles find Fairy Pool car park on L. Cross road and follow clear path down and then up valley, crossing the minor stream and then keeping the Allt Coir a' Mhadaidh river on your R for ¾ mile to find several falls and pools.
20 mins, 57.2496, -6.2547

9 SPAR CAVE, ELGOL

Remarkable cathedral-like sea cave popular with Victorian explorers. Enter by the marble-like flowstone staircase and explore giant columns formed from water dropping through the limestone for thousands of years, until you reach the real reward, the crystal clear Mermaid Pool. Bring torches and keep an eye on tide times!

→ As you drop down to Elgol on B8083, turn L signed Glasnakille as road bends R. At T junction after 1½ miles park by telephone box turning R dir IV49 9BQ and enter field downhill 100m on L, by ruined barn. Bear L down to inlet and boulder hop L along LT foreshore rocks 100m, passing another small inlet, then traverse around into Spar Cave canyon. Inside, R passage diminishes but L one bears R and rises in flowstone staircase, descending to deep Mermaid Pool.
15 mins, 57.1401, -6.0685

10 COIRE LAGAN

A perfect introduction to the Cuillin range, this impressive and lofty ice-carved bowl contains a tiny turquoise lochan surrounded by spectacular jagged peaks. If you're lucky enough to visit on a day of good weather, the natural amphitheatre is a great place to stop, eat and relax– if you're feeling brave, even plunge into the unforgivingly icy water.

→ From the car park for the Fairy Pools (see 8) follow road S to park at end by Loch Brittle, after IV47 8TA. Take path leading E uphill, ignoring path heading S along loch. When path splits, take L fork and continue climbing. After passing shore of Loch an Fhir-bhallaich, keep straight, ignoring path veering off to R, taking the steeper, rockier climb to the lip of the coire. Some mild scrambling required near top. Return same way.
2-4 hrs, 57.2073, -6.2335

11 RHA BURN, UIG

Magnificent double waterfall with large plunge pool near charming Fairy Glen in Uig.

→ Entering Uig from S on A87, bear R on A855 to Staffin (IV51 9XP), then find footpath and steps up on R, before bridge. Follow path through deep glen for 5 mins. More waterfalls up the valley. No parking at bridge, but

unrestricted parking on roads beyond in Uig.
5 mins, 57.5935, -6.3602 🅅🄻

NATURAL WONDERS

12 THE STORR & OLD MAN OF STORR

The spectacular Old Man of Storr is a
48m rock pillar, part of a dramatic ancient
landslide feature beneath the iconic cliffs of
The Storr. Explore the paths leading around
the pinnacles or climb up to the craggy
summit of The Storr to enjoy magnificent
views of the island and beyond, from the
flat-topped Macleod's Tables in the west,
sweeping south past the jagged Cuillin
mountains to a wonderful array of peaks on
the mainland.

➜ Head N from Portree on the A855 for 6¼
miles to park in car park on L side of the road
about ¾ mile before IV51 9HX. From the
information board a good path heads uphill
through a felled area, which soon turns into
woodland. Turn R at both forks in path ahead,
passing a gate which leads to open moorland
before the cliffs. From here either follow
the path to the Old Man or if you'd like to get
higher, follow a fainter path to the R of the
pinnacle which continues to the summit.
10–150 mins, 57.5069, -6.1748 🄻🄿🄼🅅

13 CAMASUNARY BAY

Small, beautiful beach on the Strathaird
peninsula, backed by the dramatic Cuillins.
Great wild camping spots and one of
Scotland's most perfectly situated bothies.

➜ Parking ¼ mile S of Kilmarie (IV49 9AX) on
the B8083 to Elgol. From the car park, cross
the road to a gravel track where a green sign
marks the route. After 25 mins you will reach
another gate, head through and continue up
path, which is steep for a while and then rises
slowly towards the Am Màm pass. From here
views open up of the Cuillin and Camasunary.
The path then drops, zig-zagging down the
hillside and over the river to reach the bay. The
farthest building is the bothy.
90 mins, 57.1905, -6.1184 🅈🄻

14 THE QUIRAING

A massive landslip that is still moving
created this fantastical landscape of
spectacular plateaus enclosed by dark basalt
cliffs and pinnacles. Distinctive features
have their own names: The Needle is a
jagged 37m high pinnacle, The Table is a
flat expanse of short grass and The Prison
is a pyramidal rocky peak that resembles a
medieval keep from some angles.

➜ Parking at summit of minor road between

Uig and Staffin at 57.6281, -6.2909.
2 mins, 57.6395, -6.2705 🄼🄼

15 THE FAIRY GLEN

Strange magical landscape formed by an
ancient landslip. It consists of many grassy
cone-shaped hills, small lochans and natural
rocky towers – the most prominent is known
as Castle Ewen.

➜ Just S of Uig IV51 9YE, turn E off A87
before bus stop onto minor road heading
steeply uphill. Continue for 1 mile and park on
L after road drops down and grassy hills at the
start of the glen are in view.
5 mins, 57.5837, -6.3289 🅇🄻🄼🄲

16 HOE RAPE, RAMASAIG BAY

Spectacular coastal views towards
Waterstein Head and Moonen Bay and an
impressive waterfall plunging over the
dramatic sea cliffs.

➜ From B884 between Glendale and Milovaig,
turn S onto minor road signed for Ramasaig
300m W of IV55 8WL. Park at road end and
walk down towards Ramasaig Bay, then follow
faint path SW along the cliff edge towards Hoe
Rape for great views. From here either return
same way or continue on to Hoe Point and
follow path on a circular route past abandoned

15

village of Lorgill to return to Ramasaig (2½ hrs walk). Bring a map.

15 mins, 57.3895, -6.7387 🖼️📷🏕️🚻🍴

17 GLEN SLIGACHAN

Narrow glen beginning at the famous old bridge in Sligachan and dividing the spectacular Red and Black Cuillin mountains. There are excellent views from the bridge itself or with time and a map, head down into the glen for up to 10 miles (6 hour walk) for a closer look.

→ Parking near Sligachan Hotel (IV47 8SW), over the A87 new bridge and next to old bridge. Also along A863 near hotel. Paths from old bridge following river up the glen, can be wet.

1 min, 57.2798, -6.1619 🖼️🔽🏕️

18 RUBHA HUNISH & THE LOOKOUT

A former coastguard watch station sits atop the high cliffs of Meall Tuath at the most northern point of the island. The front part of the building (the watch room) was built in 1928 for the coastguard but by the 1970s was no longer needed and has become a favourite haunt for whale spotters, bird watchers and those just looking to enjoy the panoramic views from the large bay window. After a bad storm in 2005, the MBA

renovated the building so it could remain available as an open shelter.

→ 1 mile W of Kilmaluag (IV51 9UL) on the A855, take R signed Shulista by a phone booth to car park just before the cattle grid. By foot, cross the cattle grid and turn L onto rough boggy path. Follow path NNW for. 1½ miles, passing through a kissing gate and eventually climbing uphill towards the bothy. From here the only way to descend to the Rubha Hunish headland is by a steep scramble, we recommend only experienced climbers take this route. From the bothy, return the same way.

60–120 mins, 57.7013, -6.3448 🔽🏕️🏠↩️

19 NEIST POINT

The dramatic headland at the most westerly point of the island is regarded the best place on Skye to spot minke whales, basking sharks and dolphins. There is also spectacular coastal cliff scenery and a wonderful lighthouse at the end of the peninsula.

→ Turn SW off the B884 at Upper Milovaig (IV55 8WY) signed Waterstein/Neist Point. Drive to the end, to find Neist Point car park. Follow concrete path down to the lighthouse.

30 mins, 57.4232, -6.7879 🔽🏔️📷↩️

20 BEN TIANAVAIG

Wonderful hillwalk which follows dramatic cliffs towards a coastal peak offering great views of the Trotternish coast and beyond.

→ Park by picnic bench at Camustianavaig IV51 9LQ. Walk N on road for 2 mins and at red post box, turn R at path next to gate (signed Hill path). Follow uphill, turning R when path splits. Continue along cliff edge to trig point.

90 mins, 57.3912, -6.1429 🏕️🔽🏔️

LOCAL FOOD

21 JANN'S CAKES, DUNVEGAN

High quality organic cake shop also serving delicious soups, sandwiches and sweets. Only a couple of tables but if full, get your food to take away and eat on one of the nearby beaches.

→ 46 Kilmuir, Dunvegan, IV55 8GU, 01470 521730.

57.4359, -6.5800 🍴

22 SINGLE TRACK, KILMALUAG

High-quality coffee, hot drinks and home-made cakes are served in this larch-clad studio building, which was once featured on *Grand Designs*. The space doubles up as a small gallery, showcasing some of the

owner's artworks inspired by the island scenery. Closed in winter.

➜ Kendram, Kilmaluag, Portree. IV51 9UL. Single-track.co.uk
57.6829, -6.2991 🍴

23 ELLISHADDER ART CAFÉ

This café on the north-east coast offers a delicious freshly prepared menu, award-winning baking, distinctive high-quality art, craft work and hand-woven interior accessories and gifts. Closed in winter.

➜ Ellishadder, Nr. Staffin, IV51 9JE, 01470 562734. Ellishadderartcafe.co.uk
57.6112, -6.1845 🍴

24 EDINBANE INN

A warming stove, an open fire and the best seasonal and local produce await you in this former farmhouse, which also hosts an array of traditional music sessions. B&B available.

➜ Edinbane, IV51 9PW, 01470 582414. Edinbaneinn.co.uk
57.4701, -6.4300 🍴🛏🏠

25 THREE CHIMNEYS, DUNVEGAN

Internationally renowned Scottish restaurant serving award-winning seasonal dishes using local produce. Rooms available.

➜ Colbost, Dunvegan, IV55 8ZT, 01470 511258. Threechimneys.co.uk
57.4434, -6.6419 🛏🏠

26 CARBOST OLD INN

Dog-friendly pub & B&B with waterfront terrace serving local produce and real ales. .

➜ Carbost, IV47 8SR, 01478 640205. Theoldinnskye.co.uk
57.3017, -6.3525 🛏🏠

27 THE ISLES INN, PORTREE

Busy pub and restaurant decorated in traditional Jacobean style and serving good selection of whiskies and ales.

➜ Somerled Square, Portree IV51 9EH, 01478 612129. Accommodationskye.co.uk
57.4135, -6.1947 🍴🛏

28 LOCH BAY, STEIN

Contemporary, Michelin-mentioned restaurant with wonderful French-influenced seafood. Small, booking recommended.

➜ Stein, IV55 8GA, 01470 592235. Lochbay-restaurant.co.uk
57.5149, -6.5712 🍴

CAMPSITES & HOSTELS

29 GLENBRITTLE CAMPSITE

Summer campsite in spectacular location at the foot of the Black Cuillins on the rugged west coast. Pitches and hook-ups available. Great spot by a lovely sheltered beach.

➜ Glenbrittle, IV47 8TA, 01478 640404. Facebook.com/Glenbrittlecampsite
57.2022, -6.2875 🏕🏠

30 SKYEWALKER HOSTEL, PORTNALONG

This award-winning family-run hostel on the Minginish peninsula is set in a former school built in the 1920s, in an area that is great for watching sunsets and stargazing.

➜ The Old School, Portnalong, IV47 8SL, 01478 640250. Skyewalkerhostel.com
57.3261, -6.4070 🏠🏕

31 SLIGACHAN SELF CATERING

20-person bunkhouse, rooms in a self-catering lodge and cottages all surrounded by incredible mountain scenery.

➜ Allt Altdarach, Sligachan, IV47 8SW, 01478 650458. Sligachanselfcatering.com
57.2893, -6.1701 🏠

32 THE COWSHED BUNKHOUSE, UIG

Boutique bunkhouse and camping pods complete with stunning sea views, large wood-burning stove and comfortable, nicely designed rooms.

→ Uig, IV51 9YD, 07917 536820. Skyecowshed.co.uk
57.5817, -6.3577

DESIGNER SHEDS

33 THE BLACK SHED, DUNVEGAN

Architectural-award-winning modern self-catering lodge, situated on a working croft at the foot of Macleod's Table.

→ 2 Skinidin, Dunvegan, Isle of Skye, IV55 8ZS, 01470 521214. Blackshed.co.uk
57.4278, -6.6312

34 THE SHED, TOKAVAIG

Architect-designed house overlooking the small isles of Rùm and Canna and set amongst native woodland on the west coast of the Sleat peninsula, the 'garden of Skye', famous for its flora, fauna and dramatic scenery.

→ 4 Tokavaig, Teangue, IV44 8QL. Skyeshed.com
57.1342, -5.9651

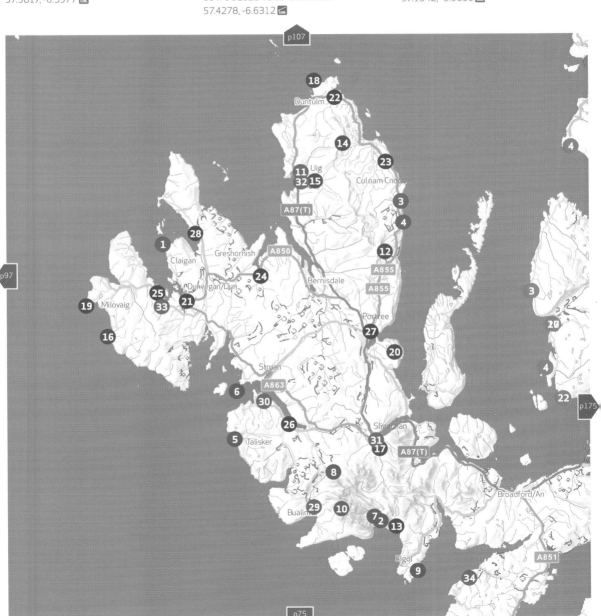

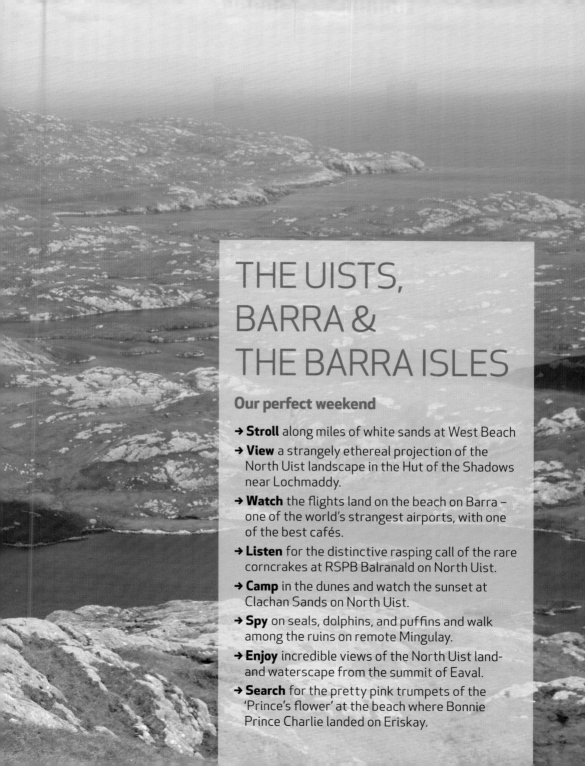

THE UISTS, BARRA & THE BARRA ISLES

Our perfect weekend

- → **Stroll** along miles of white sands at West Beach
- → **View** a strangely ethereal projection of the North Uist landscape in the Hut of the Shadows near Lochmaddy.
- → **Watch** the flights land on the beach on Barra – one of the world's strangest airports, with one of the best cafés.
- → **Listen** for the distinctive rasping call of the rare corncrakes at RSPB Balranald on North Uist.
- → **Camp** in the dunes and watch the sunset at Clachan Sands on North Uist.
- → **Spy** on seals, dolphins, and puffins and walk among the ruins on remote Mingulay.
- → **Enjoy** incredible views of the North Uist land- and waterscape from the summit of Eaval.
- → **Search** for the pretty pink trumpets of the 'Prince's flower' at the beach where Bonnie Prince Charlie landed on Eriskay.

The southern half of the Outer Hebrides is made up of a long chain of diverse islands. The Uists, which seem more water than land, are joined by a causeway, as is little Eriskay. Lying not far south of them, Barra and the Barra Isles are reached by ferry.

These beautiful remote isles are world famous for their spectacular beaches. Some are vast and stretch on for miles, like West Beach on Berneray and Tràigh Eais on Barra, and here you can take cover below high dunes and enjoy watching dramatic waves on stormy days. Others are more sheltered bays, like the Prince's Strand on Eriskay and the east beach on Vatersay, where you can enjoy picnics or wild swimming in the clear, luminescent water.

On North Uist the landscape of wild peat moors and cultivated crofts is a maze of innumerable trout-filled lochs and inlets – more than half the 'land' here is water. Further down the chain, South Uist is a rugged and mountainous island where long sea lochs indent the east coast. In the summer months there is an explosion of colourful wildflowers on the machair plains of these islands. Carpets of harebells, clovers and orchids bloom, and long coastal grasses grow despite often hostile weather conditions. If fauna rather than flora is what you seek, you will find an impressive variety of native and visiting birds both on- and offshore and at the RSPB Balranald nature reserve.

A 40-minute ferry journey south from Eriskay (the real *Whisky Galore* island) brings you to beautiful Barra, a popular island with a strong Hebridean character, where more than half of the population still speak Gaelic. Joined to its southern end by a causeway is the peaceful and remote isle of Vatersay, which is so deeply indented by the sea on both sides that only a narrow strip of land prevents it separating into two. Both islands, like the Uists, offer plenty of opportunities for wild camping or longer breaks in charming, traditional self-catering cottages. The 'long chain' is also a popular route with cyclists, who can stop overnight at many of the great hostels and campsites along the way.

The best time to visit is in May or June; this is before the midges arrive, when the machair is in bloom and you're most likely to have sunshine as you take in the glowing expanses of white sand and bright azure sea at some of the most wonderful beaches in Britain.

COAST & BEACHES

1 CLACHAN SANDS, N UIST

Tràigh Lingeigh and Tràigh Hòrnais are two beautiful beaches backed by large machair plains that come to life with an abundance of wildflowers during summer. Keep an eye out for the purple flowers and dark leaves of the Hebridean marsh orchid, found nowhere else in the world! There is a picnic area and informal camping at the south end of Tràigh Lingeigh beach (honesty box £10 per night).

→ Head N from Lochmaddy on A865 nearly 5 miles then turn R onto B893. After 1½ miles turn L onto minor road after HS6 5AY, signed Cladh a Clachainn/Clachan Sands Cemetery and beach access. Continue on road to park at cemetery and follow the rough track to the picnic area and beaches.

5 mins, 57.6719, -7.2464 ⛴🚶♿🏕⛺🎪

2 TRÀIGH EAR BEACH, N UIST

This large, curved sandy bay is a haven for a variety of birdlife. Continue on from the beach for impressive views at Àird a' Mhòrain, the 'headland of the bent-grass'.

→ Take A865 NW from Lochmaddy for 8½ miles, turn R at a red phone box (HS6 5BP) into the small village of Grenitote. Continue to a small picnic area and car park, then head along the track and onto the sandy bay at R. To reach Àird a' Mhòrain, follow the grassy headland at the far end of the beach.

10–60 mins, 57.6686, -7.3297 ⛰🏖

3 TRÀIGH IAR, N UIST

Stunning large crescent of pristine white sand and high dunes, which can be combined with a walk round Àird a' Mhòrain headland and Tràigh Ear bay (see 2) just over the dunes E. Can be rip currents here.

→ From Tràigh Ear parking (see 2) head along the track towards the beach but take a L when you can towards to the machair and dunes lying W; alternatively walk around the headland.

20–60 mins, 57.6673, -7.3454 🌊▽♿✿

4 COILLEAG A' PHRIONNSA, ERISKAY

Small, idyllic Eriskay has many claims to fame, including being the real *Whisky Galore!* island. The beautiful Coilleag a' Phrionnsa (Prince's Strand) is a lovely beach, great for both wild swimming and camping. Look out for the sea bindweed, known here as the 'Prince's flower' – local legend holds it has grown since Bonnie Prince Charlie arrived on the beach and dropped the seeds.

→ Access via causeway from S Uist, or Barra Ferry. Path to beach is between slipway and HS8 5JN; limited space to park off road.
2 mins, 57.0748, -7.3056 🏖️📷♿

5 WEST BEACH, BERNERAY

Ideal for long walks, this magnificent 3-mile, white sand beach is backed by high dunes and an impressive border of machair, home to an assortment of wildflowers in the summer months.

→ After crossing the causeway from North Uist, take the second L past the village of Borve (HS6 5BJ). Follow the minor road 1½ miles from the turning to informal car park by the fields. From here follow path towards coast. This is the S end of the beach, so follow sands N for as long as you wish. Return same way, or continue around the island in a loop back to the car park.
5–120 mins, 57.7099, -7.2210 🚶📷🏖️

6 TRÀIGH MHÒR AIRFIELD, BARRA

Barra Airport is the only airport in the world to use a beach runway for regular flights and has been voted both the world's most treacherous and its most scenic landing. Come and watch the small planes land and take off when the tide is out, or even better, fly from Glasgow yourself for truly magnificent views.

→ Turn N off the A888 at Northbay (350m W of HS9 5YQ) and follow single-track road for 2¼ miles. Space to park at small grassy area just beyond the airport buildings.
5 mins, 57.0239, -7.4495 🏞️

7 TRÀIGH EAIS, BARRA

This beautiful beach faces the full force of the Atlantic and has some of the highest sand dunes in Britain. A great place to wrap up and watch dramatic winter waves on a rough day.

→ As for Barra Airport (see 6), but from the road follow the faint trail across the grass opp the airport towards the dunes.
10 mins, 57.0265, -7.4546 🏞️📷

8 CLEAT BEACH, BARRA

Quiet white sand beach backed by the rocky summit of Ben Cleat.

→ 2 miles W from Northbay on A888, turn R onto road signed for Grithean and Cleit and continue to road end by the shore. Informal parking on grass, beach just beyond on the R.
2 mins, 57.0142, -7.5892 📷🐚🏖️

9 BÀGH BHATARSAIGH, VATERSAY

Sheltered bay of bright white sand and clear turquoise water on the small and peaceful island of Vatersay. Great spot for wild swimming and a summer barbeque or picnic below the dunes.

→ Cross the causeway at the south of Barra onto the island and follow minor road S approx 3 miles, dir HS9 5YU. There is informal parking on the grass to the L opp passing place and signed path to shipwreck monument.
5 mins, 56.9236, -7.5353 🏖️🐚🌊

WILDLIFE WONDERS

10 BALRANALD RSPB RESERVE, N UIST

Situated at the most westerly point of North Uist, this nature reserve is one of the best places in the country for wildlife. Amongst the sandy beaches, dunes, marshes, flower-rich machair and rocky foreshores you will find a variety of birds and interesting plants. Some highlights in summer are the visiting Arctic terns and corncrakes and the wild orchids and poppies growing in the machair.

→ 2¼ miles N of Bayhead on the A865, turn off dir Hougharry (HS6 5DL). After just under 1 mile take L signed visitor centre, to parking.
15 mins, 57.5969, -7.5224 🌿🏖️🏞️🌊

15

11 MINGULAY

Look out for dolphins and seals on your way to deserted Mingulay, home to some of the highest sea cliffs in Britain, a ruined village, and large colonies of puffins, razorbills and kittiwakes.

→ Boat trips from £50pp with Barra Fishing Charters, Caolis, Vatersay, HS9 5YL, 01871810679.

1 min, 56.8135, -7.6317 🚗🏕🏖🚌🚢

RUINS & SHELTERS

12 TOBHA MÒR, S UIST

This pretty village, called Homore or Howmore on maps and signs, is home to a collection of charming traditional thatched buildings and a hostel. With a wonderful mountain backdrop, sandy beach and the ruins of a castle on an island nearby, there is plenty to explore.

→ Head S from South Ford causeway 7 miles on A865. Tobha Mor is signed to R (HS5 5SH). Claim a basic bed at Howmore Hostel (white thatched cottage at end of road, see 23). The next turn N off the A865 leads to Loch an Eilein, with the island ruin of Caisteal Bheagram.

5 mins, 57.3026, -7.3854 🏔🚌🚢

13 HUT OF THE SHADOWS, N UIST

Curious camera obscura hidden inside a small stone tumulus. Enter to view the wonderful projection of the surrounding land and waterscape on the wall inside the chamber. Part of the Uist Sculpture Trail.

→ Parking at Lochmaddy Tourist Information Centre (HS6 5AA). From main street, turn R at junction signed for Uist Outdoor Centre, opp Morrison's local shop. Head down this road, taking third R on bend at Tigh Dear Hotel. Continue for ½ mile end of the track, then follow signed footpath over a suspension bridge. After the bridge turn R at the junction and continue R along causeway and shore of Loch nam Madadh where you will soon see the grass-roofed hut close to the shore on the R.

20 mins, 57.6099, -7.1535 🚌🚢

14 KISIMUL CASTLE, BARRA

Partially restored ruins of a medieval castle on a rocky islet in the sea at Castlebay (HS9 5UZ), reached by short boat trip. Small, simple, and leased to Historic Environment Scotland by the clan chief for £1 and a bottle of whisky a year.

→ Boat runs April–September (weather permitting), from pier in Castlebay.

5 mins, 56.9521, -7.4875 🚌🚢

15 BARPA LANGASS, N UIST

Remarkable Neolithic chambered cairn sitting prominently on the hill. Part of the structure has collapsed, but it is still possible to carefully climb inside one of the hidden chambers.

→ Head SW on the A867 from Lochmaddy for just over 5½ miles to reach the car park on L signed Barpa Langass, just before turn to HS6 5HA. There is a clear path uphill to the tumulus.

10 mins, 57.5705, -7.2915 🚲🚢✝

HILL WALKS

16 EAVAL, N UIST

The highest hill on North Uist is only 347m, but is surrounded almost entirely by water and the ascent is steep and pathless. Reach the summit however, and you are rewarded with outstanding views of the maze of lochans that dominates the surrounding wild land- and waterscape. Bring a map, because navigating between lochs is tricky, and check tide times.

→ From the A867 just E of Clachan, turn R onto minor road signed Loch Euphort. After 5 miles park at the road end after HS6 5EX. Head along track through gate to R of last

17

house following faint, boggy track E through gap in wall to reach stepping stones (may be covered at HT). Bear R around edge of Loch Obasaraigh to Eaval and make your way up.
4–6 hours, 57.5279, -7.1832

17 HEABHAL, BARRA

It's a short but very steep climb to the summit of the highest hill on Barra, with spectacular views, particularly towards Castlebay and the islands lying to the south. Look out on the hillside for the statue of the Madonna and child, known locally as Our Lady Star of the Sea. If you visit in early July, you may see the annual race from Castlebay to the summit and back.

→ Head NE for 1 mile on the A888 from Castlebay. There is parking on the R just beyond a modern white house, 400m after HS9 5UH. Cross the road and head into the moorland below the hill. There are several very faint paths leading to the summit.
40 mins, 56.9673, -7.4685

LOCAL FOOD

18 BARRA AIRPORT CAFÉ

Situated within the famous Barra Airport, this is as far as you can get from a typical airport café. Enjoy some great home cooking, coffee and wonderful cakes by the windows overlooking the beach runway.

→ Barra Airport, Ardmhor, HS9 5YD, 07855 143545. Hial.co.uk/barra-airport
57.0254, -7.4495

19 CAFÉ KISIMUL, BARRA

Family-run licensed restaurant specialising in a surprising mix of Indian and Italian cuisine and local seafood.

→ Main Street, Castlebay, HS9 5XD, 01871 810645. Cafekisimul.co.uk
56.9543, -7.4867

20 MACLEAN'S BAKERY, BENBECULA

Small independent bakery and butchery run by the Maclean brothers for over 15 years. Tasty traditional biscuits, pastries and meat from the onsite shop.

→ Uachdar, HS7 5LY, 01870 602659.
57.4803, -7.3329

21 HEBRIDEAN SMOKEHOUSE, N UIST

Delicious locally produced peat-smoked salmon and sea trout. Also an opportunity to watch the team preparing, smoking and slicing the fish in the shop's viewing gallery.

→ Clachan, HS6 5HD, 01876 580209. Hebrideansmokehouse.com
57.5550, -7.3396

22 THE DECK, BARRA

Outdoor café at the Hebridean Toffee Factory. Enjoy some mouthwatering tablet, home baking and wonderful views of Kisimul Castle and Vatersay.

→ Castlebay Factory, Castlebay, HS9 5XD, 01871 810898. Hebrideantoffeecompany.com
56.9550, -7.4897

CAMPING & HOSTELS

23 HOWMORE HOSTEL, S UIST

Popular hostel situated in the heart of the South Uist machair and close to both the beach and the highest hills on South Uist. No booking ahead, wardens visit daily.

→ Howmore, Tobha Mòr, HS8 5SH, 0845 2937373. Gatliff.org.uk
57.3012, -7.3732

24 THE TRACTOR SHED, N UIST

Cosy, contemporary turf-roofed camping huts and small bunkhouse with a fully

equipped communal kitchen and dining area, fire pit and peat-fired camping stoves. Open April–October.

➜ The Tractor Shed, Paible, HS6 5DZ, 0795 2163080. Northuistbunkhouse.co.uk
57.5816, -7.4406 🏕

25 BERNERAY HOSTEL

Basic mixed-dorm accommodation with camping possible by the dunes. Set in a wonderful location overlooking the Sound of Harris. Enjoy a cup of tea on the benches outside or by the coal-burning stove in the common room. No booking ahead, wardens visit daily.

➜ Berneray, North Uist HS6 5BQ, 0845 2937373. Gatliff.org.uk
57.7172, -7.1540 🏕

26 MOORCROFT HOLIDAYS, N UIST

Family-run summer campsite based on a working croft and overlooking a beautiful tidal bay. Also a small bunkhouse, 'Hobbit homes', a fully equipped campers kitchen and free wi-fi.

➜ 17 Carinish, HS6 5HN, 01876 580305. Moorcroftholidays.com
57.5182, -7.2825 🏕🏕

HEBRIDEAN COTTAGES

27 BORERAY COTTAGE, N UIST

Sweet, whitewashed highland cottage with thatched roof, yards from the beach and machair. Perfect island escape for two.

➜ 3 Clachan Sands, HS6 5AY, 01835 822277. Unique-cottages.co.uk
57.6590, -7.2456 🏕

28 NO. 1 ARDVEENISH, BARRA

Traditional red-roofed croft house nestled away in a quiet spot overlooking the water. Newly renovated modern interior. Handy for both Barra airport and Eriskay ferry.

➜ Ardveenish, North Bay, HS9 5YA, 07725 409080. Barraholidayhome.co.uk
57.0086, -7.4274 🏕

29 MONTY'S COTTAGE, N UIST

Cosy traditional thatched roof cottage with a multi-fuel stove. Tucked away in a secluded spot nearby beautiful beaches.

➜ Griminish, HS6 5DF, 01835 822 277. Unique-cottages.co.uk
57.6546, -7.4525 🏕🏕

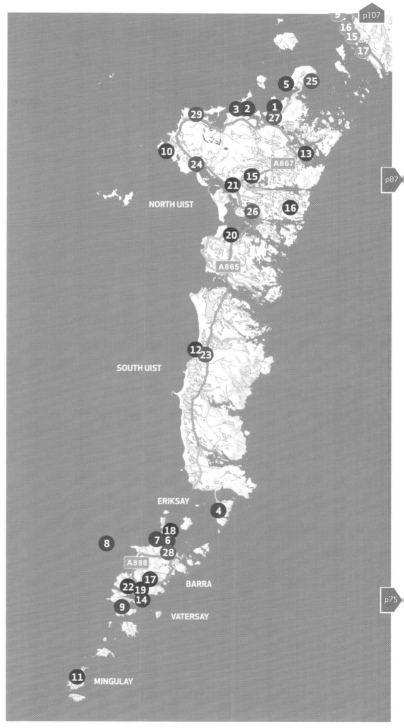

HARRIS, LEWIS & ST KILDA

Our perfect weekend

→ **Venture** to the historic and starkly beautiful archipelago of St Kilda to see vast seabird colonies and a deserted village.

→ **Indulge** in a dream island getaway at Scarista House on Harris, in the lap of luxury just a few minutes stroll from the beach.

→ **Drift** along the Golden Road of Harris, taking in the scenery and stopping off for local art and crafts.

→ **Treat** yourself to the fresh-baked goodies from the 'shack' at Croft 36 on Harris.

→ **Imagine** ancient life in the turf-roofed house at the site of Bosta Iron Age village on Bernera, Lewis.

→ **Unwind** at the tranquil Losgantir Beach, Harris.

→ **Experience** a night in a traditional Hebridean house at Gearrannan Blackhouse Village, Lewis.

→ **Watch** the sun setting over the sea from the majestic cliffs of Mangersta, Lewis.

A journey to the northernmost islands in the Outer Hebrides – Lewis and Harris and St Kilda – is a memorable experience at any time of year. These isolated, windswept and mostly treeless islands hold some of the most outstanding landscapes in the world.

Begin your Hebridean adventure by sailing to the principle island, Lewis and Harris. Commonly taken for two islands, it is in fact just one, but of two distinct characters. The northern part, Lewis, is largely a low-lying land of pool-mottled peat bogs, although it also contains Stornoway, the most populous town in the Hebrides and the centre of Gaelic culture and speech. The island is home to a lively working population with strong traditional and religious values. Many of the islanders belong to one of the five Presbyterian churches and you'll still find that almost all shops are closed on Sundays.

As you travel south into Harris there's a dramatic shift in the terrain. The landscapes suddenly become wild and rugged, the expanses of flat moorlands broken up by dark mountains and surrounded by spectacular beaches. A great place to experience all of these is at Losgaintir, where miles of pristine white sand and glassy azure-green water contrast with more distant views of the forbidding North Harris mountains.

Both areas are full of ancient treasures: step inside the magically reconstructed Iron Age house at Bosta or spend the night in one of the traditional blackhouses at Gearrannan. You can swim here before watching the sun set over the bay where women and children would have waited anxiously for their men to return from sea on small fishing boats.

If you visit between April and September and the weather is on your side, you might also make the long, rough boat journey to the islands on 'the edge of the world', the exceptionally isolated archipelago of St Kilda. These islands, lying over 100 miles west of the mainland, form one of a very few World Heritage Sites to hold status for both natural and cultural merits. They have a truly fascinating history and boast breathtakingly dramatic scenery, with a series of staggering, dark sea stacks scattered in the sea around towering cliffs. These host puffins, petrels and gannets, while rare-breed sheep descended from ancient flocks survive on the islands. You might have to make a few attempts to get there, but visiting these islands is a truly powerful experience and one you will never forget.

3

BEACHES

1 TRÀIGH MHÒR, LEWIS

Amongst the finest beaches in Lewis, Tràigh Mhòr is a long, straight stretch of pale golden sand backed by dunes. The dramatic cliff of Rubha Tholastaidh also known as Tolsta Head projects out from the southern end and it's a good place to spot minke whales or basking sharks. Beyond the northern end is the strange Bridge to Nowhere, a substantial structure from about 1920 for a road that was never completed.

→ Follow the B895 N through Tolsta/Bail' Ùr Tholastaidh to the car park signed R ½ mile after HS2 0NN. Take footpath to the beach; for the bridge follow the road another mile. For Tolsta Head (58.3449, -6.1670), leave the Tràigh Mhòr car park heading S on the B895 and take the junciton leading E signed Cuimhneachain Cogaidh/War Memorial and Slighe mun Aird/Tolsta Head Route, then R at T junction for Tolsta Head Route and L after 300m, continuing to park at the road end (HS2 0NT). Walk through the gate following the coastline path to easternmost point; 60 mins.
10 mins, 58.3592, -6.2044 🚶🏊⛱

2 BHALTOS BEACHES, LEWIS

A magnificent collection of white beaches in the community owned village of Bhaltos. Tràigh na Clibhe beach is perhaps the most spectacular of them all; a vast bay of white sand backed by steep rocky headland. East lies Tràigh na Beirigh, a mile long arc of white shell sand backed by incredible machair.

→ Heading NW on the B8011, take junction leading N signposted Cnip. Continue on road NW until a parallel slip road leads N towards a car park (HS2 9HP) for Tràigh na Clibhe. Tràigh na Beirigh can be accessed by continuing E past Bhaltos and heading briefly SW, parking at the campsite (HS2 9HS) 58.2179, -6.9368.
5 mins, 58.2212, -6.9672

3 ARDROIL BEACH, LEWIS

Also called Uig Sands or Tràigh Uige, this is one of the most unusual beach landscapes in the country – an astonishingly huge expanse of flat sand surrounded by dunes and rolling hills. Best viewed from the southern end.

→ Heading W on the B8011 towards Ardroil, take exit heading N signposted for Tràigh Eadar/Ardroil Beach just after HS2 9EU. Park at road end (campsite and toilets see 19). Continue through gate to the beach by foot.
10 mins, 58.1873, -7.0242 🚶🏊⛱⛺

1

9

4 CRABHADAIL BEACH, LEWIS

This secluded peaceful bay of bright sand is a good walk from the equally beautiful beach at Hushinish/Huisinis. The route passes under dramatic cliffs and boasts impressive views of the uninhabited island of Scarp. Look for the ridges of raised 'lazy beds', which improved crop yields when the area was farmed.

→ From the A859 at the S of Lewis, take the B887 signed Huisinis for 14 miles to the beach car park by the toilets (HS3 3AY). Follow path that leads NE from here, heading along the cliffs and then hugging the S shore of Loch na Cleabhaig. Shortly after a passing a lone cottage, Crabhadail is just over the rise.

90 mins, 58.0088, -7.0525 🐾🌊⚓🏊

5 LOSGAINTIR BEACH, HARRIS

Often rated one of UK's top ten beaches by visitors, Losgaintir (Luskentyre) lives up to the accolade. The northern part, Tràigh Rosamol, is particularly special – a long stretch of white sand sweeping down to turquoise waters from a mountainous backdrop.

→ On the A859 in the southern peninsula, take the turn signed Losgaintir and park at the car park at the end of the road after HS3 3HL. Walk through the dunes to the N shore.

5 mins, 57.8914, -6.9565 🚶🐾♨️🏕️🌊

COAST & CLIFFS

6 ST KILDA

Today dramatic St Kilda is home mostly to an abundance of wildlife, particularly seabirds, and the only humans are at a radar station in the bay, plus some scientists and restoration workers in the summer. But incredibly, Hirta was inhabited from the Late Stone Age until 1930, when the last 36 inhabitants were evacuated; much of the deserted village still stands in the bay. On the western cliffs look for the 'portal' of the Mistress Stone at Ruabhal or the pinnacle of the Lovers' Stone at Geodha na Bà Glaise, once the sites of young men's agility dares. On the sea voyage you will pass rarely visited Boreray (57.8675, -8.4910), the most isolated part of the archipelago and the smallest Scottish island to have a summit over 300m. Spectacular sea cliffs are unforgettable seen from below as birds circle over the tops. A truly unique piece of Scotland.

→ Kilda Cruises (4 hrs) leave most days' midweek (Apr–Sept) from Leverburgh, South Harris, 01859 502060. Take a day trip or camp at the NTS site (see 22).

1 day, 57.8126, -8.5692 ❓🐾🌊✈️⚓🏊🌲🗻🔻

7 MANGERSTA CLIFFS, LEWIS

Majestic cliffs and wild Atlantic views. A truly magical place, especially at 'golden hour', as the sun sets on the horizon. Keep an eye out for a remarkable private shelter that's nestled into the cliffs at the S end of the kidney-shaped headland. This was lovingly hand built by a local family, all adding to the unique appeal of this place.

→ Follow the B8011 N and then as minor road W past turning signed Aird Uig, pass by bay of Tràigh Ùige on R and follow signs for Mangarstadh/Mangersta past HS2 9EY, parking at road end. Retrace steps on foot for 100m, heading through gate up on L, following the faint path heading NW towards the cliffs.

30 mins, 58.1738, -7.1008 🌊📷

8 GOLDEN ROAD, HARRIS

Winding through the glorious scenery of the east coast of Harris is the Golden Road, beginning at Meavag and ending at Grosebay/Greosabagh or Rodel/Roghadal, depending on whom you ask. Apparently the single-track road is jokingly named for its cost, but it should be so-called for the landscape. This is a sublime drive or cycle through bays, lochans and rocky outcrops, with the chance to visit local tweed and craft shops along the way.

→ On A859 in South Harris, take turn (dir HS3 3DZ) signed 'The Golden Road' and begin. If sunny, starting from Grosebay (HS3 3EF) or Rodel (S of HS5 3TW) will put the sun behind you. 60 mins, 57.8449, -6.7600 🎿

9 CEAPABHAL, HARRIS

A steep ascent up Ceapabhal is rewarded with panoramic views of the shores of South Harris and, on a clear day, St. Kilda. You might detour to visit the medieval chapel on the machair at Rubha an Teampaill, where you can also find cup marks on nearby rocks and the foundations of an Iron Age tower.

→ On the A859, take turning signed An Taobh Tuath/Northton NW of Leverburgh. Car park at (HS3 3JA) near the road end. Walk NW towards Ceapabhal. Pick up path from the road end and take L fork towards the dunes. Where path forks, the L through a gate leads to the chapel, visible ahead (adding 30 mins). The R through another gate leads uphill to the summit. 90 mins, 57.8179, -7.1004 🔲🖼️✝🚲

10 EILEAN GLAS LIGHTHOUSE, HARRIS

One of the first four lighthouses built in Scotland, Eilean Glas has shone since 1789, although the original construction was replaced in 1824. The red-and-white-banded

tower sits on the eastern shores of Scalpay, now joined by a bridge to the Isle of Harris.

→ After crossing the bridge to Scalpay follow road S which soon leads SE (HS4 3YF). Bypass the sign for Aird Aghanais and head to the SE point at Kennavay. Park at road end and walk back 60m to pick up faint path on E of road, opp storage building. The path, with some marker posts, heads back S and continues to lighthouse. 60 mins, 57.8573, -6.6428 🏔️

SACRED & ANCIENT

11 CALLANISH, LEWIS

One of the most significant megalithic sites in Britain, the Callanish stones date back to 2900–2600BC, in the late Neolithic. Most spectacular is the main group, Callanish I, arranged in a cross with a circle at the heart of it, and a chambered tomb within that. Two simpler circles are easily reached nearby.

→ On A858 heading NW from Garynahine, take L signed Ionad Tursachan Chalanais and follow signs for Callanish. Park at visitor centre (past turning to HS2 9DY). Other circles along signed paths a little back down A858 – Callanish II is at 58.1942, -6.7288, Callanish III at 58.1955, -6.7242, visible from the road. 30 mins, 58.1975, -6.7451 🚲🍴🏔️

12 BOSTA IRON AGE VILLAGE, HARRIS

In 1993 severe gales revealed the remains of several Iron Age houses by the beach, dating back to 400AD. After the site was explored and smaller finds removed, it was covered again, but on empty ground nearby a careful reconstruction of a house was built. Open weekdays May–Sept, but subject to change.

→ Cross onto Great Bernera on B8058 and continue N all the way eventually to signs for Tràigh Bostadh, past the turning to HS2 9LZ. Car park at road end, walk beyond cemetery. 10 mins, 58.2554, -6.8818 🚲🧍🏔️

WILDLIFE WONDERS

13 EAGLE OBSERVATORY, HARRIS

Harris is home to one of the highest densities of breeding golden eagle pairs in Europe, and this observatory is located in the heart of their territory. A walk through a marvellous glen leads to the wooden shelter, perfectly placed for watching their activity. Visit on a bright and breezy day, and bring binoculars. In autumn rutting deer may also be seen, and in winter sea eagles visit.

→ Leave the A859, take the B887 signposted for Huisinis. Park at N end of Loch Mhiabhaig (car park ½ mile E of HS3 3AW). Follow track

1½ miles N up the glen and over the bridge.
30 mins, 57.9735, -6.9060 🏊🚣

LOCAL FOOD & SEAFOOD

14 AUBERGE CARNISH, LEWIS

A menu rooted in traditional French cuisine, fused with local produce. Sited almost on the shore of Ardroil Beach (see 3), it combines fine dining with a stunning location.

➜ Uig, HS2 9EX, 01851 672459.
Aubergecarnish.co.uk
58.1765, -7.0487 🍴🛏

15 CROFT 36, HARRIS

A charming self-service 'shack' croft shop run by a local family. Baked goods, vegetables and seafood with an honesty box for payment. A catering business delivers meals to holidays homes and campsites.

➜ 36 Northton, HS3 3JA, 01859 520779.
Croft36.com
57.7974, -7.0661 🍴

16 TEMPLE CAFÉ, HARRIS

What used to be the MacGillivray Centre – built in celebration of the famous naturalist and ornithologist who grew up here – is now a beautiful little café with incredible views overlooking the Sound of Harris, serving freshly made food. Walls of stone and a wooden ceiling give it an almost temple like feel (hence the name). Closed in winter.

➜ 41 Northton, HS3 3JA, 07876 340416.
Facebook.com/TheTempleCafe
57.8000, -7.0700 🍴🛏

17 THE ANCHORAGE, HARRIS

Specialising in locally caught seafood landed at the pier right outside, the restaurant at The Anchorage has a great reputation and splendid views of the Sound of Harris. Informal and frequently busy, the restaurant is closed in winter, but the convivial bar stays open, with regular live music.

➜ Leverburgh, HS5 3UB, 01859 520225.
57.7668, -7.0240 🍴

BUNKHOUSES & CAMPING

18 GEARRANNAN BLACKHOUSE VILLAGE

A unique self-catering and hostel on the Atlantic coast of Lewis. This croft village (also called Garenin) uses traditional stone houses modernised inside to provide a historic setting with comfort. Open all year. Or simply to visit the living museum on site.

➜ 5a Gearrannan, Carloway, Lewis, HS2 9AL, 01851 643416. Gearrannan.com
58.2965, -6.7927 🛏

19 UIG/ARDROIL CAMPSITE, LEWIS

Nestled in the sandy dunes of the enormous bay of Ardroil (see 3) is this beach campsite, so low key it has no firm name. A wild spot with basic facilities; toilet and shower, no booking, pay at the house.

➜ 6 Ardoil, Timsgearraidh, Isle of Lewis, HS2 9EU, 01851 672248.
58.1847, -7.0259 ⛺

20 NO 5 DRINISHADER, HARRIS

A log fire and comforting atmosphere makes this self-catering hostel a popular stopover along the Golden Road (see 8). Normally open all year, but call ahead in winter/spring. Also bikes and kayaks to hire.

➜ No 5, Drinishader, HS3 3DX, 01859 511255. Number5.biz
57.8530, -6.7699 🛏

21 LIKISTO BLACKHOUSE CAMPING

A remote, quirky campsite. As well as camping, it offers two 2-person yurts with futons, wood burners and cooking stoves. A

blackhouse on site allows for communal cooking. Washrooms are in converted byres.

→ 1 Likisto, HS3 3EL, Harris 01859 530485. 57.8316, -6.8574 🖼

22 NTS CAMPSITE, ST KILDA
Those seeking the ultimate in off-grid isolation can stay on Hirta, St Kilda (see 6) for up to five nights. The tiny NTS campsite only accommodates six and must be booked in advance. Showers and toilets, but no phones or shop. Bring what you need plus three days extra in case of bad weather.

→ NTS, 01463 732645, or packaged trips with Go to St Kilda, 07789 914144. 57.8122, -8.5656 ▲▼

COTTAGES & HOTELS

23 AMHUINNSUIDHE CASTLE, HARRIS
This grand hideaway offers remarkable accommodation and delicious meals set in a traditional Hebridean sporting estate, popular for deer stalking and fishing.

→ HS3 3AS, 01859 560200. Amhuinnsuidhe.com 57.9614, -6.9906 🖼

24 BLACKHOUSE AT BORVEMOR COTTAGES

A romantic self-catering black house on the coast of Southern Harris. Surrounded by machair, 200m from the beach, the house is beautifully located with fine views out to sea and includes exclusive use of an outdoor hot tub. Suitable for a couple and one child.

→ Scarista, Isle of Harris HS3 3HX, 01859 550222. Borvemorcottages.co.uk/blackhouse 57.7887, -7.0103

25 SCARISTA HOUSE, HARRIS

This remote hotel is one of the most beautiful places to stay in the country, overlooking a vast golden beach and backed by heather-coated hills. The former manse provides B&B, restaurant and a large self-catering cottage.

→ Sgarasta Bheag, HS3 3HX, 01859 550238. Scaristahouse.com 57.8248, -7.0413

26 LIOSBEAG COTTAGE, LEWIS

This open-plan timber building has all the modern comforts and a woodburner. It sits just 200m from a pair of lovely sandy coves, and the large windows and outdoor sitting area make the most of the location.

→ Valtos, HS2 9HR, 07785 723108. Unique-cottages.co.uk 58.2243, -6.9511

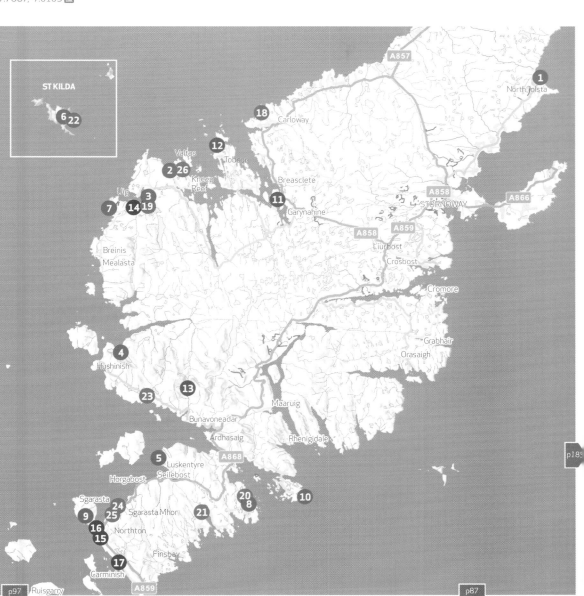

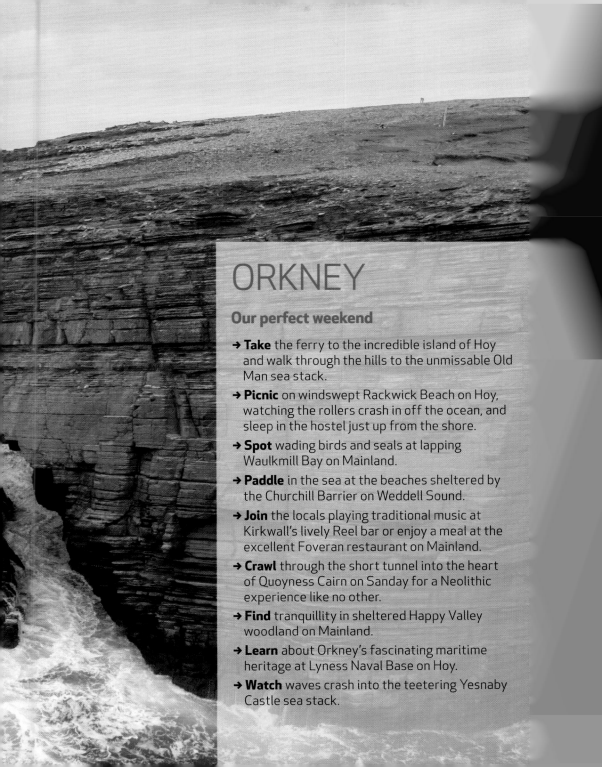

ORKNEY

Our perfect weekend

→ **Take** the ferry to the incredible island of Hoy and walk through the hills to the unmissable Old Man sea stack.

→ **Picnic** on windswept Rackwick Beach on Hoy, watching the rollers crash in off the ocean, and sleep in the hostel just up from the shore.

→ **Spot** wading birds and seals at lapping Waulkmill Bay on Mainland.

→ **Paddle** in the sea at the beaches sheltered by the Churchill Barrier on Weddell Sound.

→ **Join** the locals playing traditional music at Kirkwall's lively Reel bar or enjoy a meal at the excellent Foveran restaurant on Mainland.

→ **Crawl** through the short tunnel into the heart of Quoyness Cairn on Sanday for a Neolithic experience like no other.

→ **Find** tranquillity in sheltered Happy Valley woodland on Mainland.

→ **Learn** about Orkney's fascinating maritime heritage at Lyness Naval Base on Hoy.

→ **Watch** waves crash into the teetering Yesnaby Castle sea stack.

Orkney is a confusing explosion of islands, each with their own personality. It is often unfairly lumped in with Shetland as the 'north isles', but these varied islands have their own rich and fascinating history that informs their character, landscape and archaeology. Orkney lies in sight of the mainland but feels more unique than its geographical closeness to Scotland suggests, perhaps because the Pentland Firth, the body of water one needs to cross to reach Orkney, is notoriously rough and wild.

Though Orkney is a group of islands, many are joined by man-made Churchill barriers. These causeways were built during the Second World War to defend and enclose the naval base at Scapa Flow, the expanse of water in the centre of the island group. The half-submerged block ships that protected the waters before the barriers were built can also still be seen, and it was here that the crews of the impounded German fleet scuttled their ships in 1919 rather than see them shared out among the victors of the First World War. There is world-famous diving around the wrecks, and fascinating maritime history to immerse yourself in, from sad tales of ships lost at sea recorded in Longhope lifeboat station to discovering Orkney's proud Royal Naval heritage.

The land is a paradise for lovers of ruins and archaeology too, and a Neolithic World Heritage Site. There are amazing examples of ancient burial cairns, some of the finest in Europe. The most famous is Maes Howe, dating back to 2800BC, but Quoyness Cairn is similarly fascinating, and much quieter. The most interesting and exceptional landscape is on Hoy, which features larger hills, several steep valleys and the famous Old Man, a withered sandstone sea stack which defiantly stares down the turbulent sea.

Orkney is reached via Scrabster, Gils Bay, John O'Groats and Aberdeen on the ferry that continues through the night to Shetland. There are also flights from Glasgow, Edinburgh, Aberdeen, Inverness and Shetland. Once on Orkney many of the islands are connected by the Churchill barriers, making getting around quick and efficient, and ferries serve the outlying islands.

CLIFFS & SEA STACKS

1 THE OLD MAN OF HOY

One of the principle attractions of the
Orkney Islands, and with good reason. This
towering 137m sandstone sea stack faces
proudly out to sea, staring down the crashing
waves with defiance. Much photographed
and filmed, it is nonetheless awe-inspiring to
visit, and nothing is quite like the impression
it makes at first hand. The Old Man is a big
part of Scottish climbing history, and on a
good day climbers can be seen ascending the
stepped sandstone ledges.

→ From the B9047 just SE of KW16 3NJ take
the road signed Rackwick and follow past the
Dwarfie Stane (see 16) to the rough car park in
the centre of Rackwick Bay; there is space for
a few tents here, and campervans can stay for
a week. The Old Man walk is well signed from
here, heading towards the sea on a good track.
Follow the excellent path around the headland,
and the Old Man comes in to view
90 mins, 58.8864, -3.4307

2 BROUGH OF BIGGING, MAINLAND

Yesnaby is a wild place. Blasted by easterly
winds and ravaged by the sea, the cliffs have
eroded to form magnificent natural arches
and teetering sea stacks. The passage at the
Brough of Bigging is a powerful example:
watch the sea funnel and crash through the
natural arch, and even catch an interesting
glimpse of the distant Old Man of Hoy (see 1)
to the south. The remains of walls here are
taken by some for a promontory fort; better
documented are the several old military
fortifications at the road end in to Yesnaby.

→ Take turning signed Yesnaby from B9056
S of KW16 3LP to car park at end. Facing the
sea, head L and walk round the inlet to Brough
of Bigging.
10 mins, 59.0214, -3.3622

3 YESNABY CASTLE, MAINLAND

South along the cliffs from the Brough of
Bigging (see 2), Yesnaby Castle is a crazy
sea stack, teetering impossibly with a hole
through in its base. Look out for abseil ropes
from its summit, and imagine having to swim
out to the stack, as Joe Brown did in 1967
when he was the first to climb it.

→ Start from the car park as for Brough of
Biggin (see 2). Simply head S along the cliff
top, following a well-worn in path about ½
mile. The castle is unmissable, several inlets
along the coast.
15 mins, 59.0181, -3.3620

4 SKIBA GEO, MAINLAND

A geo is an eroded cleft in a cliff – there are
a great many in these isles. This one, also
called Skipi Geo, is a great example, and you
can clearly see where the sea has eroded the
rock to leave dumpy sea stacks and slanted
rock formations. This easy walk takes in
an interesting stretch of coastline and a
picturesque fisherman's hut. Part of a whale
skull fixed atop a jawbone stands on the cliff,
possibly as a navigation aid – all that remains
of a whale that beached here in the 1870s.

→ Park as for Brough of Birsay (see 14) and
head R along the cliff top, signed for Skiba
Geo. Follow the cliff top for a short distance
till the fisherman's bothy is reached, just
beyond the dumpy sea stack.
15 mins, 59.1351, -3.3113

5 HERSTON HEAD, SOUTH RONALDSAY

Though smaller than others in Orkney, this
quiet and seldom-visited stretch of coast is
an excellent place to watch the sun go down
over Hoy. The nearby hamlet of Herston is
an interesting place as well, its picturesque
houses with perfect little gardens arranged
along the sea front, and there are the
remains of an anti-aircraft battery atop the
hill.

→ Starting from the end of the minor road that passes through Herston (along seafront beyond KW17 2RH), walk round the edge of the field and cross a fence to access the cliff top. From here simply follow the coast round as far as you wish.

20 mins, 58.8060, -3.0217 🐦❓🏞🗺

BEACHES & BAYS

6 RACKWICK BAY, HOY

Absolutely stunning bay with giant cliffs, a beach of sand and great rounded boulders, and original croft houses. Reminiscent of the coast of Iceland, this is an incredible place to watch the turbulent sea interact with a mountainous landscape. It is also the starting point to visit the famous Old Man of Hoy (see 1). Not to be missed.

→ Starting from the car park for the Old Man of Hoy (see 1), head L along the road that leads to the beach.

10 mins, 58.8696, -3.3837 🏞🚻

7 BAY OF CREEKLAND, HOY

This pretty little bay has great views over to Graemsay and the bonus of an excellent little café above the dunes. A great place to spend the day relaxing.

→ Park at the Beneth'ill Café 350m from Moaness Pier, cross the road and explore the pretty bay.

2 mins, 58.9184, -3.3242 🏞🏊🍴🚻

8 SANDS OF EVIE, MAINLAND

This gentle sandy beach is a great place for a picnic. Combine it with a visit to the nearby Broch of Gurness, the well-preserved remains of an Iron Age tower and settlement.

→ Broch of Gurness is signed off A966 along minor road past KW17 2NH. Large car park at end and then for Broch walk back to beach. Also limited layby parking above beach.

2 mins, 59.1201, -3.0890 🐦🏊🐟🏊

9 WAULKMILL BAY, MAINLAND

Beautifully gentle lapping bay, set in the middle of an RSPB reserve. A great place to paddle and observe wading birds.

→ Turn S off A964 550m W of KW17 2RA for layby opp public toilets (limited parking). Take the steps down to the bay and wander along the beach; it is much more extensive at low tide.

5 mins, 58.9405, -3.0800 ❓🏞🚗🏊

NAVAL & MARITIME

10 LYNESS NAVAL BASE, HOY

The naval base on the shores of Scapa Flow was a hugely important base for the north Atlantic and is central to the recent history of Orkney. It was here that 52 of the 74 interned German battleships were scuttled by their crews in 1919; seven remain as diving sites (permit required). There are gun emplacements, interesting old naval buildings and an excellent free museum.

→ Lyness Naval Base, Lyness, Stromness, K16 3NT, 01856 791300. Orkney.gov.uk

2 mins, 58.8337, -3.1951 🚗🍴

11 BIRSAY LIGHTHOUSE, MAINLAND

On the tidal island of Birsay (see 14) stands a distinctive white lighthouse. Built in 1925, its unique castellated design might reflect Orkney's role in the First World War. It is one of the last three to be erected by the Stevenson family, responsible for nearly 100 Scottish lighthouses over three generations. Since 2002 it has been powered by solar cells and wind turbines.

→ As for Brough of Birsay (see 14), walk on past the ruins to the far side of the island.

5 mins, 59.1367, -3.3388 🚶🔽🐦❓🌊🐚✝

12 LONGHOPE LIFEBOAT MUSEUM, HOY

The Longhope lifeboat is responsible for the Pentland Firth, one of the most treacherous seas in the British Isles. The new vessel operates from across the bay, but the traditional boat has been lovingly kept and the 'shed' transformed into a museum that preserves the history of the lifeboats and crew of the area. This touching museum is a must to understand any seafaring island community.

→ Signed from B9047 at the causeway SE of KW16 3NZ.

1 min, 58.7794, -3.2283 🚇

SACRED & ANCIENT

13 HEART OF NEOLITHIC ORKNEY

Four Neolithic sites on the mainland carry this World Heritage status. The incredible chambered cairn of Maes Howe (59.0487, -3.3416) and the coastal settlement of Skara Brae (59.0487, -3.3416) are very popular, which lessens the atmosphere, but are nonetheless rightly celebrated. Between them lie the towering circles of the Ring of Brodgar (59.0015, -3.2295) and the Stones of Stenness (58.9941, -3.2077), plus several other remains.

→ Start at the Maes Howe visitor centre car park on the A965 just S of turning to KW16 3HH. Follow the B9055 and then B9056 NW from here to Skara Brae visitor centre (KW16 3LR). The stone circles, with layby parking, are visible from the road on the way.

5 mins, 59.0487, -3.3416 🚇🚇✝🚇

14 BROUGH OF BIRSAY, ORKNEY

The tidal island of Birsay is connected to the mainland via a causeway, although it can only be reached at low tide. At high tide the crossing is submerged, cutting off the island completely. The extensive ruins on the isle range from a 6th-century monastic settlement through a Pictish fortress and Viking farmsteads to a 12th-century church that remained a pilgrimage site until the Reformation. Also a lighthouse (see 11).

→ Accessible only at low tide, so plan ahead. From the A966 just N of KW17 2LX take the minor road W and N along the bay to park at the end. Head down to the beach and out across the concrete causeway.

5 mins, 59.1367, -3.3306 🚇🔽🚇🚇❓🚇🚇🚇✝

15 QUOYNESS CAIRN, SANDAY

Avoid the crowds at the most popular Neolithic Orkney sites (see 13) and have a more original Neolithic experience, by heading to Sanday. This 5000-year-old chambered burial cairn is excellently preserved, and is an atmospheric place to quite literally crawl inside history.

→ From corner on B9069 just S of KW17 2BL follow rough track to parking area at end, then head S along the coast on foot.

20 mins, 59.2254, -2.5681 ✝🚇🚇🚇🚇

16 DWARFIE STANE, HOY

Lying on the south side of the deep glen that carves its way across Hoy, the Dwarfie Stane is a giant glacial erratic (an unusual rock slab) deposited in the last glaciation. Extraordinarily, and uniquely in Britain, there is a substantial chamber cut into it. Opinion differs on its use, but it is generally regarded as a Neolithic tomb, dated some 500 years before the Great Pyramid at Giza was built, and it features heavily in the mythology of the islands.

→ On the road to the Old Man of Hoy (see 1) there is a layby. Follow the path to the obvious boulder a short distance beyond.

5 mins, 58.8844, -3.3143 🚇🚇✝🚇🚇

WALKS & WOODS

17 BINSCARTH WOOD, MAINLAND

Mostly either barren or used as arable farmland, Orkney does have a few woods. Binscarth is lovely, a peaceful haven if the desolate seascapes get too much. Also home to much of Orkney's birdlife.

→ Start from the W end of Finstown (KW17 2EL), and walk W along the main road out of town. Go through a kissing gate R, and follow path through the valley to the trees ahead. Pass through another kissing gate to enter the forest.

10 mins, 59.0086, -3.1303 🌳📷

18 HAPPY VALLEY, MAINLAND

Happy Valley is a beautiful and unusual woodland garden created over 50 years from bare land by local man Edwin Harold, and now kept up by the council and volunteers. Waterfalls, bridges, steps and benches make it an enchanting woodland walk. Woodland of any sort is unusual in these isles, so this oasis of tranquillity is well worth a visit.

→ There is a small amount of parking not far beyond the junction in Bigswell before you enter Stenness heading W (58.9774, -3.1721). The trees (a rare sight in Orkney) are visible

from this road. Simply head into the trees and explore on several trails.

Time variable, 58.9768, -3.1726 🌳📷♻️🥾

19 WEE FEA, HOY

The Wee Fea is a great viewpoint to get a sense of the often-confusing island topography of Orkney, and to see how all the islands fit in with one another. This gentle walk heads uphill past an attractive wood, and onto the hillside overlooking some derelict naval communication buildings.

→ Signed from the Hoy Hotel (KW16 3NT), uphill past the L side of the hotel. Follow this road as it passes on the R of a wood, and then bends L past the old naval buildings. A brilliant panoramic view S and picnic tables beyond.

25 mins, 58.8302, -3.2267 📷♿️

20 SANDY LOCH TO RACKWICK, HOY

Take a short stroll to a peaceful little reservoir or an excellent longer hike through the glens to Rackwick, passing Berriedale Wood, the most northerly native woodland. Watch out for rain goose (red-throated divers) and bonxies (great skuas) at the loch.

→ From Moaness Pier, head W past turning to KW16 3NJ. About ¾ mile later road bends right, pull off for parking and a RSPB sign.

Follow the track for a few minutes until Sandy Loch is reached. Keep following the clear path SW for Rackwick; in summer you should be able to catch a minibus service back.

5–120 mins, 58.9075, -3.3568

21 CHURCHILL BARRIER NO 3, WEDDELL SOUND

The islands of South Ronaldsay are connected to the Mainland by Churchill Barriers, causeways built to defend the naval base at Scapa Flow. Originally 'block ships' were sunk to hinder entrance to the bay, and these can be seen lying half-submerged from the pretty beach and dunes that have built up against the barriers.

→ Park either end of the barrier linking Glimps Holm to Burray (N of KW17 2SY); beaches have built up on both sides, and both have easy roadside access.

2 mins, 58.8727, -2.9149

LOCAL FOOD

22 BENETH'ILL CAFÉ, HOY

A welcome rest spot in a quiet area of Hoy, this friendly café overlooks the pretty Bay of Creekland.

→ Hoy, Stromness, KW16 3NJ, 01856 79119. 58.9161, -3.3190

23 BIRSAY BAY TEAROOM, ORKNEY

Modern and refreshing tea room tucked away at the end of Birsay in a great elevated position overlooking the Brough of Birsay. Finalist in Orkney Food and Scottish Baking awards in 2016.

→ Birsay, KW17 2LX, 01856 721 399. 59.1259, -3.3157

24 THE FOVERAN, ORKNEY

Stunning and popular Michelin-listed restaurant showcasing the very best of local Orcadian produce. Often busy, so call ahead.

→ St Ola, KW15 1SF, 01856 872 389. 58.9552, -3.0078

BARS & PUBS

25 THE REEL, ORKNEY

Lively and welcoming traditional and occasional jazz music venue in Kirkwall. Show up in the evening and you might even join in.

→ 6 Broad Street, Kirkwall, KW15 1NX, 01856 871000. Wrigleyandthereel.com 58.9820, -2.9595

SLEEP WILD

26 KIRKWALL YOUTH HOSTEL, ORKNEY

Though visually unassuming from the outside, this excellent hostel is a great budget base from which to explore. The staff are incredibly friendly and knowledgeable about all aspects of Orkney and have great recommendations about things to see or do.

→ Old Scapa Road, Kirkwall, KW15 1BB, 01856 872243. Syha.org.uk 58.9750, -2.9686

27 WHEEMS FARM, S RONALDSAY

Wheems is a small organic farm producing fruit, vegetables and eggs for the local market. They have pitches for up to 20 tents, cosy wooden pod-like bothies and a yurt, on a lane to a sandy beach.

→ Wheems/Weemys, Eastside, South Ronaldsay, KW17 2TJ, 01856 831556. 58.8085, -2.9255

28 RACKWICK OUTDOOR CENTRE, HOY

Small hostel situated at Rackwick. Ideally placed to explore the rugged wonders of Hoy, particularly the Old Man. Open Apr–Sept.

→ Rackwick, KW16 3NJ, 01856 873535 Ext. 2901. Stromnesscs@orkney.gov.uk 58.8774, -3.3898

29 CANTICK HEAD COTTAGES, HOY

These whitewashed cottages were homes for the lighthouse keepers in the days before automatic lights. They now provide romantic and interesting accommodation next to a fully working lighthouse.

→ Longhope, Hoy, KW16 3PQ, 07810 414753. 58.7872, -3.1312

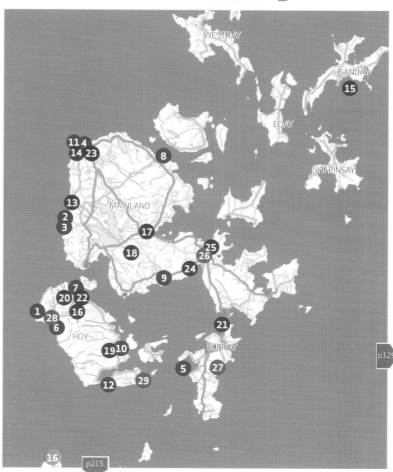

p129

p215

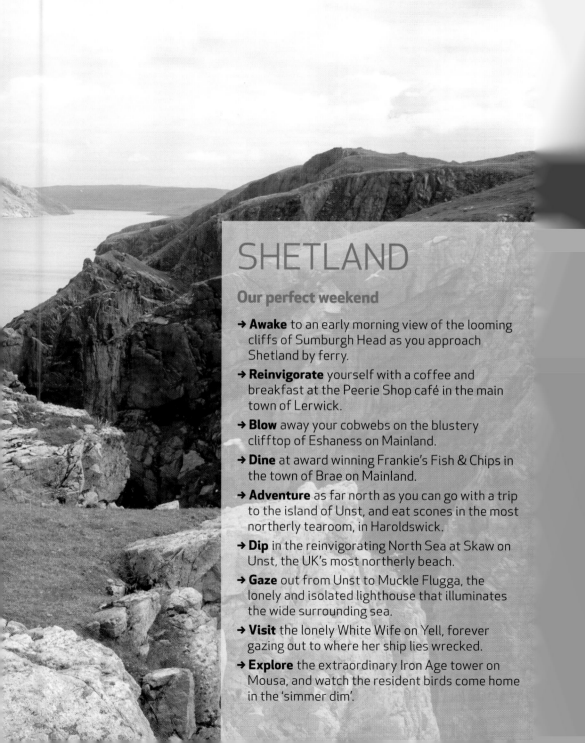

SHETLAND

Our perfect weekend

→ **Awake** to an early morning view of the looming cliffs of Sumburgh Head as you approach Shetland by ferry.

→ **Reinvigorate** yourself with a coffee and breakfast at the Peerie Shop café in the main town of Lerwick.

→ **Blow** away your cobwebs on the blustery clifftop of Eshaness on Mainland.

→ **Dine** at award winning Frankie's Fish & Chips in the town of Brae on Mainland.

→ **Adventure** as far north as you can go with a trip to the island of Unst, and eat scones in the most northerly tearoom, in Haroldswick.

→ **Dip** in the reinvigorating North Sea at Skaw on Unst, the UK's most northerly beach.

→ **Gaze** out from Unst to Muckle Flugga, the lonely and isolated lighthouse that illuminates the wide surrounding sea.

→ **Visit** the lonely White Wife on Yell, forever gazing out to where her ship lies wrecked.

→ **Explore** the extraordinary Iron Age tower on Mousa, and watch the resident birds come home in the 'simmer dim'.

Often romantically referred to as Ultima Thule, 'beyond the borders of the known world', the Shetland Islands are 100 miles north of the mainland and unlike anywhere else in Scotland. Lying 60 degrees north – a position local businesses are proud to promote – Shetland is classified as a sub-arctic archipelago and is almost as close to Norway as it is to Scotland. This has endowed it with a strange Scottish-Nordic culture that doesn't quite fit in anywhere. It gives Shetlanders a unique sense of identity, and they refer to themselves as Shetlanders first and Scottish second.

The islands themselves – over 100 of them, although only 15 are inhabited – are rugged, barren, windswept and completely in thrall to the sea. The landscape is startling at first, the peaty soil and salty air making trees and foliage sparse, and giving the islands an empty feel. The sea dominates here everything here; the weather, employment, leisure and attitude to life are dictated by strongly maritime influences. The summers are long and lazy and the sun doesn't really set, instead the day takes on an eerie veil that the locals call the 'simmer dim'. One can swim in the sea in sunshine at ten o'clock at night. Winters are the opposite, of course, with extremely short days and a relentless night-time atmosphere that draws locals in around their warm peat fires.

Shetland is a mecca for bird watchers, sea-life enthusiasts, sailors and anyone willing to put in the extra effort on an adventurous trip to an unusual destination. The islands are increasingly popular as a cycling destination, and wonderful provided you aren't heading into the wind! Walking and camping is likewise straightforward and accessible. Wild swimming takes a bit more courage than on the mainland – the rough North Sea is not quite as forgiving as a placid Highland loch.

Shetland is reached either by a 12–14 hour ferry crossing via Aberdeen and Orkney, or by a 90 minute flight from Aberdeen, Glasgow or Edinburgh. Decent roads and inter-island ferry services, the result of lucrative oil investment, form a network over and between the islands and make travel up and down the archipelago straightforward and easy.

BEACHES & WILD SWIMMING

1 UYEA, MAINLAND

Undoubtedly a contender for Shetland's greatest beach, although you need a low tide to see it at its best. This remote and wild tombolo beach links jagged sea stacks and cliffs with pristine white sands, beset by the sea on both sides. Seals play in turquoise surf that looks almost Caribbean. The beach is reached by a scramble down the rough cliff side. In recent years erosion and rock fall have made this more difficult, and is not recommended unless you are confident and the tide is out. However, the cliff top overlooking the beach is an excellent spot for a picnic in its own right.

→ Uyea is reached by a 3½ mile walk in on a good off-road track to a farm close to the beach. Start from the small village of North Roe (ZE2 9XG), take first L after the primary school, heading N. Follow track until ½ mile before it ends at a farm, then break off the path on L heading over flat grass to the shore.

90 mins, 60.6157, -1.4184

2 BRAEWICK BEACH, MAINLAND

An interesting dark-red sandstone beach with a lagoon behind it and a stream to one end. It has a wild feel and stunning view over to the fearsome Drongs – jagged sea stacks that lie out to sea.

→ Park at Braewick Caravan Park (ZE2 9RS, see 28) and spend some time in the excellent café. From here cross the stile at the lower L hand side of the car park and walk down to the beach.

10 mins, 60.4902, -1.5547

3 ST NINIAN'S ISLE, MAINLAND

Located in the south Mainland, St Ninian's is the quintessential Shetland beach and the best example of a tombolo beach anywhere. The sea comes in on both sides, swim on whichever is calmest. Very popular with tourists and locals out walking their dogs. The island features an interesting ruined chapel, where a local boy helping on a dig found Viking treasure in 1958. Usually accessible at all tide levels in summer, but winter seas sometimes scour the sand away.

→ Near Bigton (ZE2 9JA), the Isle is signed from the B9122 at the S of the village. Car park above the beach, head down the dunes to reach the sand.

5 mins, 59.9712, -1.3460

4 DOCK OF LINGNESS, MAINLAND

This secluded and sheltered little bay is a peaceful spot and a good area to view otters. An attractive cottage completes the scene.

→ From the B9075 take minor roads past Nesting school (ZE2 9PS). Start from a rough layby beside some farm sheds on the public road that ends in Eswick (ZE2 9PS). There is a red Reliant Robin with 'Welcome to Lingness' painted on the side. Go through the gate here, head R past a farm and then N on a good farm track that winds down to the shore. Climb the small hill on the Lingness promontory for a good view of the bay. Limited parking space.

20 mins, 60.2738, -1.1169

5 WOODWICK, UNST

Woodwick is a bizarre inlet on Unst that accumulates large amounts of wood and other debris washed up from the sea. The entire bay is scattered with logs of all shapes and sizes, and locals have taken to arranging odd shoes and other interesting beach-combing finds. A fun family place.

→ Start from the end of the public road at Houlland on the W side of the island (NW from ZE2 9DZ), where there is a car park. Woodwick lies 1¾ miles NW from here over a rough hill with little in the way of a path at

times. Head NW for 1 mile to reach the Dale of Woodwick, a valley that leads to the beach.
40 mins, 60.7813, -0.9320 ⬇️🚶🏕️♿🅿️⛴️

6 WEST SAND WICK, YELL

This tranquil little sandy beach is a brilliant stopping off point for those travelling north to Unst. Wild camp on the banks above.

→ From the A968 heading N through Yell, turn L after 5 miles from the ferry pier signed West Sandwick (ZE2 9BH). Take first L and follow signs for Beach, R then L to reach the car park.
5 mins, 60.5821, -1.1868 🏕️🏕️♿

7 SKAW, UNST

The UK's most northerly beach. Idyllic and peaceful place for a swim with the seals. A Russian trawler shipwrecked itself on this promontory, prompting suspicion that the sailors were spies observing the RAF base at Saxa Vord. The trawler's lifeboat is used as a shed roof on the cottage at Skaw.

→ From Norwick (ZE2 9EF) head N on the only road, following signs for Skaw. Park next to a small white cottage and fish farm in sight of beach and walk down.
5 mins, 60.8252, -0.7886 🚶🏕️♿⛴️🅿️

8 NORWICK, UNST

Popular and picturesque sandy beach on the island of Unst. A great place to camp or park a caravan. Plenty of rock pools and boulders to scramble over.

→ Accessed via the hamlet of Norwick (beyond ZE2 9EF). Beach car park is two gravelly tracks from junction at S of hamlet.
5 mins, 60.8082, -0.8029 ⬇️🏕️♿🅿️

9 LUNDA WICK, UNST

Pristine white beach with an interesting medieval chapel and a graveyard overlooking it. Inside St Olaf's chapel there are two Hanseatic merchants' graves and a Pictish carved stone incorporated into a lintel.

→ From the A968 in the S of the island, take turn signed Westing just S of ZE2 9DW. After ½ mile take L signed standing stone and follow past standing stone to car park at end.
5 mins, 60.7152, -0.9622 🚶🏕️♿⛴️🅿️✝️

CLIFFS & SEA STACKS

10 WESTER WICK CLIFFS, MAINLAND

Shetland is almost entirely ringed with cliffs, so there are a lot to choose from, but the wild formations at Westerwick on the west side of the Mainland are a real hidden gem.

Jagged stacks, knife edge arêtes and rough seas all combine to create an epic scene.

→ From Wester Skeld (ZE2 9NL) follow the roads SW to the small village of Westerwick. The bay and cliffs are visible from the end of the road, where there is limited parking space. Either head L along the cliff top for a sea stack shaped like a church, or head R up the steeper cliff top to view a promontory still attached to the mainland via a narrow ridge.
15–30 mins, 60.1669, -1.4901 🏕️🚶❓🅿️

11 RONAS VOE, MAINLAND

A hidden gem of a spot. Lonely Ronas Voe has cliff scenery as good as anywhere, and you probably won't see another soul. Classic Shetland landscape of sea, sea-stack and sky. As a calmer inlet, also a good place to kayak through arches and passages.

→ Start from the end of the public road at Heylor (ZE2 9RL, limited parking) and continue NW along the clifftop to reach a towering set of stacks and broken cliff. Beyond a visible geological change in the landscape occurs, with granite replacing red sandstone.
45 mins, 60.5339, -1.5212 🚶♿🅿️

12 ESHANESS, MAINLAND

A guide to Shetland would not be complete without a mention of Eshaness. Much photographed and the star of several television advertisements, this classic expanse of cliff is an undeniably impressive scene. One truly feels at the edge of the world. The walk to the Grind o' da Navir takes in amazing scenery and amazing geology. Keep an eye out for the impressive blow holes and subterranean passages.

→ From Braewick (ZE2 9RS) head W on the B9078 and take R to park by beautiful Eshaness lighthouse. Head N along the cliff top, avoiding the in-cut cliffs. Continue for 1½ miles to reach the Grind of the Navir (locally Grind o' da Navir), a dramatic, rocky 'storm beach' blasted by centuries of turbulent sea.
60 mins, 60.4896, -1.6265

13 THE WHITE WIFE, YELL

The White Wife is the figurehead (now a replica of the original) of the German barque Bohus which foundered off the coast of Yell in 1924. Some of the dead are buried in a nearby cemetery. The figurehead was erected within sight of where the ship sank as a lonely monument to the perils of Shetland's coastline.

→ Located at the sea shore below Queyon on the E side of Otterswick. From the B9081 turn towards ZE2 9AX, but then take first R and drive to the end of the minor road. Continue on foot along the track towards a farm, and from here head R and walk down to the shore.
10 mins, 60.5476, -1.0372

HILLS & VIEWS

14 RONAS HILL, MAINLAND

At 450m Ronas Hill is the highest hill in Shetland, and as such, a commanding viewpoint on a good day. The vistas extend over the entire Shetland Isles. Barren and rocky, it has a wild plateau feel to it, strewn with pink granite and crowned by a Neolithic chambered cairn. The weather can be atrocious however, and good navigation skills could be needed.

→ From Collafirth Hill take unsigned track L off A970 1 mile NE of ZE2 9RX, park near the signal masts. From here head NW to reach Mid Field after 1¼ miles – this is often mistaken for Ronas Hill on the walk in. Descend to a tiny lochan, before ascending another ½ mile to the summit of Ronas Hill.
90 mins, 60.5337, -1.4455

15 MUCKLE FLUGGA, FROM UNST

The most northerly point of the UK, Muckle Flugga is a rocky island lying off the north coast of Unst. Perched on top is a whitewashed lighthouse dating to 1854, and built by the Stevenson brothers (father and uncle to Robert Louis Stevenson, who also visited the island). This long walk visits the land nearest the island, although it can be seen from nearby Saxa Vord hill.

→ From Hermaness Nature Reserve car park at end of B9086, past ZE2 9EQ. Follow gravel path N, then a wooden boardwalk to reach the clifftop at Toolie, after 1½ miles. From here follow cliff top N for 1¼ miles until the tip of Hermaness is reached, offering the closest views of Muckle Flugga.
90 mins, 60.8446, -0.8852

16 SAXA VORD BASE, UNST

Relive Cold War paranoia at this decommissioned RAF radar listening station, situated atop Saxa Vord, the highest hill on Unst. The base itself is still MOD property and is completely fenced off, but a walk around the site is an eerie and fascinating experience. The views over to distant Muckle Flugga and back to the Mainland of Shetland are simply incredible.

16

→ From the crossroads near ZE2 9TN, a good road signed Housi Field leads on from there over a cattle grid (the access sign refers to the fenced area at the top) and up Saxa Vord, unmissable on Unst as the giant hill with the radar masts on top. From here simply circumnavigate the outer fencing.
30 mins, 60.8261, -0.8433 🟥🟨❓🌄

BROCHS & ANCIENT SITES

17 BROCH OF MOUSA
Shetland has an incredibly rich Pictish heritage, and features the best example of an Iron Age broch, or fort. This lies in the south of the small island of Mousa. Storm petrels live in the double walls – visit at night for the best chance to see them. There are also mysterious burnt mounds on Mousa, two at the head of the nearby lochan.
→ Reach Mousa by boat, leaving from Sandsayre pier. Operates regularly, but phone ahead to check The boat crew offer info on walks, and run night-time storm petrel sailings. Mousa Boat, Sandwick, Shetland ZE2 9HP, 07901 872339. Mousa.co.uk
15 mins, 59.9954, -1.1818 🏚️⛵🏞️🎣♿⚡

18 CULSWICK BROCH, MAINLAND
Less well-preserved than Mousa, but wilder and easier to get to as it sits atop a hill overlooking the sea on the west side of the main island. An incredible viewpoint. There are also ruins and standing stones nearby.
→ Take the B9071 past L turn to ZE2 9NL, following signs to Culswick. Limited parking close to end near a red phone box. Take uphill path from phone box past tiny Culswick Methodist Chapel and round the N side of the Loch of Sotersta and then to Loch of the Brough (ruins and standing stones down path to S here). The broch is visible on a hill just beyond, go through a gate and cross a causeway at N end of the loch and head uphill.
30 mins, 60.1867, -1.5439 🟨🏞️🌄🏚️✝️♿

LOCAL FOOD

19 FRANKIES FISH & CHIPS, MAINLAND
Most northerly fish and chip shop. Frankies has won countless awards, and is very popular with the locals, so you know it will be great.
→ Brae, ZE2 9QJ, 01806 522700.
60.3930, -1.3508 🏚️🍴

20 BONHOGA GALLERY, MAINLAND
Brilliant café and exciting art gallery well situated on the road out to the west of the Mainland. The gallery has ever changing, high quality exhibitions.
→ Weisdale, ZE2 9LW, 01595 745750. Shetlandarts.org
60.2602, -1.2883 🍴

21 VICTORIA'S VINTAGE TEA ROOMS, UNST
Charming vintage tea room serving amazing home-baked scones with jam and clotted cream. Also a shop for local produce. Closed in winter.
→ Haroldswick, ZE2 9ED, 01957 711885.
60.7884, -0.8294 🏚️🍴

22 PEERIE SHOP CAFÉ, MAINLAND
Modern and popular, this friendly little café, tucked behind the shop, is one of the best in the capital Lerwick.
→ Esplanade, Lerwick ZE1 0LL, 01595 692816.
60.1541, -1.1431 🍴

23 SUMBURGH HEAD LIGHTHOUSE & CAFE
Excellent 'pop-up' summer café inside a refurbished lighthouse in a stunning location

atop huge cliffs on the very southern tip of Shetland. An exceptional place to see puffins in season, and keep an eye out for whales too.

→ Sumburgh Head Lighthouse, Virkie, ZE3 9JN, 01950 461966.
59.8542, -1.2746 ⛰🏖🍴

SLEEP WILD

24 BURRASTOW BOTHIES

Basic, wild and remote – the perfect getaway. Pick a bothy perched on the shoreline and a brilliant place to spot otters, or a pod with high views over the sea. B&B also available

→ Bo's B&B, Muckleburgh View, Burrastow, Walls, ZE2 9PD, 01595 809258.
60.2135, -1.6007 🍲🛏🛁🐾🚿🏕🏠

25 JOHNNIE NOTIONS BÖD

Economy bunkhouse in a traditional Shetland 'böd' or bothy, with very basic amenities. Named after local well-known inventor and maker of nostrums, John Williamson. Close to the incredible Eshaness cliffs (see 12).

→ Shetland Amenity Trust, Garthspool, Lerwick, ZE1 0NY, 01595 694688. Camping-bods.com
60.5083, -1.5698 🏠

26 NESBISTER BÖD

Perched adventurously on the tip of a small peninsula, this very basic böd is an incredibly atmospheric place to stay. Lie in bed and listen to the waves, which can crash up to the front door in bad weather!

→ Shetland Amenity Trust, Garthspool, Lerwick, Shetland ZE1 0NY, 01595 694688. Camping-bods.com
60.1865, -1.2901 🏠

27 WADDLE SELF CATERING, MAINLAND

Beautifully and simply restored former croft house on the west side of Shetland. Close to the peaceful hamlet of Walls, it is the perfect base to explore the west side.

→ Walls, ZE2 9PD, 01595 809319.
60.2217, -1.5939 🏠

28 BRAEWICK CARAVAN PARK, MAINLAND

Much more than the name implies. Pitch your tent on the grass as well, or book a wooden eco wigwam overlooking stunning Braewick Beach and Bay. Highly rated family-friendly café using local produce.

→ Braewick, Eshaness, ZE2 9RS, 01806 503345. Eshaness.moonfruit.com
60.4934, -1.5585 🏠🍴

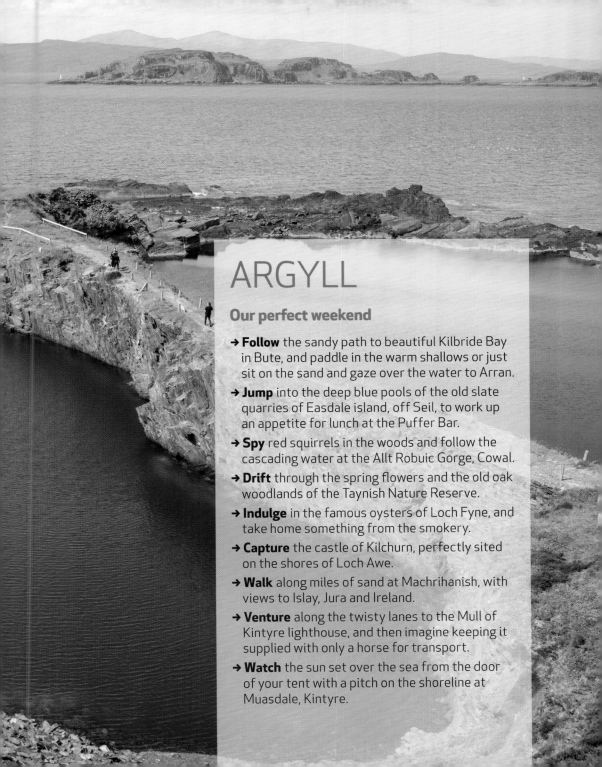

ARGYLL

Our perfect weekend

→ **Follow** the sandy path to beautiful Kilbride Bay in Bute, and paddle in the warm shallows or just sit on the sand and gaze over the water to Arran.

→ **Jump** into the deep blue pools of the old slate quarries of Easdale island, off Seil, to work up an appetite for lunch at the Puffer Bar.

→ **Spy** red squirrels in the woods and follow the cascading water at the Allt Robuic Gorge, Cowal.

→ **Drift** through the spring flowers and the old oak woodlands of the Taynish Nature Reserve.

→ **Indulge** in the famous oysters of Loch Fyne, and take home something from the smokery.

→ **Capture** the castle of Kilchurn, perfectly sited on the shores of Loch Awe.

→ **Walk** along miles of sand at Machrihanish, with views to Islay, Jura and Ireland.

→ **Venture** along the twisty lanes to the Mull of Kintyre lighthouse, and then imagine keeping it supplied with only a horse for transport.

→ **Watch** the sun set over the sea from the door of your tent with a pitch on the shoreline at Muasdale, Kintyre.

Go west to explore a gloriously diverse area of luxuriant glens, lush forests and gardens, rolling hills and mountains, sparkling sea lochs and unspoilt beaches. Rich in biodiversity, Argyll has some of the best land, coastal and freshwater habitats and species in the country.

Head up the A83 past the rugged Arrochar Alps and through the famous Rest and Be Thankful pass into Argyll Forest Park. Established in 1935, this is Britain's oldest forest park, and within it there are stunning fertile landscapes to explore, such as the mesmerizing Puck's Glen where, dripping ferns hang off the rocky gorge walls and a peaceful burn tumbles downstream.

In spring and summer much of the landscape erupts with colour – bluebells flood the lichen-and-moss-carpeted woodland floors, and rhododendrons bloom creating vibrant banks of colour amongst the trees of Black Gates Forest and the stunning hillside and coastal gardens of Crarae and Arduaine.

Make your way to Oban, the bustling 'seafood capital of Scotland' and sample delicious freshly caught shellfish at the famous green Oban Seafood Hut by the pier. From here follow the coast south and cross the perfect stone arch of the 'bridge over the Atlantic', which is hung with fairy foxgloves in summer, and you will soon arrive at the slate island of Seil. Whitewashed stone cottages are lined up by the harbour, where you can jump on the tiny ferry to charming Easdale and swim in the magnificent turquoise pools that lie in the old quarries, surrounded by glorious views of the blue sea and the Isle of Mull.

Further south, below the National Scenic Area of Knapdale, lies the Kintyre peninsula – a less dramatic landscape perhaps, but its coastline carries both long beaches and dunes like Machrihanish and calm bays like Carradale, whose shallow waters are great for bathing on sunny days. From Tayinloan on the west coast, take your bike on the ferry to the delightful Gigha Island to enjoy quality local food by Ardminish Bay before cycling north to the idyllic Twin Beaches, where there is glorious turquoise water to swim in and carpets of wildflowers nudging the sand in spring.

BEACHES & WILD SWIMMING

1 EASDALE SLATE QUARRIES

Magical old steep-sided slate quarries now filled with Mediterranean-blue sea water, on the beautiful car-free Easdale.

→ Off A816 S of Oban, follow B844 to Seil and Easdale (PA34 4TB). From conservation village Ellenabeich, where free car park is signed at N end, cross to island by ferry and walk NW to quarries, 400m. The L-shaped pool is the usual swimming one.

20 mins, 56.2939, -5.6595

2 TWIN BEACHES, GIGHA

Two beautiful, secluded white sand beaches on the tombolo linking Eilean Garbh to the north end of the community-owned Isle of Gigha. Magnificent in spring when bluebells cover the land by the beaches.

→ 20 min Calmac ferry service to Gigha from Tayinloan (PA29 6XJ) then on foot or bike head up from ferry terminal and turn R to follow road N for 3½ miles until you reach a sign for footpath on L that leads to the beaches.

60 mins, 55.7226, -5.7351

3 FINART BAY, COWAL

Attractive pebbly beach on the west shore of

Loch Long backed by Ardentinny forest, with many pleasant coastal woodland trails.

→ From Ardentinny village (PA23 8TU), head N past caravan park and turn R 300m later at Forestry Commission sign. Follow minor road around bay towards shore, passing bowling club before reaching large parking area at road end. Quieter coves further N around bay.

5 mins, 56.0561, -4.9057

4 MACHRIHANISH BAY, KINTYRE

Beautiful west-coast beach, 6 miles long and backed by the wild Machrihanish dunes, the biggest dune area in Argyll, which manages to be both an SSSI and a golf course. Rip currents can develop.

→ Parking by A83 as it turns inland 5 miles N of Campbelltown (1½ miles N of PA28 6QF), signed Westport Beach.

5 mins, 55.4715, -5.7124

5 CARRADALE BAY, KINTYRE

Sweeping sandy bay stretching out to Carradale Point and overlooked by Torrisdale Castle, which is home to an organic tannery, and the Garden Cottage (see 35). The shallow water warms up well on a sunny day.

→ From Carradale at crossroads W of PA28 6RY on B879, turn S onto minor road signed

for Port Righ. Where it bends L continue straight through gate to grassy parking area at E end of bay.

5 mins, 55.5809, -5.4777

6 KILMORY BAY, KINTYRE

Fine sandy beach where you can swim in crystal clear waters and enjoy views out across the Sound of Jura.

→ Head S along E shore of Loch Sween, passing caravan park to reach Kilmory 4 miles S of PA31 8PT. Park near the chapel in the village and follow footpath down to beach.

15 mins, 55.9094, -5.6834

7 DUNAVERTY BAY, KINTYRE

Fine sandy crescent beach curving round to Dunaverty Point, where an old boathouse stands under Dunaverty Rock. Caravan park behind the bay, but at the NW end where you park, so walk along beach beyond it.

→ Head S from Southend village (PA28 6RW) to reach parking in large layby on L just past caravan park, with track down to beach.

2 mins, 55.3095, -5.6454

8 LETTERMAY BURN, LOCHGOILHEAD

Plunge into some refreshing waterfall pools

with rockslides. Best when the water levels are high enough to jump and the midge count low, so before June or after August.

→ Park in Lettermay and follow gravel track E about 150m N of PA24 8AR – part of Cowal Way. After 100m the track splits, go R another 100m and down track through gate to river. Walk up river ½ mile for three waterfalls. Path on S side is tricky; cross for an easier path.
20 mins, 56.1612, -4.9317 🏊📖🍴

WOODS & GLENS

9 PUCK'S GLEN, COWAL

A truly enchanting deep gorge, which is darkened by a canopy of dense trees and enclosed by rocky walls. The shaded walls are covered in moist, sparkling forest undergrowth.

→ From car park off A815 300m N of Rashfield (PA23 8QT) follow clear waymarked trail winding along a Victorian walkway up the gorge.
30 mins, 56.0159, -4.9724 🚶‍♀️🍴

10 GLEN NANT NATURE RESERVE

Explore the verdant woodland of native oak, ash, birch trees and colourful lichens and look out for otters by the river in this delightful nature reserve.

→ From Taynuilt take B845 dir Kilchrenan, past PA35 1HP. After approx 3 miles, turn R into Glen Nant National Nature Reserve and over the small bridge to car park.
5 mins, 56.3960, -5.2102 🐾🅿️🚶

11 ALLT ROBUIC GORGE, COWAL

Cascading waterfalls, native oak woods and red squirrels at an impressive gorge within Glenbranter Forest.

→ Glenbranter is signed off the A815 2½ miles SE of Strachur (PA27 8DJ). Info centre, waymarked paths and cycle routes from the carpark. Follow Waterfall trail signs to gorge.
40 mins, 56.1259, -5.0590 🅿️📖🍴

12 TAYNISH NATURE RESERVE

One of the largest native oakwoods left in Britain. There are also wildlife-rich grasslands and loch shores to explore. Best visited in spring or early summer, when wildflowers cover the woodland floor and you can see dragonflies and maybe even a marsh fritillary butterfly. Paths everywhere, including to picnic tables SE.

→ Head S from Tayvallich (PA31 8PJ) on B8025 and take L road signed for Reserve, continuing for 1 mile past loch to parking area.
5 mins, 56.0066, -5.6311 🅿️🌼🅿️🚶🏞️

13 ARDCASTLE POINT, LOCH FYNE

Pleasant hillside woodlands where red squirrels and deer roam. Enjoy a picnic on one of the pebbly beaches on the shore of Loch Fyne, and keep an eye out for seals too.

→ Park in Ardcastle Forestry Commission car park 1.5 miles N of Lochgair (PA31 8UJ). Cross road to enter woods and bear S and E for beaches.
5 mins, 56.0676, -5.3016 🏖️🍴

14 BLACK GATES FOREST, COWAL

The circular, waymarked Big Tree Walk leads uphill through a series of grand Douglas firs, Californian redwoods and western hemlocks, where many red squirrels hide. Colourful rhododendrons bloom during spring and early summer. The magnificent Benmore Botanic Gardens across the road is also well worth a visit, particularly the Victorian glass fernery and spectacular rows of redwoods at the entrance.

→ Park at Benmore Botanic Gardens carpark (PA23 8QU). Cross main road to information board and Black Gates forestry sign, and from here follow blue waymarked trail.
40 mins, 56.0263, -4.9796 🅿️🌼🚶🅿️

9

15

ANCIENT & SACRED

15 KILCHURN CASTLE, LOCH AWE

Delightful ruined castle, romantically situated on a rocky peninsula at the end of Loch Awe. A perfect gift to photographers.

→ Turn S off A85 onto unsigned track near head of Loch Awe between the turning for Inverary and bridge over River Orchy, ½ mile E of PA33 1AJ. Park here and follow track taking a R at the fork to pass through gate and under railway bridge before rejoining older path. Continue straight to castle.

20 mins, 56.4042, -5.0279 ⊠🅿🏊🐾

16 KILMARTIN GLEN, LOCHGILPHEAD

With some 800 cairns, cists, standing stones and a henge monument, this is one of the richest archeological areas in the country. There are too many to detail here: it is best to start with a tour of the museum, which has artefacts from the locations, information about them, and an excellent café.

→ Park by Kilmartin Museum, Kilmartin, PA31 8RQ, 01546 510278. Kilmartin.org.

10–90 mins, 56.1334, -5.4868 🚲†

17 ELLENABEICH HILL, ISLE OF SEIL

Fine views of dramatic coastal scenery on Mull, nearby Easdale and over the pretty Ellenabeich village itself.

→ Start as for Easdale Slate Quarries (see 1). Paths up the hill start over a stile the back of the Highland Crafts shop car park, but are faint so you may have to make your own way to the top; the W side is less steep.

30 mins, 56.2972, -5.6453 ⛰🅿📷🐾

WILD GARDENS

18 CRARAE GARDEN, INVERARAY

Exotic Himalayan-style woodland garden magnificently positioned on the hillside and centered around the Crarae burn. There are over 600 types of rhodedenron here, plus camellias and magnolias, pretty waterfalls and pools and a wild forest garden above.

→ 10 miles S of Inveraray on the A83, ½ mile W of PA32 8YA, 01546 886614.

5 mins, 56.1258, -5.2421 🅿

19 KILMUN ABORETUM

Explore an exotic mix of over 150 species of tree, including little monkey puzzles, in this beautiful forest garden. There are three waymarked trails leading through the woodland, including one that is suitable for prams.

→ Signed off A880 in Kilmun, 500m NW of PA23 8SD.

5–60 mins, 55.9978, -4.9447 🅿🐾

20 ARDUAINE GARDENS, OBAN

Victorian coastal garden on the south slope of the Arduaine peninsula. The peaceful woodland and gardens are a delight to stroll through at any time of year, but it is most wonderful in spring and summer when many gorgeous rhododendrons and azaleas burst into colour. Refreshments at Loch Melfort Hotel next door.

→ Signed off the A816 at Arduaine approx 600m N of PA34 4XQ, 01852 200366.

5 mins, 56.2347, -5.5610 🌼🍴🐾

SCENIC VIEWPOINTS

21 MULL OF KINTYRE

Extreme southwestern tip of the Kintyre peninsula, reached by a very steep and challenging single track. The end of the headland is the site of Scotland's second lighthouse, built in 1788 and rebuilt in the 1820s, and on a clear day there are views over to Ireland.

→ From Southend head W turning inland on minor road for 2½ miles then L signed Mull of

Kintyre lighthouse, past PA28 6RU. Take care following the steep road for 6½ miles and park car at road end. From here follow steep track to the lighthouse.

40 mins, 55.3104, -5.8029 🏕️📷🔺

22 REST & BE THANKFUL, ARROCHAR

The summit of this spectacular mountain valley pass is a welcome pit-stop for weary travellers. The name comes from the words inscribed on a stone erected after the completion of the original military road, which can be seen below from the viewpoint.

→ 6½ miles W of Arrochar on A83, 3½ miles W of G83 7AS.

5 mins, 56.2258, -4.8558 🏔️⛩️

LOCAL FOOD

23 INVER RESTAURANT

Award-winning restaurant with small shop and wilder camping area on the shores of Loch Fyne. Their contemporary take on traditional and forgotten Scottish dishes uses local wild and farmed ingredients. Opening hours vary, booking recommended.

→ Stracthlachlan, Strachur PA27 8BU, 01369 860537. Inverrestaurant.co.uk

56.1056, -5.2071 🍴🏕️🚣🏃

24 LOCH FYNE OYSTERS

Considered a pioneer of Scottish food and drink, this independent restaurant and oyster bar serves exceptionally good seafood from the loch outside, prepared in their in-house smokery.

→ Loch Fyne PA26 8BL, 01499 600264. Lochfyne.com

56.2722, -4.9272 🍴

25 OBAN SEAFOOD HUT

Famous green takeaway shack by the ferry terminal selling outstanding fresh and cooked shellfish. Try as much as you possibly can by ordering the very reasonably priced seafood platter.

→ 1 Railway Pier, Oban PA34 4LW. Obanseafoodhut.co.uk

56.4123, -5.4754 🍴

26 THE PUFFER BAR, EASDALE

Charming, cosy bar and restaurant serving fresh, local, homemade food on the delightful little island of Easdale.

→ Easdale Island, Oban PA34 4TB, 01852 300022. Pufferbar.com

56.2915, -5.6555 🍴🍺

28

27 SKIPNESS SEAFOOD CABIN

Wonderful local seafood and fine wines served throughout summer within the grounds of Skipness Castle.

→ Skipness, Tarbert, PA29 6XU, 01880 760207. Theseafoodcabin.co.uk
55.7676, -5.3380

28 INVERARAY CASTLE TEA ROOM

Traditional tea room within an iconic castle and overseen by the Duchess herself. Homemade baking, lunches, local cheeses, ice creams, teas and coffees.

→ Inveraray, PA32 8XE, 01499 302203. Inveraray-castle.com
56.2372, -5.0735

29 THE BOATHOUSE, GIGHA ISLAND

Delightful beach front restaurant by Ardminish Bay. Local produce, fresh seafood and a small basic campsite. Cash only.

→ Ardminish Bay, Gigha Island, PA41 7AA, 01583 505123. Boathousegigha.co.uk
55.6758, -5.7364

CAMP & SLEEP

30 MUASDALE HOLIDAY PARK, KINTYRE

Beachside pitches, cabin, apartments, campfires and sunsets over the sea. Camping closed in winter, apartments open all year.

→ Muasdale, Tarbert, Argyll, Scotland, PA29 6XD, 01583 421559. Muasdaleholidays.com
55.5976, -5.6836

31 THE GALLEY OF LORNE INN

Well regarded Inn with great food and sweeping views over Loch Craiginsh.

→ Ardfern, Lochgilphead, PA31 8QN, 01852 500284 Galleyoflorne.co.uk
56.1801, -5.5379

32 FOREST HOLIDAYS ARDGARTAN

Luxury family- and dog-friendly modern cabins with outdoor hot tubs, set in forest and lochside. One wheelchair-adapted cabin.

→ Ardgartan, Arrochar, G83 7AR, 03330 110495.
56.1885, -4.7813

33 GLENDARUEL HOLIDAY PARK

Family-friendly campsite in woodlands at the heart of the Cowall peninsula. Hard standing, tent pitches, a camping lodge and cabins.

→ Glendaruel, PA22 3AB, 01369 820267. Glendaruelcaravanpark.com
56.0349, -5.2096

COSY COTTAGES

34 CLAN COTTAGES, OBAN

Cluster of delightful thatched self-catering cottages by the shore of Loch Nell.

→ Dalnabreac, Kilmore, Oban, PA34 4XU, 01631 770372. Clancottages.com
56.3833, -5.4295

35 GARDEN COTTAGE, TORRISDALE

Perfect romantic getaway overlooking the former walled garden of Torrisdale Castle. With a wood burner and wood-fired hot tub.

→ Carradale, Argyll, PA28 6QT, 01583 431233. Torrisdalecastle.com
55.5688, -5.5013

36 SHORE COTTAGE, CARSKIEY

Restored sea captain's cottage right by Carskiey Bay. Open fireplace and sea views.

→ Carskiey, Campbeltown, Kintyre, Argyll PA28 6RU. Carskiey.com
55.3060, -5.6913

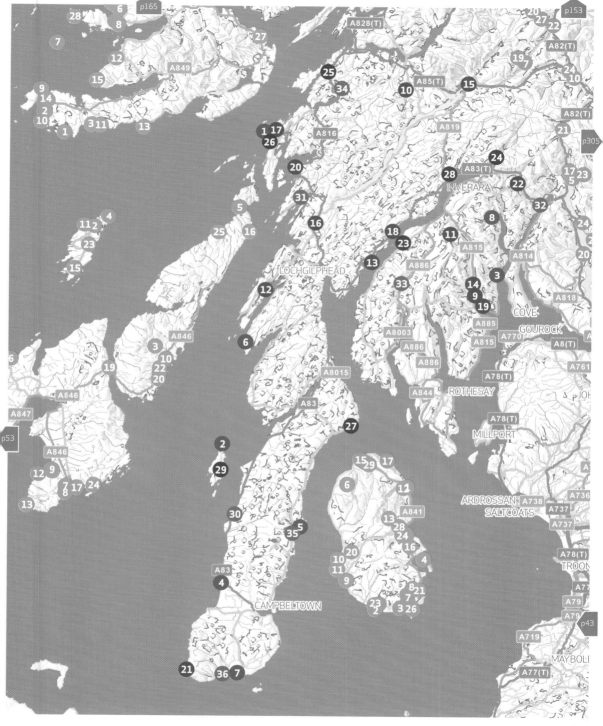

FORT WILLIAM, GLEN COE & GLEN ETIVE

Our perfect weekend

→ **Wake** up properly with an early morning dip in fresh Eas Urchaidh Falls, Glen Orchy.

→ **Soak** up the brooding atmosphere of Glen Coe with a walk into the Lost Valley.

→ **Unwind** in the friendly atmosphere of the Clachaig Inn.

→ **Gaze** in awe at the alpine grandeur of the north face of Ben Nevis.

→ **Wild** camp in the upland meadow of Glen Nevis, beneath the crashing waterfalls.

→ **Plunge** into the lonely River Roy, watching for eagles flying overhead.

→ **Dare** to cross the cable bridge at Steall Falls, a test of balance but more of nerve.

→ **Reflect** on a perfect weekend, stopping off at the Bridge of Orchy hotel on the way home.

The area from Glen Orchy north to Fort William offers an easily accessible and instantly rewarding outdoor lifestyle to anyone who lives there, holidays or passes through. Glen Coe, Glen Etive and Glen Nevis sing a siren call to walkers, and the area is justifiably world famous for its mountains, rivers, lochs and glens. It is the closest thing Scotland has to a European Alpine landscape, with high mountains, ski resorts and climbing huts.

Like many regions in the Highlands and Islands, this is an area of contrasts. Straddling the districts of Argyll and Lochaber, and changing dramatically as you head north between them, this is a place of drama and grandeur. Glen Orchy is a wide, sparsely populated and often-bypassed area that deserves more recognition than it gets, bordered on the east by the stark and desolate wastelands of Rannoch Moor. Beyond, the ranges of Glen Coe rear up like huge, dark castle ramparts, the moody landscapes evocative of its tragic history. Renowned among photographers and outdoor enthusiasts, Glen Coe is high on the 'must see' lists of many visitors to Scotland, and justifiably so; even if its sights have become over-familiar through photographs, nothing compares to the living landscape. Beyond Glen Coe lie Fort William and Lochaber, dominated by the vast bulk of Ben Nevis. This is unquestionably the most awe-inspiring mountain in Scotland, especially when viewed from the path up to its north face.

This area is a mecca for hillwalkers, climbers, campers, mountain bikers, skiers, photographers and wild swimmers, and its popularity is indicative of the vast array of activities on offer for the traveller. These pursuits are all well catered for by guides and tour companies, or they can be enjoyed in a wilder, unplanned way.

It is easy to think of Scotland in terms of transport links – major roads and rail lines are few and often far between, and the main routes resemble arteries, pumping people up and down. The A82 is the main artery here, offering instant and easy access, but also at times a great deal of traffic. This double-edged sword of access and popularity is nowhere more present than in places like Glen Etive and Glen Coe, so if you are planning to visit these on a sunny Saturday you may not get the solitude you hoped for. Many quieter options exist however, and Glen Roy, Clashgour and Rannoch Moor offer options for escaping the crowds.

6

RIVERS & LOCHS

1 WATER OF NEVIS

Beautiful river set in breathtaking scenery. Set inside a steep-sided gorge, with Ben Nevis behind and An Steall waterfall (see 2) in front, this is truly one of the most beautiful locations in Scotland. Just beyond the famously minimal wire bridge the river widens and deepens enough to swim in. Perfect for a morning dip after camping in the meadows.

➜ From Fort William take the road that winds up the glen (PH33 6SY) to the Upper Falls car park at the end. Follow the rocky but obvious path up into the higher reaches of Glen Nevis, following the river as you go.

20 mins, 56.7723, -4.9814 🏔🗑🏊🛶🎒🌀🌀

2 AN STEALL WATERFALL

One of the most picturesque and spectacular waterfalls in Scotland. Justifiably popular, this 120m cascade is the perfect backdrop to an already stunning glen. It occasionally freezes, an extremely rare occurrence which is not to be missed!

➜ Start as for Water of Nevis (see 1). Visible as soon as you enter the upper meadows. Also cross wire bridge and walk to foot of the falls.

20 mins, 56.770, -4.9794 🏔🏕🏊🏊🌀🌀

3 GLEN COE LOCHAN

This tranquil little spot is a great, easily reached gem that requires no effort to visit, but repays the visitor in abundance of beauty. North American trees such as sequoia and Douglas fir grow in abundance here, planted by Lord Strathcona in the 1890s for his homesick Canadian wife.

➜ Leave A82 at Glencoe village (PH49 4HX) and take L signed for lochan immediately after crossing river. From car park at end, follow well-signed Lochan Trail. Wheelchair friendly.

30 mins, 56.6890, -5.0968 🌀🚶🏔🏕🏊🌀

4 GREY MARE'S TAIL

Impressive waterfall, with water cascading for 50m in a single leap. For the thrill-seekers looking for a different view, Vertical Descents run a via Ferrata next to the falls (01397 747111).

➜ From the car park next to the church in Kinlochleven (PH50 4QT), follow signed Grey Mare's Waterfall path out of the park. Take a L at a T-junction and follow this to the falls.

30 mins, 56.7167, -4.9627 🌀

5 COIRE ARDAIR & CREAG MEAGAIDH

Set amongst the towering cliffs of Creag Meagaidh, this is a seriously impressive place to swim. Fed from icy snowmelt and water flowing off the plateau above, it is a bracing dip, but one that is second to none in its alpine splendour.

➜ Park as for the All Abilities Trail, Creag Meagaidh (see 11). Head out of car park on well-constructed paths, past a whitewashed farmhouse with picnic tables outside. At fork, follow sign for Coire Ardair. A good path hugs the N side of the Glen, with ever-increasing views of the cliffs ahead.

2 hours, 56.9593, -4.5677 🗑🏊🎒🌀

6 RIVER ETIVE

Superlative wild swimming spot, with easy access. Set in stunning Glen Etive, there are numerous spots that are perfect for swimming and lounging on warm rocks in the summer sun. Extremely busy on hot days.

➜ Turn off the A82 at the head of Glen Coe shortly W of PH49 4HY and follow single-track road down Glen Etive. Pools exist all along the river, and there are places to pull off.

1 min, 56.6218, -4.9151 🌀🏔🏕🏊🛶🌀

7 EAS URCHAIDH FALLS

On a tranquil day this provides a lovely spot for a leisurely picnic or swim, set amongst beautifully preserved woodland. Easy

145

Fort William, Glen Coe & Glen Etive

13

access to the water on interesting rock formations. Not recommended if the river is in spate!

→ Park as for Allt Broigleachan forest (see 19). Best swimming is on the downriver side of the bridge when viewed from the car park.
1 min, 56.4477, -4.8530

8 RIVER ROY

This winding and crashing river often widens to create incredible plunge pools and deep bowls, perfect for swimming. Following a period of hot weather, the river becomes reasonably warm, making it an excellent and easily accessible wild swimming spot.

→ Continue up Glen Roy from the viewpoint for the Parallel Roads (see 12). There are numerous spots along the river, particularly by the bridge near the end of the public road, where there is space to pull off.
5 mins, 56.9776, -4.7511

9 ACHADERRY LOCHAN, ROYBRIDGE

This tranquil little lochan with a picnic table by the water's edge makes a lovely spot for rest and reflection.

→ Leave the car in the centre of Roybridge, next to the shop (PH31 4AE), head E over the river and follow signs for Bohenie, then at a R

into Achaderry estate and finally Lochan Walk.
30 mins, 56.8946, -4.8251

10 RIVER FILLAN PLUNGE POOLS

These secluded and little-visited plunge pools lie just off the West Highland Way, but attract little attention, partly because they are hidden slightly further upstream.

→ Turn off the A82 for Dalrigh (FK20 8RX) and follow the road swinging L to car park. Head R out of car park and take L past several houses. Take a further L following track down to a small beach by the River Fillan. Pools lie a short distance upstream on the main river.
10 mins, 56.4236, -4.6934

GLENS & MOUNTAINS

11 CREAG MEAGAIDH ALL ABILITIES TRAIL

Wild Creag Meagaidh is topped by a vast, windswept plateau and famous among ice climbers, but for the less intrepid, the all-abilities trail at its foot is gentle and even suitable for wheelchairs. The route winds up to a viewpoint with a great outlook.

→ From the car park at Creag Meagaidth reserve at Aberarder on the A86 (approx 4 miles SW of PH20 1BX). Follow the path off to the L of the car park which works its way

around the Aberarder meadow in a loop.
60 mins, 56.9516, -4.4959

12 PARALLEL ROADS OF GLEN ROY

Glen Roy becomes increasingly empty and wild beyond Roybridge, a mysterious setting for these bizarre and fascinating parallel terraces carved into the hillsides. In Gaelic folklore they were roads built by Fingal the Giant, but they are really a glimpse into the Ice Ages, the last imprint of an ancient frozen loch; each 'road' is a marker etched where the waterline once sat. Head on up the River Roy for swimming spots (see 8).

→ Excellent viewpoint and car park overlooking the glen 1¼ miles N of PH31 4AH. Information board explains the phenomenon. Head up the hillsides at the back of viewpoint, then contour the hillsides N to the 'roads'.
90 mins, 56.9278, -4.7981

13 GLEN NEVIS

Glen Nevis is an incredibly special place that combines rugged, breathtaking scenery with easy access. A steep-sided gorge hemmed in by the tallest mountains in the UK, it has it all – beautiful river, cascading waterfalls, plunge pools and perfect places for wild camping. The flat grass of the upper meadow

is great for camping, just watch out for the midges in high summer.

→ Head S out of Fort William for Claggan and then Achintee (PH33 6TE). Follow this road to its end, and then continue on foot on the single rocky trail that leads out of the carpark.
20 mins, 56.8107, -5.0771 🚗🏕️🔦✛🏕️

14 DUN DEARDAIL

Rising above the west side of Glen Nevis is the ancient Iron Age fort of Dun Deardail. Called a 'vitrified fort' due to the fusion of rocks by intense heat, today Dun Deardail is reduced to a grassy bank around the summit, although summer excavations to investigate it began in 2015. It is an incredible viewpoint looking down on Glen Nevis and across to Ben Nevis itself, and easy to see why it was chosen as a defensive structure.

→ Park at the Glen Nevis visitor centre car park (PH33 6SY) and head S on the road before turning R up a track signed for the fort. Follow excellent tracks rising through the forest, with good signs for the fort all the way.
60 mins, 56.7850, -5.0675 📷🖼️🐾🔺🏕️

15 BEN NEVIS

The north face of Ben Nevis is a truly stupendous place: the site of an ancient

volcano that fell in on itself. This has created towering 700m cliffs, and climbers the world over flock to the crags in all seasons. Though the North Face is extremely dangerous, with several deaths each year, the path as far as the CIC hut is safe and excellent. Take some binoculars and see if you can spot any climbers!

→ From the A82 at Torlundy (PH33 6SN) take the road signed for the North Face car park. From the car park follow all signs for Allt a' Mhuillinn. The path winds up through a forest before breaking out into open moorland with fantastic views of the cliffs ahead.
90 mins, 56.8055, -5.0033 🔻🖼️🏕️

16 THE LOST VALLEY

The other-worldly and atmospheric hanging valley of Coire Gabhail has a dark past: it was here that many members of Clan MacDonald took refuge in the immediate aftermath of the massacre in Glen Coe in 1689. It is an incredible place, full of suspense and drama, and completely hidden from Glen Coe itself. Hemmed in on all sides by towering peaks, it is the perfect place to camp, with a flat alpine meadow, picturesque stream and giant boulders to shelter behind.

→ Park in one of the National Trust car parks

on the A82 in Glen Coe, 3½ and 5 miles E from PH49 4HX (busy as the day goes on). The Lost Valley is the L of two valleys between the Three Sisters, the giant prong-like ridges jutting out into the glen. A decent path heads down into the valley floor, crosses the River Coe and winds up into the Lost Valley itself. Some mild scrambling is required to gain the upper valley.

60 mins, 56.6549, -4.9940 🚶🥾⛰️🏕️💧🔁

17 THE PAP OF GLEN COE

This steep and prominent peak offers an incredible viewpoint that is well worth the ascent. Though short in stature compared with the surrounding hills, its position is the perfect place to look out on Ballachulish and Loch Leven.

➜ Leave A82 at Glencoe village, pass through the village and park at the car park on your L 400 metres after crossing river, next to an electricity substation. (PH49 4HX). Take the path that leads L out of the car park parallel to the road. The path eventually joins the road for a bit. Turn L at the second of 2 gates (second is signed for the Pap), and begin the ascent uphill. Further up, a bridge is reached, take a R and cross this. From here the path varies in quality, but follow it steeply uphill

towards the ever more visible Pap, which rears up in front of you. Boulders and rocks are encountered on the final summit cone, but the going is straightforward.

2 hours, 56.6888, -5.0626 🚶🥾🏕️💧🔁🏞️

18 LAIRIG GARTAIN & LAIRIG EILDE

These parallel glens offer a great loop walk that takes you between some of Glen Coe's finest mountains, with a stunning view down Glen Etive in the middle.

➜ Starting from the large parking area on A82 at Altnafeadh (2½ miles W from PH49 4HY) head up into the obvious U-shaped valley between Buchaille Etive Mòr and Buchaille Etive Beag. Continue up this on a good path to a stupendous viewpoint looking down over Glen Etive. Continue on the path curving R up into the Lairig Eilde, passing an impressive waterfall. From here the path loops back and returns to Glen Coe on the other side of Buchaille Etive Beag parallel to your walk in. Return up the glen to the carpark.

5 hours, 56.6522, -4.9267 🚶🏞️

19 ALLT BROIGLEACHAN

This gentle and tranquil walk winds through recent forestry plantations before arriving at a beautifully preserved remnant of

ancient Scots pine woodland – one of the best examples.

➜ Start at the carpark at Eas Urchaidh Falls in Glen Orchy (see 7), on B8074 (½ mile N from PA33 1BD). From the new car park next to the bridge cross the bridge and follow the forestry track, ignoring turn offs and following signs for the pine reserve.

45 mins, 56.4559, -4.8759 🚶🏞️

20 BLACK MOUNT AND CLASHGOUR

The Black Mount estate is a quiet and lonely area. Glen Orchy is much photographed at the Loch Tulla end, passed by the A82, but these lands around Clashgour beneath the Black Mount/Monadh Dubh range feel remote and wild.

➜ Start from the end of the public road (PA36 4AH) at Victoria Bridge, parking at signed car park 500m before. Turn L at Victoria Lodge and follow track out into Clashgour, along the N bank of the Abhainn Shira river. Numerous beautiful picnic spots along the river.

30 mins, 56.5419, -4.8371 🚶🥾🏕️💧🔁

26

LOCAL FOOD

21 CLACHAIG INN, GLEN COE

This lively inn is justifiably well known, and has provided a welcome sanctuary and post-mountain pints for decades. Head around the back to the Boots Bar, order one of the hundreds of malt whiskies and dry yourself by the stove. Dog friendly; there is a separate family-friendly lounge, B&B/self-catering also available.

→ Glencoe, Argyll, PH49 4HX, 01855 811252
56.6644, -5.0569 🍴🚻🛶

22 BRIDGE OF ORCHY HOTEL

Popular, walker-friendly and well-placed old inn, serving excellent food. An extremely handy base for walks in the Bridge of Orchy area, on the A82 just north of Tyndrum.

→ Bridge of Orchy, Argyll, PA36 4AD, 01838 400208. Bridgeoforchy.co.uk
56.5174, -4.7686 🍴🚻🛶

23 CORROUR STATION HOUSE

Inaccessible by road, this wonderfully situated café is served only by a train line or a very long walk, and is Scotland's highest station at 408m. Located on the West Highland Line, Corrour is 50 minutes' by train from Fort William, 3 hours from Glasgow. Closed over winter. Rooms available in the Signal Box, or Loch Ossian SYHA is close (see 29 and 30).

→ Corrour Estate, Fort William, PH30 4AA, 01397 732236.
56.7600, -4.6903 🍴🚻🛶

24 REAL FOOD CAFÉ

Hearty and welcoming café busy with outdoor types on the way back from long days on the hill. Award-winning fish and chips.

→ Tyndrum, Crianlarich, FK20 8RY, 01838 400235.
56.4359, -4.7106 🍴

25 THE GROG AND GRUEL

Unusual and lively Highland pub with strong emphasis on Scottish ales and local single malt whisky. Also separate restaurant.

→ 66 High Street, Fort William, PH33 6AD, 01397 705078.
56.8172, -5.1124 🍴🚻

SLEEP WILD

26 LAIRIG LEACACH BOTHY

This tiny half-house bothy sits alone on the ancient drove road of the Lairig Leacach, the 'pass of the flagstones', which ran south from the Great Glen. It is the only outpost in a wild land, and has a brilliant Munro, Stob Ban, up a cairned path that leads off just beyond the bothy when approached from Spean Bridge. Initially boggy, a decent path leads to the obvious conical summit.

→ Turn off A82 at Spean Bridge and follow signs up quiet road to Corriechoille (PH34 4EY). After bridge, turn R past Corriechoille farm. Continue on rough track through unlocked gate; find parking further up track by a second, locked gate. Leave car here and follow decent vehicle track up through the obvious glen beyond, passing a wooden sculpture of a minister along the way. 90 mins.
56.8226, -4.8157

27 INVERORAN

Designated wild-camping spot near the Inveroran Hotel. The are no facilities at the hotel to support camping here, but it is tolerated and is often used by West Highland Way walkers. The hotel itself is a great place to eat and drink.

→ Rough area of grass just W of the Inveroran Hotel (PA36 4AQ), next to the bridge over the Allt Tolaghan river. Hotel is closed in winter.
56.5323, -4.8131 ⛺🚻🛶

28 RED SQUIRREL CAMPSITE

Unique and attractive campsite situated in stunning Glen Coe. Swimming loch, fire pits and amazing views over to the west face of Aonach Dubh. Open all year, and anyone other than groups can just turn up, plenty of space.

→ Glencoe, Argyll PH49 4HX
56.6699, -5.0705 ▲ ⚠

29 CORROUR SIGNAL BOX

Three B&B rooms in the former signal box at Corrour Station (see restaurant entry 23), plus a sitting room with panoramic views. For lovers of quirky and unique holiday accommodation. Closed over winter.

→ Corrour Estate, Fort William, PH30 4AA, 01397 732236.
56.7600, -4.6903 🚂 🍴 🎒 ⚐

30 LOCH OSSIAN YOUTH HOSTEL

Hydro and solar power ensure that this little eco-hostel now has hot showers. Right on the shore of the loch, it once served as a waiting room for estate guests crossing the loch by steamer, and is unrivalled for a remote getaway from everything but the midges. Not normally open in winter.

→ Corrour, Fort William, PH30 4AA, 01397 732207. Syha.org.uk
56.7666, -4.6662 🏴 🚂 ⚐ ⚠

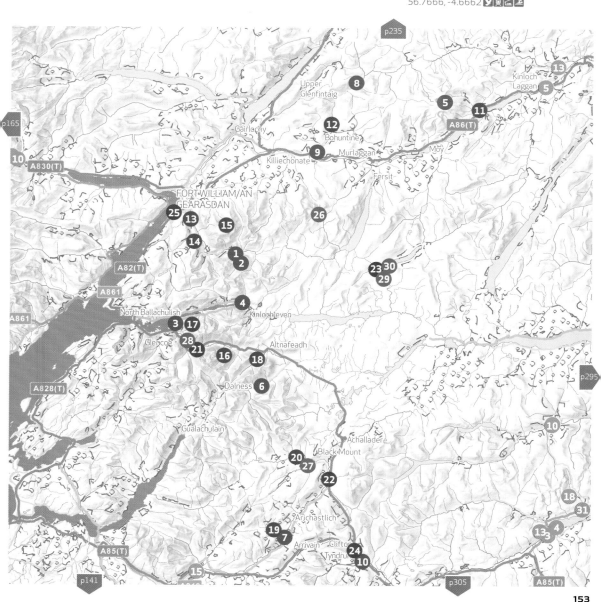

MORAR, MOIDART & ARDNAMURCHAN

Our perfect weekend

→ **Pitch** your tent and enjoy a campfire on the beach at Invercaimbe Campsite.

→ **Watch** the sunset between the Small Isles & Skye from Tràigh beaches.

→ **Swim** in crystal clear water and relax by the dunes at Camusudarach Beach.

→ **Kayak** or canoe surrounded by wonderful mountain scenery in Loch Morar.

→ **Explore** the tiny lanes of the wildly beautiful Ardnamurchan peninsula.

→ **Relax** on the silvery sands and enjoy the spectacular views at Sanna Bay.

→ **Travel** back in railway time with a lunch in the Glenfinnan Dining Car and take a tour around the railway museum.

→ **Discover** a white cove hidden beyond the ancient crofting township of Smirisary.

Long sea lochs break up the west of Lochaber into a series of beautiful peninsulas that are famous for their magnificent beaches, rough rocky coastlines and wildlife-rich woodlands and forests.

You can travel there by car or bike via the scenic A830 'Road to the Isles', or take the renowned West Highland Railway line. This passes through wonderful Scottish hill scenery and over the spectacular Glenfinnan viaduct to end in the busy fishing port of Mallaig, which is also a gateway to Skye and the Small Isles.

The Morar peninsula is cut deeply through its heart by the lonely freshwater Loch Morar, which reaches depths of over 300m. Largely surrounded by wild mountain scenery, it's surprising to find that its western head lies only a few hundred metres away from the North Atlantic.

The coastline here is home to the charming harbour village of Arisaig and silvery white sands of Camusdarach and Traigh beaches, where you can take a swim in crystal-clear azure sea before warming up with a picnic in one of the rocky coves. The Morar peninsula is also one of the best places to go camping on the mainland, whether it be at a pleasant campsite like Invercaimbe, where you can enjoy a campfire on the beach, or in remote, hidden bays like Peanmeanach and Camas Ghaodeil, where you can pitch your tent amidst the remnants of lost villages. If you're not much of a camper, retreat to a highland cottage on the peaceful wooded island Eilean Shona or a cosy turf-roofed building on the wildly beautiful and remote Ardnamurchan peninsula.

Ardnamurchan's diverse and unspoilt landscape is home to an abundance of wildlife and the most westerly point of the British mainland. Along the shores of the island-studded and seal-filled Loch Sunart are peaceful ancient woodlands carpeted in wildflowers, and beautiful nature trails to explore between Strontian and Glenborrodale. Here you have high chances of spotting otters, red deer, red squirrels and a variety of birdlife, perhaps even a golden eagle! Follow the single-track road further on to the wind-lashed lighthouse at Ardnamurchan point and you also have a chance of seeing dolphins and whales, before ending the day on the soft white sands at Sanna Bay to watch the sun set behind the magical Small Isles.

BEACHES, COAST & BAYS

1 CAMUSDARACH BEACH

One of Scotland's most beautiful beaches and a popular swimming spot. Walk along the white sand, swim in the crystal water and enjoy panoramic views of Rùm and Eigg.

→ On the B8008 in Glenancross the beach car park is signed shortly N of the turning to PH40 4PN and on the opp side. Footpath to beach.
10 mins, 56.9575, -5.8427

2 PORT NAM MURRACH

Lovely secluded beach with great views at the end of the Rhu peninsula. Swim in the beautiful blue water and explore the rock pools, wonderful machair and the other small beaches around the point. There is also good wild camping by the beach.

→ From Arisaig follow dead-end road dir Rhu past PH39 4NU to end. Park in layby next to boathouse. Follow track into Arisaig Estate and along coast eventually reaching Rhu house. Turn L at house, follow fence, pass shed and go through gate. Continue on path curving R by a stone wall and then L through second gate. Continue on damper grassy section, then path bears L before rocky descent to bay.
2 hours, 56.8831, -5.9183

3 SMIRISARY WHITE SANDS BEACH

Small hidden white beaches at Port Achadh an Aonaich, sitting opposite Eilean Coille with the wild and rugged hills on Eilean Shona to the S. On a good day enjoy great views of the Small Isles and a bracing dip in the beautifully clear waters.

→ From Smirisary Township (see 11) turn R at end of field towards a white cottage, then L at a small sign. Follow path uphill along a ridge, passing a ruined house on L. Continue along coast until path drops down to two beaches.
90 mins, 56.8171, -5.8638

4 SINGING SANDS BY KENTRA

The whistling sands of remote Camas an Lighe are set in a bay lined with birch trees, with further coves to the E and views of Eigg and Rùm. Good wild camping near the beach.

→ From A861 at Acharacle take B8044 dir Kentra/Arivegaig/Ardtoe, and L again after ½ mile dir Arivegaig. From the car park at end, past PH36 4LE, go through gate and follow the clear track a mile, hugging the shore, bearing R past Gorteneorn House, then into forest. After further 1½ miles, bear R at sign for beach.
90 mins, 56.7527, -5.9045

5 ARDNAMURCHAN POINT

A wild and lonely place with fine views of the nearby islands and the chance to spot basking sharks, dolphins and other sealife. Often called the westernmost point of the mainland, it is just beaten by Corrachadh Mòr, a little over ½ mile S and just 30m or so further W – you can walk there along the coast. In summer you can pay to visit the lighthouse, dated 1849 and the only one in the UK built in an 'Egyptian' style, more obvious in the details seen close up.

→ From Kilchoan (PH36 4LH) follow the B8007 NW, take a L signed Grigadale/Lighthouse and continue until the road end where you will find a small car park.
10 mins, 56.7260, -6.2240

6 TRÀIGH BEACHES

Delightful silvery sands in sheltered bays sitting against a backdrop of machair. There are excellent views of the Small Isles and Skye, and great spots for swimming, picnics, beachcombing and exploring rock pools.

→ Head N from Tràigh Golf Course (PH39 4NT) to reach small car park on L after ½ mile.
5 mins, 56.9449, -5.8545

7 SANNA SANDS

Stunning bay situated at the tip of the British mainland's most westerly peninsula, with great views of the Small Isles. Around a series of coves and rocky islets, clear turquoise water laps beautiful white sands.

→ Follow B8007 from Kilchoan W dir Portuairk but turn R after 1 mile for Sanna (PH36 4LW). Car park at road end. Good sand and coves at Portuairk, too, but limited space to pull off.

10 mins, 56.7479, -6.1859 🏊🚶⛺🏖️📷

8 CAMAS NAN GEALL

This small sandy beach, sheltered in a grassy bay on an attractive stretch of coastline, is a lovely spot for a swim. For added interest find archaeological remains on the path down, including the remnants of a chambered cairn, two later burial grounds and ruined buildings. On the headland R are fragments of an Iron Age fort. Further along are the larger ruins of Bourblaige township.

→ Parking at large bay on B8007 above beach, 4 miles W of Glenborrodale, 2 miles past PH36 4JG. Follow farm track downhill, through kissing gate and across fields. From the beach continue to fort and Bourblaige via a rough path past stream at far R end of the beach.

90 mins, 56.6837, -5.9862 🏊🚶⛺🏛️

LOCHS & WILD SWIMMING

9 LOCH MORAR

Wildly beautiful 12-mile long loch surrounded by natural woodland and open hillside. The deepest loch in the British Isles and a great place to swim, fish or explore by small boat.

→ Turn L off the B8008 from Mòrar and park in one of the laybys between on the N Shore and Bracara (PH40 4PE).

10 mins, 56.9718, -5.7900 🏊🚶⛺🛶

10 LOCH SHIEL

Wonderful loch surrounded by spectacular Highland scenery and sweeping glens. At the head of the loch stands the Glenfinnan monument to the Jacobite rising that started here. From here follow the River Finnan NE to the Glenfinnan railway viaduct, most famous for appearing in four Harry Potter films.

→ Park at the pay & display NTS car park, just off A830 opp turning to PH37 4LT, and cross the road towards the loch.

10 mins, 56.8692, -5.4370 ⛺🚶🏛️

RUINS & ANCIENT REMAINS

11 SMIRISARY TOWNSHIP

Ancient village only accessible by foot in a quiet plot of land by the sea. Some of the charming cottages in the formerly deserted crofting community have since been restored and are used as holiday homes. From the village you can follow a rough coastal path to White Sands Beach (see 3).

→ From the A861, turn W into Glenuig Village (PH38 4NG) continue onto the minor road signposted to Smirisary and park in the car park L near road end, 1½ miles in all. Walk to the road end and enter a gate on your R, follow path down small fields and up through another gate to the village. Return by same route.

20 mins, 56.8271, -5.8577 🚶♿🏛️🚶

12 PEANMEANACH

A lonely stone bothy stands between the ruins of an abandoned village in this small bay on the Ardnish peninsula – emptied after the railway inland replaced boats as transport. The flat turf plateau and lovely sand and shingle beach also make it a great spot to camp for the night. The interesting coastline here is popular with kayakers.

→ Drive N on A830 from Lochailort for 2 miles and park in large layby on L before PH38 4NA. Follow path signposted right-of-way. Ignore paths leading L and follow the path downhill, crossing a humpback bridge over the

13

railway line and a footbridge over a burn. Beyond here the route to Peanmeanach is perfectly clear.

90 mins, 56.8594, -5.7546 🅱️🦪♻️⛺️🏊

13 CAMAS GHAOIDEIL

Deserted township on a secluded bay with fine views over the Sound of Arisaig to the hills of Moidart. Wonderful wild-camping. Enjoy a swim and a campfire on the quiet stony beach and visit a remarkable little cabin perched on a cliff edge above the bay.

→ Park in Arisaig and start as for Port nam Murrach beach (see 2). Where road swings R at PH39 4NU follow a clear vehicle track straight ahead. Pass Glen Cottage on R and through two gates (close gates). Continue through a wooded glen with burn on L then turn R through a deer fence gate. At fork, keep R and go through another gate. Clear route to shore.

75 mins, 56.8883, -5.8269 🏞️🏖️⛺️🏊

14 CASTLE TIORAM

Ruined, turreted castle on the rocky tidal island of Eilean Tioram, where the waters of Loch Moidart and the River Shiel meet. It is no longer safe to go inside the castle, but you can visit the island. Alternatively follow the Silver Walk route from the car park,

which offers great views of the castle

→ Turn W off A861 dir Dorlinn along E of the River Shiel past PH36 4JY. The road soon forks, turn R and follow to parking area at end.

10 mins, 56.7845, -5.8289 🏞️🚶

ANCIENT WOODLAND

15 ARIUNDLE OAKWOODS

Sometimes referred to as Scotland's rainforest, Ariundle is a peaceful woodland featuring remnants of the ancient coastal oak forest that once spanned the Atlantic coasts of Europe. The ferns, primitive plants, lichens and mosses growing over the damp woodland floor are a fascinating reminder of some of the oldest vegetation in the world. Look out for its rare butterflies.

→ From Strontian on the A861, head past PH36 4JA then turn R signed Aryundle where road forks. Follow for 2 miles to the signed Airigh Fhionndail car park.

2 hours, 56.7106, -5.5516 🍽️🚶♻️🏃

LOCAL FOOD

16 GLENFINNAN DINING CAR

Enjoy a unique experience dining in a 1950s railway carriage with a veranda viewpoint at

Glenfinnan Station Museum. Tea, coffees, light lunches and traditional meals every day, and diners are entitled to a free tour of the museum exhibition. Closed in winter.

→ Station Cottage, Glenfinnan, PH37 4LT, 01397 722300. Glenfinnanstationmuseum.co.uk 56.8722, -5.4494

17 THE BAKEHOUSE & CRANNOG, MALLAIG

Fantastic artisan bakery and pizzeria serving up tasty bread, pizzas, handmade cakes, pastries and great coffee.

→ Old Quay, Mallaig PH41 4QF, 01687 462808. Facebook.com/oldquaybakehouse 57.0046, -5.8272 🍴

18 THE BOATHOUSE, ARDGOUR

Varied highland cuisine including fresh local produce from the Kingairloch Estate, served in a restored Victorian boathouse in a fantastic location.

→ Kingairloch Estate, Ardgour, PH33 7AE, 01967 411242. Kingairloch.co.uk 56.6172, -5.5173 🍴

19 LOCHAILORT INN

Small hotel and bar with great traditional Scottish character amidst stunning scenery.

25

Situated on the doorstep of a natural larder, the Inn serves fantastic fresh meals made with locally sourced produce. Seasonal dishes, particularly game- and seafood-based, are their specialty.

→ Lochailort, PH38 4LZ, 01687 470208. Lochailortinn.co.uk
56.8788, -5.6654 🍴

20 KITTIWAKE'S KITCHEN, ARDNAMURCHAN

The café is part of the Sonachan Hotel and bunkhouse, and serves up hearty local food, drinks and good coffee, which can all be enjoyed by a wood burner. Take time to visit the little garden hut shop across the road outside which sells a selection of wonderful local produce. Closed in winter.

→ Sonachan, Kilchoan, Acharacle, PH36 4LN, 01972510211. Sonachan.com
56.7198, -6.1643 🍴🏕

CAMPING & BUNKHOUSES

21 INVERCAIMBE CAMPSITE, ARISAIG

Beachside campsite within a working croft, in the same family for 270 years. A perfect place for a coastal camping trip with swimming and campfires allowed on the beach and stunning views of the Small Isles. Electric hookups, showers, laundry & wifi.

→ Invercaimbe, Arisaig PH39 4NT, 01687 450375. Invercaimbecaravansite.co.uk
56.9398, -5.8625 🏕🚿🚻🧺📶

22 MALLAIG BACKPACKERS LODGE

Homely hostel in the oldest croft house in Mallaig with a great onsite café/restaurant, the Tea Garden. Home cooking, baking and good coffee in the flower garden by day and bistro-style food using local meats, seafood and farm vegetables by the original croft fireplace by night. Great base for exploring the Road to the Isles.

→ Station Roadd, Mallaig, PH41 4PU, 01687 462764.
57.0054, -5.8290 🏕🍴

23 ARDNAMURCHAN CAMPSITE

Charming camping and caravanning site with great views across the north of Mull. Semi-wild camping by the shore is a good place for spotting porpoises and other interesting wildlife. Closed in winter.

→ Ormsaigbeg, Kilchoan Acharacle PH36 4LL, 01972 510766. Ardnamurchanstudycentre.co.uk
56.6897, -6.1324 🏕🚿🚐

COSY COTTAGES

24 THE SEASHELL, GLENBORRODALE

Unique luxury self-catering hidden in the hills in Ardamurchan. A timber, stone and glass house shaped like a shell perches above the sea. With a huge open fire, spa bath and beautiful views it's the perfect intimate highland getaway.

→ Glenmore Holidays Glenborrodale, Acharacle, PH36 4J, 01972 500254. Holidayardnamurchan.co.uk
56.6908, -5.9445 🏠🚐

25 TIORAM HOUSE, EILEAN SHONA

Stunning stone cottage with an open coal fire and views of Castle Tioram (see 14). The cottage is set by the shore of Loch Moidart on the private and peaceful wooded island of Eilean Shona. Author JM Barrie leased Eilean Shona in the 1920s and is thought to have written a screenplay of *Peter Pan* while here. Utterly magical!

→ Eilean Shona, Acharacle, PH36 4LR, 01967 431249. Eileanshona.com
56.7923, -5.8182 🏠🚐🚣☕

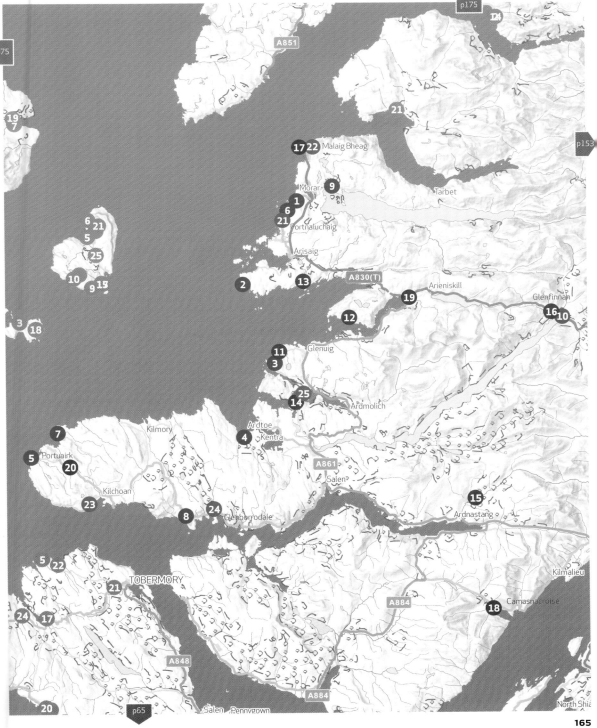

A851

19
7

17 22 Malaig Bheag

Tarbet

21

6 21
5

9

25

10
9 15

1

6
21 Portnaluchaig

Arisaig

2

13

A830(T) Arieniskill

Glenfinnan

12

19

16
10

3
18

11
3 Glenuig

25
14 Ardmolich

7 Kilmory

Ardtoe

4 Kentra

A861

Salen

15
Ardnastang

5 Portuairk
20

23 Kilchoan

8

24 Glenborrodale

A884 Kilmalieu

Camasnacroise

18

5 22
TOBERMORY

21

24
17

A848

A884

20

Salen Pennygown

North Shia

APPLECROSS, KINTAIL & LOCHALSH

Our perfect weekend

→ **Warm** up with a walk to the plunging white Falls of Glomach, some of the highest in the country.

→ **Enjoy** breakfast at the lovely Sheena's Tea Hut and explore the Corran coast path.

→ **Play** on the white sands of stunning Sandaig Bay and swim in the bright waters.

→ **Relax** with a coffee or a pint and waterside views at the Glenelg Inn.

→ **Catch** the sunset at remote Camban Bothy, a welcome overnight break in the Bealach an Sgàirne circuit.

→ **Refresh** in the morning with a swim at a remote plunge pool on the Allt Gleann Ghnìòmaidh.

→ **Rise** to the challenge of a cycle up and over the twisting Bealach Na Bà, pausing at the top for breath – and breathtaking views.

→ **Descend** to a well-earned pint, or fresh local ice cream at the Applecross Inn.

These unique peninsulas are sometimes seen as merely a gateway region for their larger, more popular neighbour to the west – Skye. The Skye phenomenon looms large here, and most travellers bypass these areas in favour of the short trip across the bridge. That is not to say that Skye isn't amazing, but there are other pleasures in this area that are often overlooked. Like most of the Western Highlands, this region packs a huge variety of landscapes into a relatively compact area. However, the sparsity of roads in and out of the three promontories give Applecross and the Glenelg peninsula in particular a wild and untouched atmosphere; there is little of the unsightly development or mass tourism that at times affects Skye. Resist the urge to travel further west, and stay a while – this is an area of hidden jewels and well-kept secrets.

Applecross, to the north, feels like a miniature country in itself, with remote villages linked by lofty mountain roads, often snow-bound in winter. Until the early 20th century the village that gives the headland its name was only accessible by boat, after that the only road in was over the tortuous Bealach Na Bà. Cycle it and see for yourself! This isolation has endowed Applecross with an independent mindset and a real community feel.

Kintail and Lochalsh are less inaccessible, but both a real mecca for walkers and a brilliant stop off en-route to Skye. Some of the grandest mountain scenery and most popular Munros are situated here – The Five Sisters of Kintail and the Saddle. Deep glens, soaring ridges and dark mountain passes characterise the landscape, and the long-distance Bealach an Sgàirne circuit is an absolute must if time, fitness and weather allow.

Like Applecross, Glenelg has limited access; there is only one road in. A peaceful peninsula, it is a lazy place to soak up the delights of the West Highlands, away from the crowds. Some of the best hospitality is to be found at Sheena's Tea Hut in Corran, a place you should plan adventures around. Arnisdale and Corran are simply stunning on a hot summer's day, and the local atmosphere of the sleepy villages is the perfect antidote to the fast pace of modern life.

BEACHES & THE SEA

1 SANDAIG BAY AND ISLANDS

Intense turquoise bay with a white beach and a Mediterranean feel, dotted with little rocky islets. Immortalised by Gavin Maxwell in his classic book, *Ring of Bright Water* under the disguising name of Camusfearna. A stunningly beautiful place for a swim.

→ Start from the layby (limited space, also a passing place) next to the Forestry Commission track in Upper Sandaig on the Glenelg to Arnisdale road (IV40 8JB). The beaches are visible below. Follow the main Forestry Commission track down to bay, ignoring any turnings R.

60 mins, 57.1689, -5.6877 ▼●▲♨

2 CORRAN COASTAL PATH

This interesting ramble from the beautiful village of Corran along the shore of Loch Hourn takes you through some of the most unspoilt and grandest scenery in the Highlands, with numerous swimming opportunities from the pebbly beaches. Initially easy, the path takes on a rugged character the further you go.

→ In Corran park at car park N of the bridge (IV40 8JH). Cross the bridge and follow the path that weaves its way along the shore, which is rough and rocky in places. The path ends 2½ miles along the coast; return the same way. Up to 60 mins to path end.

5–60 mins, 57.1239, -5.5539 ▼●▲

3 SAND BEACH, APPLECROSS

Fine sandy beaches with excellent views over to Skye, Raasay and Rona. An ideal wild camping spot.

→ From Applecross (IV54 8ND) head N 2 miles to turning into Sand car park overlooking the beach on L. Follow track down to the beach.

5 mins, 57.4700, -5.8649 ●▲♨

4 CULDUIE CORAL BEACHES

Two beautiful coral-like maërl beaches with tranquil turquoise water. An amazing place for a swim.

→ Heading S from Applecross to Toscaig, there is parking at the junction of the road that leads to Aird Dhubh (500m S from IV54 8LX). Walk along the Aird Dhubh road a short way and take signed footpath over the moor towards beaches. This forks, the branches visiting different beaches, both extremely attractive.

30 mins, 57.3823, -5.8270 🐚▲

5 FALLS OF GLOMACH

This magnificent and remote 113m cataract is one of Britain's highest and often called Scotland's best. It is well worth the walk in, which passes through a steep-sided gorge impressive in its own right.

→ Start at the NTS car park at Morvich (IV40 8HQ). Follow the road upriver, ignoring two L branches to cross the bridge at Innichro/ Innis a' Chròtha and follow signs from here. Keep L then R at two forks as the path passes through forestry. After crossing a bridge and leaving forestry the path follows a well-worn stalkers' route up to the falls.

3 hours, 57.2786, -5.2890 🌊▼

6 ALLT GLEANN GHNÌOMAIDH

The Allt Gleann Ghnìomaidh river features an incredible plunge pool that provides a refreshing dip and a welcome rest spot. The pool is deep, crystal clear and easily reached. It also makes for an outstanding wild camping spot.

→ Follow directions for the Bealach an Sgàirne circuit (see 9). The plunge pool is roughly halfway up Gleann Ghnìomaidh and marked by a free-standing fin of detached rock. 2½ hrs from Camban Bothy (see 24)

2½ hrs, 57.2312, -5.2507 ▼▲▼

24

7 LOCH A' BHEALAICH

Large and tranquil loch in a remote setting of grand mountain scenery. A great spot for secluded wild swimming.

→ Follow directions for the Bealach an Sgàirne circuit (see 9). The loch is further up Gleann Ghniomaidh from the plunge pool. 3–4 hours from Camban bothy (see 24).

3–4 hrs, 57.2347, -5.2716 🟡🔵🔷Ⓥ

ANCIENT WOODLAND

8 RASSAL WOOD

This 6000-year-old ash woodland is also a wildflower paradise.

→ Start from the small lay-by N of Tornapress on the A896, halfway between two National Nature Reserve signs (½ mile S of IV54 8UY). Pass through a gate with information boards on the walk 100m up road to N. Continue R to the woodlands. The path is boggy in places.

30 mins, 57.4266, -5.5918 🟡🔷🔵🚶

MOUNTAINS & GLENS

9 BEALACH AN SGÀIRNE CIRCUIT

Incredibly wild and remote circuit through lonely glens and over lofty mountain passes. This extended trip passes through some of

the most dramatic scenery in the central Highlands, becoming increasingly wild. It is too long to enjoy in one day; break the journey with a stay at Camban bothy (see 24) or Glen Affric hostel (see 25), or simply by wild camping. The circuit incorporates points of interest detailed further in the chapter. There are extremely well-made paths almost all the way, with some indistinct sections heading up Gleinn Gniomhaidh, but this is one for the adventurous and properly equipped – help is a long way off.

→ Start at the NTS car park in Morvich (IV40 8HQ). Follow signs for Glen Affric via Gleann Licht, taking the wide track along the River Croe up Gleann Licht (or Lichd), passing a red-roofed mountaineering hut. Ignore a path off R and cross two well-made footbridges. Follow the excellent path over the Alt Grannda gorge past the waterfall and down the other side of the pass to Camban Bothy. Follow the path to a confluence of rivers (57.2285, -5.1940). Cross the first footbridge (the second leads to Glen Affric hostel), and follow the path L into Gleann Ghniomaidh. The path can be indistinct and boggy here, but the way up the glen is obvious, passing a plunge pool on the Allt Gleann Ghniomaidh. Eventually the path reaches Loch a' Bhealaich (see 7), before continuing up and over Bealach an

Sgàirne (see 1) between Meall a' Bhealaich and A' Ghlas Bheinn. Gleann Chòinneachain has well-ordered forest cultivation and leads back to Morvich.

8–10 hrs, 57.2285, -5.1940 🟡Ⓥ🔵❓🔷Ⓑ🔺

---

10 BEALACH AN SGÀIRNE

An impressively steep-sided mountain pass and subsequent gorge. An excellent path winds up and over this rugged notch between towering peaks – a truly stunning finale to an action packed walk with breathtaking mountain scenery.

→ Follow directions for the Bealach an Sgàirne circuit (see 9). For a shorter but steep trip to just the bealach, head up Gleann Chòinneachain from the start point and return the same way; this will still be a half-day round trip. 30 mins from Loch a' Bhealaich.

30 mins, 57.2405, -5.29523 Ⓥ🟡🔵🔺

---

11 BEALACH NA BÀ

An amazing road to drive, cycle or run. Peaking at over 600m, it is one of the highest roads in the UK and is a marvel of engineering. There are plenty of places to stop and take photographs of the towering cliffs, hairpin bends or far-reaching views in all directions. A tough but rewarding ride.

13

→ Turn off the A896 1½ miles N of Kishorn at Tornapress Bridge junction, dir IV54 8XF. Cross the River Kishorn, and where the single-track road forks follow R up and through the obvious mountain pass to Applecross.
1 min, 57.4187, -5.7085 🎿🏔️⛺📷

12 SGURR A' CHAORACHAIN
An easily accessible mountain summit, making use of good tracks and one of the highest car parks in the country. Enjoy lofty summit fever with minimal input.
→ Start at the viewpoint car park at the summit of Bealach na Bà (see 11). There is a trig point with information here, and brilliant views over to Skye. Follow the excellent vehicle track to the television mast visible from the car park. From the mast head S then E along rough and rocky ground following the undulating ridge – no path here. There are incredible views down to the Cioch Nose spur to the N side of the ridge.
2 hrs, 57.4128, -5.6706 🏔️📷

CASTLES

13 LOCH DUICH & EILEAN DONAN CASTLE
Extremely picturesque, this much-photographed restored castle on a tidal island is an easy stop just off the road. A great example of picture-postcard Scotland and a perfect backdrop for a dip in the loch. The castle can be visited too.
→ Car park on the loch side off the A87 just S of turning for Dornie (IV40 8DX).
5 mins, 57.2741, -5.5157 🦢⛺♿

LOCAL FOOD

14 SHEENA'S TEA HUT
A warm, charming and generous café situated in a beachy wooden shack, beautifully situated on the coast at the very end of sleepy Corran. Very dog friendly; closed in winter.
→ Cullin View, Arnisdale, IV40 8JH, 01599 522336.
57.1239, -5.5538 🍴

15 KISHORN SEAFOOD BAR
Delicious local seafood served in a friendly and welcoming atmosphere. People travel great distances on a weekend to visit this place. Highly recommended.
→ Kishorn, Strathcarron, IV54 8XA, 01520 733240.
57.3989, -5.6005 🍴

16 THE BEALACH CAFÉ & GALLERY
Friendly café, featuring local food and an interesting art gallery. Ideally situated for fuelling up for a cycle over the Bealach na Bà (see 12) or celebrating its completion if you've just come the other way. Limited opening in winter.
→ Bealach Café and Gallery, Tornapress, IV54 8XE, 01520 733436.
57.4191, -5.6029 🍴

17 APPLECROSS INN-SIDE OUT
Delicious ice creams served from a Freedom Jetstream caravan opposite the Applecross Inn in the heart of the village. Perfect if you've just cycled the Bealach na Bà (see 12). Closed in winter – refreshment available in the inside Inn instead.
→ Applecross, IV54 8LR, 01520 744262.
57.4328, -5.8161 🍴🍺

18 KINLOCHHOURN FARM
Located at the end of a 22-mile winding road through spectacular scenery and then opening up to a dramatic valley, where Kinlochhourn Farm is perfectly placed. Offering tea and cakes with breathtaking views to the Head of Loch Hourn. The ideal

starting point of a hike through Knoydart.

→ Kinlochhourn, Invergarry, PH35 4HD, 01809 511253 Kinlochhourn.com
57.1046, -5.3859 ⊞

INNS & PUBS

19 GLENELG INN

Cosy pub serving local food with an emphasis on seafood, with outstanding views from its garden. Regular music night, B&B and rooms available.

→ Kirkton, Kyle IV40 8JR, 01599 522273.
57.2122, -5.6227 ⊞⊟⊟⊟

20 THE APPLECROSS INN

Local food, excellent atmosphere and lovely outdoor seating with views over to Skye. A focal point for the community. Rooms available.

→ Applecross, IV54 8LR, 01520 744262.
57.4328, -5.8161 ⊞⊟

21 THE OLD FORGE

Britain's remotest pub situated in the stunning landscape of Knoydart, often referred to as Scotland's last wilderness. Accessible only by ferry from Mallaig or an 18-mile hike through rough country, The Old Forge is a place full of charm and character.

→ Inverie, Knoydart, Mallaig, PH41 4PL, 01687 462267 Theoldforge.co.uk
57.0387, -5.6840 ⊞⊟

BOTHIES & OFF-GRID

22 UAGS BOTHY

A wild and lonely bothy, right on the seashore at the southern tip of the Applecross peninsula with fantastic views across to Skye.

→ Park at the end of the road at Toscaig (IV54 8LY) head for a footbridge and follow the path signed Airigh-Drishaig and Uags to the L. At a metal signpost take R fork and follow the rough, often indistinct path S over moorland, keeping the coastline on your R. 4 hours walk.
57.3486, -5.7874 ⊞⊟⊟

23 SUARDALAN BOTHY & GLENELG BROCHS

This easy scenic walk to an often-overlooked bothy takes you back in time past Dun Telve (57.1944, -5.5994) and Dun Trodden (57.1947, -5.5865) brochs, remarkably well preserved Iron Age forts. Dun Telve is one of the best preserved in the country.

→ Start from the centre of Glenelg and walk S on the main road. After 2km head E up Gleann

Beag to IV40 8JX; brochs are visible by the road. Follow the public road to a farmhouse, pass through the gate on R and follow a track up the glen. At a fork head L and continue on to the bothy. 3 hours walk.
57.1969, -5.5060 ⊞⊟

24 CAMBAN BOTHY

One of the most remote bothies in Scotland, Camban is 10 miles from anywhere and as such is an extremely welcoming and reassuring shelter set in incredible scenery. With stunning views over to the Five Sisters of Kintail, this is a place of savage beauty.

→ Follow directions for the Bealach an Sgàirne circuit (see 9). 3 hours walk.
57.2143, -5.2252 ⊟⊟⊟⊟

25 GLEN AFFRIC YOUTH HOSTEL

Still known familiarly as Alltbeithe, the place name on the OS map, this tiny eco-hostel is a former estate hunting bothy. It is only accessible on foot or mountain bike, and there are no signs to it, but it is a good place to break the Bealach an Sgàirne circuit (see 9) about halfway around.

→ Allt Beithe, Glen Affric, 0345 2937373. Shya.org.uk
57.2325, -5.1838 ⊟⊟

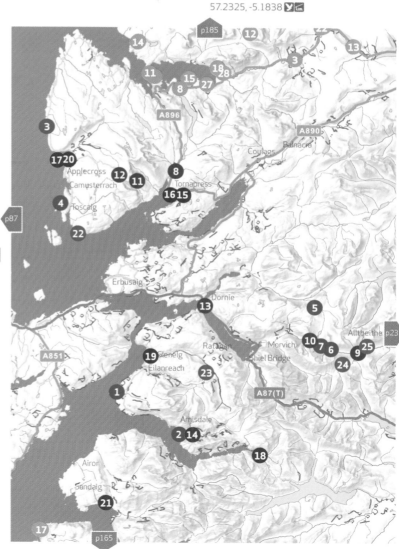

TORRIDON & GAIRLOCH

Our perfect weekend

→ **Sip** your morning coffee at the bustling Torridon Stores and Café, checking the local events and planning a weekend of adventures.

→ **Marvel** at the dramatic buttresses of Coire Mhic Fhearchair on Beinn Eighe.

→ **Wander** amongst venerable pine trees and the ancient rocks of Torridon in the Wood of the Grey Slope.

→ **Swim** and relax in the remarkable turquoise waters of Gruinaird Bay, not to be missed.

→ **Dine** at the small and dedicated Ghillie Bridghe restaurant in Diabaig, and feel like you've been let in on a local secret.

→ **Sleep** in peace at the little loch-side campsite at Badrallach, or wake beneath the barrel-vaulted metal ceiling of the cottage.

→ **Watch** salmon on their epic autumnal journey upstream leaping the Falls of Balgy.

The unusual juxtaposition of savage mountains, rough-hewn geology and tranquil bays characterises the dramatic landscape of Torridon and Gairloch. The area is famous for its rugged mountains, with three giant Munros – Liathach, Beinn Eighe and Beinn Alligin – dominating the area like a trio of brooding brothers. Composed of ancient Torridonian sandstone, capped with quartzite screes and arranged on linear terraces, their vast bulk and form are instantly recognisable and attractive to hill-walkers and photographers. Contrast this with the small, peaceful villages and gentle turquoise seas that lap the inlets of Grunaird Bay and Gairloch and you have a spectacular and unique area, one of the finest in the Highlands.

Torridon and Gairloch form a broad peninsula on the north-western seaboard, with a fjord-cut coastline that looks out over to the Outer Hebrides. To the south the tiny village of Torridon nestles at the foot of mighty Liathach – the scale of the hulking mountain beside the small cottages is an impressive sight. Further north the promontory is split by Loch Maree and Loch Ewe and before Little Loch Broom, with Ullapool on the northern shore. The area gives its name to Torridonian sandstone, a rough, red rock that is around 500 million years old and gives many of the cliffs and mountains in the area their distinctive appearance.

Like much of the north-western Highlands, this is a paradise for wilderness activities. The area is a hill-walking mecca, but has managed to retain an air of remoteness and even mystery. The turquoise bays and pristine white sand beaches make simply beautiful wild swimming spots, while canoeing and kayaking in the reasonably sheltered bays and coves is also great fun. Swimming in Gruinard Bay in March with snow on the hills is an unforgettable experience!

The area is quickly reached on the A832 winding west from Inverness, but for those with time to spare the most scenic approach is from the south, up the A82 and west through dramatic Kintail and Glen Shiel before coming over the high pass overlooking Loch Carron.

BEACHES, COAST & ISLANDS

1 GRUINARD BAY

Limpid, aquamarine waters, a pristine sandy beach and rugged mountainous backdrop make Gruinard Bay one of the natural wonders of Scotland. A gorgeous place for a wild swim or camp. On a hot day, you could imagine it's the Caribbean.

→ From Little Gruinard beach car park on the A832 (½ mile E of IV22 2QY) cross the road and descend the wooden steps.

5 mins, 57.8521, -5.4520

2 CAMAS AN LÈIM

Secluded and peaceful little pebble beach just north of Shieldaig (see 11).

→ Park at N end of Shieldaig (IV54 8XN) off A896 and walk up past the school and tennis courts. Bear R off the path after 0.6 miles.

20 mins, 57.5359, -5.6462

3 LOCH CLAIR

Panoramic views of Liathach from this loch. There is a good spot to camp on a spur that juts out into the water.

→ Start from a layby either side of a cattle grid on the A896 (½ mile W of turning to IV22 2ES) E of Torridon. Head S over rough ground to the spit of land.

5 mins, 57.5641, -5.3569

4 RED POINT SOUTH BEACH

Lovely sandy beach surrounded by machair where flowers grow in abundance in summer.

→ Park at the end of the road to Red Point (IV21 2AX), go through the gate at the end of the farm and follow the track to another gate. Stay R after the gate and continue to beach.

15 mins, 57.6402, -5.7990

5 GAINEAMH MHÒR BEACH

Clear waters, a long sweep of soft sand and easy access – perfect for a quick swim.

→ From Gairloch golf club car park (just N of IV21 2BE), head down the boardwalk to beach.

5 mins, 57.7142, -5.6885

6 MELLON UDRIGLE BEACH

Great views across the water from this easily accessible beach with turquoise sea and a crescent of pure white sand.

→ There is a parking area R just before the small hamlet of Mellon Udrigle (IV22 2NT) with a path to the beach.

5 mins, 57.9026, -5.5588

LOCHS & WATERFALLS

7 LOCH MAREE

A vast loch scattered with 66 wooded islands, home to remnants of the original ancient Scots pine forest. All are conservation areas, important for the preservation of many native species of flora and fauna. The waters are supposed to have healing powers – a hermitage and monastery were established here in the 8th century. Good for canoeing, contact Ewe Canoe (07980 588467).

→ The Tollie Path runs aside Loch Maree for 5 miles, but you can take it as far as the loch. Park at layby off A832 (opp IV22 2JZ), walk uphill several metres to the start of the path, which winds to reach Loch Maree after 3 miles.

90 mins, 57.7146, -5.5594

8 FALLS OF BALGY

This turbulent waterfall is a great place to watch salmon leaping upstream in autumn. It can be combined with the Àird Mhòr peninsula (see 15) to provide a varied circuit.

→ Park as for Àird Mhòr. Take path on E of the bridge S along River Balgy, with river on your R. The falls are about ½ mile S.

10 mins, 57.5231, -5.5933

3

9 FAIRY LOCHS, BADACHRO

Tranquil little lochans in the hills, more properly called Lochan Sgeireach, and the crash site of a USAAF Liberator in 1945. A propeller and other wreckage remains, there is a memorial plaque and the area is classed as a war grave.

→ From a layby just W of the Shieldaig Hotel (IV21 2AW), take the public signed path. The route is marked by cairns; turn L at the first cairn sign, and again at the next. Path is boggy in places. Stay on the track following the cairns, it reaches a high point with good views before descending to the Fairy Lochs.

30 mins, 57.6783, -5.6760 🏊⛪🔆

10 LOCH KERNSARY

Quintessential north-western Highland loch, with great views over to Fisherfield and the Torridon hills.

→ Walk N from the centre of Poolewe (IV22 2JX). At the end of the speed restriction, after a long white house there is a footpath signed for Loch Kernsary. This passes through the Cnoc na Lise woodland to reach the shores of the loch. It is possible to make a complete circuit of the loch, but only on much rougher paths.

30 mins, 57.7673, -5.5759 🏕🐾🔆

MOUNTAINS & PENINSULAS

11 SHIELDAIG

Romantic whitewashed cottages set in front of mountains and facing out to sea make Shieldaig a contender, along with nearby Diabaig, for the most picturesque village in Scotland. This short walk takes you out to Camas Ruadh beach on the peninsula, a good place to spot otters.

→ Park in Shieldaig (IV54 8XN), head N uphill through town to the school, up the road to the R of school, through a gate and below sports pitch. Take R fork at sign for Rubha Lodge and continue N. Track becomes a path and forks; keep L to follow coast all the way.

40 mins, 57.5396, -5.6569 🏊🐚🔆🔆🏊

12 COIRE MHIC FHEARCHAIR, BEINN EIGHE

The towering triple buttress of Coire Mhic Fhearchair is a stupendous sight, dominating a lochan in the centre of the corrie, and the site of an RAF crash in 1951. This path leads into the corrie with Liathach on the left and Beinn Eighe on the right and stops at the lochan, where the views are best. Beyond this the way becomes hazardous; the difficulty of reaching the crash site changed both RAF practices and the mountain rescue.

Atmospheric and even more so in winter.

→ Start from layby on A896 W of the bridge over the Allt a'Choire Dhuibh Mhoir (2 miles E of IV22 2ET). Take path signed for Coire Mhic Nobuil. After 1¼ miles take R fork and keep following path as it contours R around.

2½ hrs, 57.5918, -5.4529 🔆🏊🏊🔆🏔

13 KINLOCHEWE ROAD VIEWPOINT

Famous viewpoint over a perfect scoop of valley looking down towards Loch Maree. Great picnic spot, with no effort at all.

→ 3 miles SE of Kinlochewe (IV22 2PB) on A832.

5 mins, 57.5827, -5.2357 🏔🔆

14 DIABAIG

The pretty lochside hamlet of Lower Diabaig is sleepy and very seductive. At the end of the road, tucked in between cliffs it overlooks a crescent bay with views over Loch Torridon. There is much to do, from poking around the rapidly diminishing wreck of a fishing boat on the shore to walking the rugged circular coastal path to Inveralligin. Finish your day at the Gille Brighde (see 19).

→ Pass through Torridon continuing on minor road, following all signs to Diabaig (IV22 2HE). Park at Lower Diabaig, beside the pier. Coastal path starts just before the last

house at end of the village and heads S around the peninsula to rejoin the road you drove in on at Alligin Shuas. The going is rough and rugged at times, and the circuit is 7½ miles in total.
5–180 mins, 57.5746, -5.6863 ⛺🏄🚿⛴🍴🏪🚻

15 ÀIRD MHÒR
Small peninsula and easy walk that offers fine views of Beinn Alligin and Liathach – the Torridon 'big beasts'.
→ Park at Balgy Bridge on the A86; there is a limited room for cars either side of the bridge (IV54 8XP). Take gravel path signed for Annat E of the bridge and follow E for about 1¼ miles before taking a L up the peninsula. This path forks into a loops clockwise around the end of the peninsula, so either fork will eventually re-join this path to return to the start.
40 mins, 57.5359, -5.5750 🚶🚻🏪🚻

FORESTS & GARDENS

16 WOOD OF THE GREY SLOPE
Beinn Eighe was Britain's first National Nature Reserve, due in part to its Caledonian pine woods. It is a commanding mountain, with rugged corries that are a testing ground for winter climbers. This lower walk takes in the awe-inspiring forest scenery as well as

the geology of the Torridon area – these trees are a remnant of 8,000-year-old forest, and the rocks are amongst the oldest in Europe.
→ 2½ miles NW of Kinlochewe (IV22 2PB) on A832 park in dedicated Coille na Glas Letire Trails car park. Walk through underpass, cross bridge and head L at the junction. After a while the path meets the Mountain Trail; keep R. At next fork take a R to viewpoint overlooking Loch Maree and a plinth detailing the various rock. Return to path, R and follow back to start.
30 mins, 57.6302, -5.3570 🚗🚶🏕🏪🚻

17 INVEREWE GARDENS
A lush, sub-tropical oasis incongruously situated amidst rugged, unforgiving scenery. Started on bare rock and scrub in 1862 and now owned by NTS, it features everything from Wollemi pines to Himalayan blue poppies.
→ Just north of Poolewe on the A832 (IV22 2LG). Many trails head around the estate.
2–3 hrs, 57.7752, -5.5963 🚗🚶🏕🏪🚻🍴

FOOD

18 TORRIDON STORES & CAFÉ
Torridon is a tiny, picturesque hamlet nestled in the shadow of Liathach. The village shop and café is a bustling, lively place, where

locals catch up on news and tourists enjoy coffee. Limited opening in winter.
→ Torridon, IV22 2EZ, 01445 791400. Torridonstoresandcafe.co.uk
57.5496, -5.5163 🍴

19 GILLE BRIGHDE
Highly recommended restaurant run with a great deal of passion. Local food, friendly hosts. Closed in winter and limited hours in summer, with booking essential for evenings; the emphasis is on keeping up the quality.
→ The Old Schoolhouse, Diabaig, IV22 2HE, 01445 790245. Gille-brighde.com
57.5755, -5.6848 🍴🚻

20 ISLE OF EWE SMOKEHOUSE
Artisan smokehouse specialising in mouth-watering smoked salmon.
→ Ormiscaig, Aultbea, IV22 2JJ, 01445 731304. Smokedbyewe.com
57.8535, -5.6181 🍴

21 BADACHRO INN
Real ales, real fires, fine wine, 50 malts, delicious food with an emphasis on local seafood, and great views from outside seating and a conservatory.

→ Badachro, IV21 2AA, 01445 741255.
Badachroinn.com
57.6983, -5.7236 🍴🛏

22 WHISTLE STOP CAFÉ
Excellent café with a woodburner. A real gem.
→ Kinlochewe IV22 2PF, 01445 760423.
57.6030, -5.30482 🍴

SLEEP WILD

23 SANDS CAMPING & CARAVAN PARK
Set in front of a pristine beach with views
over to Skye and the Outer Hebrides, Sands
has separate caravan and tent areas, heated
wooden wigwams and a house. Well regarded
café and playground on site. Closed in winter.
→ Gairloch, IV21 2DL, 01445 712152.
Sandscaravanandcamping.co.uk
57.7405, -5.7652 🚐🏕🛶

24 KINLOCHEWE HOTEL & BUNKHOUSE
A hotel and old-fashioned Scottish bar with
a cheap and cheerful bunkhouse adjoining.
Booking advisable in summer.
→ Kinlochewe,IV22 2PA, 01445 760253.
Kinlochewehotel.co.uk
57.6040, -5.3007 🍴🛏

25 SHENAVALL BOTHY
One of the more famous bothies in the
Highlands, Shenavall has unrivalled
views over the remote wilderness of the
Fisherfield Forest estate. You are unlikely to
get this place to yourself.
→ From the long layby at Corrie Hallie on A832
(just S of IV23 2QN). Take track opp, signed for
Gruinard, Poolewe and Kinlochewe. Follow good
track for several miles to a R fork for Shenavall.
Follow this with An Teallach on your R. After 5
miles/2hrs, you will reach the bothy.
57.7767, -5.2541 📹🐦🏕🅱

26 BADRALLACH CAMPING & BOTHY
Quiet and small lochside camping bounded
by meadows with orchids and Little Loch
Broom. Also a low cost 'bothy-plus' and
quirkily renovated cottage.
→ Dundonnell, IV23 2QP, 01845 613240.
Badrallach.com
57.8733, -5.2652 ⛺🥾

27 THE TORRIDON BOATHOUSE
Very secluded shoreside cottage, with its own
road and jetty. A Torridon Hotel offshoot.
→ By Achnasheen, IV22 2EY, 01445 791242.
Thetorridon.com
57.5300, -5.5371 🛶🌀🚣🍴🛏

28 TORRIDON YOUTH HOSTEL
Conveniently located for exploring the area.
A modern hostel and a great budget base.
→ IV22 2EZ, 01445 791284. Syha.org.uk
57.5439, -5.5042 🥾

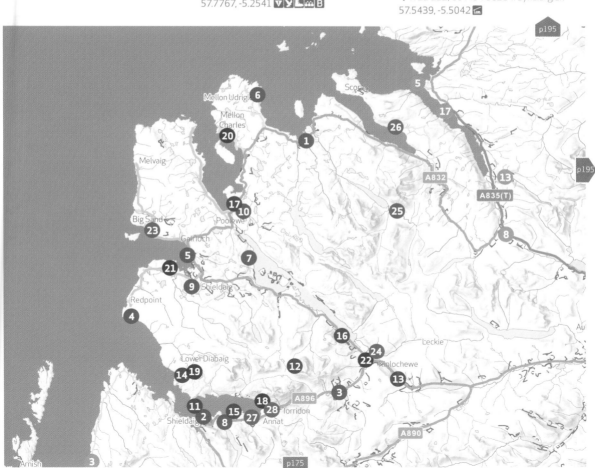

ULLAPOOL & ASSYNT

Our perfect weekend

→ **Walk** along the sea cliffs of Assynt to view The Old Man of Stoer.

→ **Marvel** at the tumbling white 'tresses' of Eas a' Chùal Aluinn, the UK's highest waterfall.

→ **Dare** to look down while walking across the suspension bridge over the Corrieshalloch Gorge.

→ **Explore** the wilds of Assynt along a hike around or up Stac Pollaidh.

→ **Pause** for a coffee in the Rock Stop Café and deepen your understanding of the landscape around you at the Exhibition Centre.

→ **Wander** under the unique tree canopies of Lael Forest, linking hands around a giant redwood.

→ **Sleep** next to the sands and wake with a swim at Achmelvich Beach.

→ **Luxuriate** in a fine-dining experience in the award winning Kylesku Hotel.

→ **Watch** the sunset from the comfort of your seat in the Stoer Lighthouse.

→ **Wake** up to unmatchable loch views from Glendhu Bothy.

Within this region, somewhere between Ullapool and Assynt lies an intriguing, invisible boundary that separates the colloquial 'north' from the true Highland north. You feel the change as you leave the pretty fishing village on the shore of Loch Broom and head boldly into a region that 'on the map' looks at first glance to be more water than land, punctuated by compelling mountains with names to suit – Suilven, Canisp, Conival and Quinag. The roads become twistier, the traffic recedes and the distance between settlements increases. You are entering the furthest wilderness of the country; you have crossed the Rubicon.

The bustling fishing village of Ullapool is on the A835, which winds up along the shores of Loch Broom, through the village and onwards to Assynt and north-west Sutherland beyond. Ullapool is an important gateway village for the Outer Hebrides, with busy ferry sailings and island traffic adding to its importance in the area. But it is charming in its own right, and is a good place to pause before heading into the wilderness beyond.

To the south lie the remote Fannichs and further west the mighty ridges of An Teallach. This is seriously high country, beloved of Munro-baggers and climbers, but there is more to the area than the challenge of the heights; the valleys contain gems like the redwoods of Lael and the Corrishalloch Gorge. To the north lie the intriguing, almost Martian landscapes of Assynt and Coigach. The hills here aren't particularly high, but each has its own unique character and stands completely alone in an otherwise flat expanse. It is quite unlike anywhere else in Scotland.

There are tremendous opportunities for cycling, wild camping, coastal exploration and hill-walking in this area, particularly because it is relatively sparsely populated and the roads are quiet. There are so many places where you can walk a short distance to a brilliant loch-side pitch or pull up a campervan in a deserted layby with a stunning view. Assynt is excellent for cycling and cycle touring; cycle companies know this, and come here to shoot promotional films. The coast is also brilliant for canoeing, with little inlets and hidden beaches perfect for paddling and exploring dotted along its wrinkled, crooked shoreline.

BEACHES & LOCHS

1 ACHMELVICH BEACH

One of the most enticing beaches in the north of the country – and there's a fair amount of competition. Achmelvich is a paradise of multiple small beaches with crystal clear water and pure white sands, nestled amongst the rocky bays of Assynt's coastline.

→ From the A837 just N of Lochinver take the B869 NW, then turn L after 1½ miles signed Achmelvich, past IV27 4JB to park at the road end next to the beach.

5 mins, 58.1703, -5.3069

2 CLACHTOLL BEACH

A truly exquisite bay of perfect sands lapped by turquoise water. There is another beautiful inlet just northwest formed of dramatically sloping rock strata either side of the sand, making the Bay of Clachtoll a popular spot for geologists.

→ From the A837 just N of Lochinver take the B869 NW and follow it to the small settlement of Clachtoll (IV27 4JD), turning L to park at the campsite.

5 mins, 58.1896, -5.3380

3 LOCH LURGAINN

A large, deep loch in spectacular surroundings, especially the iconic Stac Pollaidh (see page 14), which dominates the landscape to the north, and Sgòrr Tuath to the south. Plenty of wild camping options.

→ On the A835 N of Ullapool, head W at Drumrunie signed for Achiltibuie. Continue on this road 5 miles to car park (past IV26 2XY).

5 mins, 58.0352, -5.2066

INCREDIBLE COAST

4 THE OLD MAN OF STOER

A walk over rugged coastline to reach an incredible 60m sea stack, with fine coastal views over to Sutherland's mountains and the Western Isles. This is also a great place to catch sight of dolphins or whales – and maybe climbers on the stack.

→ From the B869, take the minor road NE signed Stoerhead lighthouse/Point of Stoer. Continue through the small settlement of Raffin past IV27 4JH to park at road end in sight of the lighthouse. Walk to the lighthouse and follow wide footpath signed Old Man of Stoer/3km. Follow this path running parallel to the cliff to the sea stack.

1.5 hrs, 58.2610, -5.3828

5 RHUE LIGHTHOUSE

Walk across a beautiful pebble beach to reach Rhue Lighthouse. Perched low on the coast of Loch Broom, this is a great viewpoint of the surrounding landscape and a lovely spot to watch the sun set. The Gaelic name, Rubha Cadail, means 'headland of the sleepy people', said to be from shipwrecked sailors found asleep and unharmed on the rocks.

→ From the A835, take the minor road heading NW dir Rhue. Park at the end of the road (beyond IV26 2TJ) and walk on the path towards the coast. Continue through the gate above a pebbled beach and to the lighthouse.

10 mins, 57.9257, -5.2234

WATERFALLS

6 EAS A' CHÙAL ALUINN

The UK's highest waterfall, the 'fall of the beautiful tresses' plunges 200m into the dramatic valley floor and flows down the valley into Loch Beag, an extension of the fjord of Loch Glencoul. The walk to this ribbon of white water takes you through the rocky landscape of Assynt to the best vantage point at the top of the falls.

→ From the A837 take the A894 N, dir Kylesku and IV27 4HW, to the car park at

Loch na Gainmhich after 3 miles. Walk NE over the outflow of the loch, following the shore gradually uphill. The route becomes rocky, passing Loch Bealach a' Bhùirich and finally descending to the lip of the waterfall. There is a small plateau under the cliff, which provides fine views of the falls and glen. Bring a map.

2 hrs, 58.2048, -4.9280 🚶🏻‍♂️💛📹📷

7 FALLS OF KIRKAIG

A delightful walk through a shrouded woodland glen leads to the Falls of Kirkaig, impressive even at just 20m. A mountainous landscape is visible over the heather, with Stac Pollaidh and the extraordinary shape of Suilven coming into view as height is gained.

➜ From Lochinver, take the minor road S to Inverkirkaig (IV27 4LR) and on around the shore and inland to car park on R at sharp R bend and bridge. Walk E, taking the R/ lower path that leads towards the forest and following Inverkirkaig Falls sign.

1.5 hrs, 58.1092, -5.2061 🚶🏻‍♂️💛

8 CORRIESHALLOCH GORGE

The mile-long Corrieshalloch Gorge is one of the finest examples of a box canyon in the country. The 61m drop is spanned by a suspension footbridge, with fine views of the

Falls of Measach, the diminished remnant of the river that carved the canyon. An extremely dramatic walk with minimal effort.

➜ From the A835, take the A832 signed for Corrieshalloch Gorge (IV23 2PJ), and park at the car park R after ½ mile. Walk through the gate and down the zig-zag track to the bridge.

15 mins, 57.7555, -5.0234 🚶🏻‍♂️🏛️📷

RUINS & CASTLES

9 ARDVRECK CASTLE

Built by the MacLeods of Assynt, Ardvreck castle dates back to the 16th century. The ruins are in a magnificent setting, standing on a grassy promontory that projects into the east end of Loch Assynt.

➜ On the A837 N from Inchnadamph (IV27 4HN) park at a car park after 1½ miles on E shore of Loch Assynt.

10 mins, 58.1664, -4.9944 🚴🚶🏻‍♂️

10 HERMIT'S CASTLE

Hermit's Castle lays claim to being the smallest castle in Europe. Built as a folly by an architect in the 1950s, it once had glass windows and doors. Today this little wonder is sometimes used as a bothy or by sunset watchers.

➜ Follow directions as for Achmelvich Beach (see 1). From the car park, head W past the caravan site and over the stile. Go through gate to the rocky peninsula, where the castle stands on rocks near the water.

15 mins, 58.1687, -5.3137 🚶🏻‍♂️🏖️

CAVES & FORESTS

11 BONES CAVES

Named after a staggering number of animal bones that were discovered here over a century ago; northern lynx, Arctic fox, brown bear and even polar bear have been excavated. There are three main cave entrances in the limestone valley under the northern crags of Beinn an Fhuarain, named Badger, Reindeer, and Bones from west to east. Bring a torch, and do not dig into the cave floor, scientific work continues here.

➜ On the A837 2½ miles S of Inchnadamph (IV27 4HN), park at the signed car park. Follow path E through the gate upstream past the waterfall. As the valley narrows the caves become visible on the cliff. Cross the river bed (usually dry) and follow path up to caves – steep in places.

90 mins, 58.1080, -4.9411 🚴📷💛🚶🏻‍♂️📷

12 TRALIGILL CAVES

The largest cave system in the country, Traligill has imposing entrances and an impressive mountain backdrop. Three large openings can be visited, including a waterslide streaming from the pothole above into a deep abyss. Take care when approaching the pothole, as footing may be slippery.

→ Park at the car park near Inchnadamph Hotel (IV27 4HN). Walk N on the A837 over the bridge and turn R on a track to a gate with an information board. Follow the track over another bridge, turn R at junction, cross a footbridge over the River Traligill, and continue along the path as it gradually climbs to the caves.

90 mins, 58.1406, -4.9323 🔲🔲

13 LAEL FOREST GARDEN

Started as an arboretum in the 19th century, Lael Forest is home to trees from all over the world. It boasts a unique collection of over 200 species, including some magnificent redwoods almost 8m around. Surrounded by wonderful mountain scenery; the peaks of An Teallach and Beinn Dearg can be occasionally glimpsed from the many paths, along with lovely waterfalls. You might spot a golden eagle or pine marten here.

→ On the A835 heading N towards Ullapool, park at Lael Forest car park (just N of IV23 2RG). There are clearly signed routes from here. 30 mins, 57.8210, -5.0302 🔲🔲🔲🔲🔲

MOUNTAIN SCENERY

14 STAC POLLAIDH

A short circular walk with spectacular views over Assynt. There is the option of climbing to the summit ridge, and even to take a tricky scramble along the fine ridge to the true summit.

→ Park as for Loch Lurgainn (see 3). Cross the road and go through the gates to begin the almost immediate ascent. Ignore the path L, continuing uphill to eventually curve around the base of Stac Pollaidh. A junction is your opportunity to either ascend to the summit ridge L, descending to re-join the circuit further round, or simply continue the circuit back to the start.

2 hrs, 58.0443, -5.2081 🔲🔲🔲🔲🔲🔲

15 SUILVEN

One of the finest and most identifiable mountains in the country, Suilven is a distinctive shape, with the dome-like peak of Caistel Liath at the north-western end standing at 731m. Its remoteness makes climbing it a challenging day out. Travelling through Assynt's moorland you are rewarded with a fabulous vantage point of sea views and miles of wild rugged landscape. You can do this in a day, or spend the night in Suileag Bothy (see 22), which you pass en-route.

→ In Lochinver, continue S on the A837 and head E on the single-track road past IV27 4LH. Parking after just under 1 mile on L. Walk on past Glencanisp Lodge at road end, to footpath through a gate on R. After around 1½ miles continue straight at junction; L leads to Suileag Bothy. Cross a bridge, turn R at the cairn and continue along path directly up the gully of Suilven. On reaching the ridge, turn R for the summit.

4 hrs, 58.1157, -5.1365 🔲🔲🔲🔲🔲🔲🔲

16 KYLESKU BRIDGE

A distinctively curved road bridge over Loch a' Chàirn Bhàin, connecting Kylestrome and Unapool. The bridge replaced a ferry which made the short journey across this fast-moving tidal water until 1984, and its curve was designed to mimimise the impact of the approach roads on the landscape.

15

26

16

22

→ On the A894 N of Unapool, shortly after IV27 4HW.
1 min, 58.2574, -5.0234 🖼

LOCAL FOOD

17 THE ARCH INN

Enjoy fresh local food with outdoor waterside seating in the heart of Ullapool. On the shores of Loch Broom, with magnificent views over the Fannich Hills. B&B available.

→ 10–11 W Shore St, Ullapool, IV26 2UR, 01854 612454. Thearchinn.co.uk
57.8944, -5.1631 🖼🍴🛏

18 THE KYLESKU HOTEL

Award-winning and popular contemporary restaurant in a modern hotel, using high-quality local ingredients. Packed lunches can also be arranged for guests.

→ Drumbeg, Kylesku, Lairg IV27 4HW, 01971 502231. Kyleskuhotel.co.uk
58.2569, -5.0181 🍴🛏

19 LOCHINVER LARDER

A wide variety of dishes including comforting homemade pies in a welcoming atmosphere. Ideal for a lunch in the bright conservatory or the restaurant with shorefront views; food is also available to take away, including dishes to heat at home.

→ Main St, Lochinver IV27 4JY, 01571 844356. Lochinverlarder.co.uk
58.1530, -5.2405 🍴

20 ROCK STOP CAFE AND VISITOR CENTRE

Not just for the geologists, the cafe serves locally made hot food, sandwiches and hot drinks, with great views form the picture window over Loch Glencoul. All this is paired with an exhibition where you can learn how the surrounding landscape was formed.

→ Unapool, Lairg IV27 4HW, 01971 488765. Nwhgeopark.com
58.2499, -5.0091 🍴

21 PEET'S RESTAURANT

Situated in the quiet fishing village of Lochinver, expect to see freshly caught fish and meats on the menu. A comfortable and relaxing atmosphere to enjoy fine food at good value. Also enjoy dining outside on the patio during summer months.

→ Harbourside, Lochinver, Culag Road, IV27 4LE, 01571 844085. Peetsrestaurant.com
58.1474, -5.2430 🍴

22 SUILEAG BOTHY

Wonderfully remote bothy with spectacular unspoilt views of Suilven (see 15).

→ Follow directions as for Suilven. 3 hrs walk.
58.1401, -5.1446 🅱️💬🚶

23 GLENDHU BOTHY

Amid this sparsely populated region sits Glendhu Bothy, in a stunning location looking down Loch Glendhu. Given its remoteness, there are surprisingly clear tracks all the way via the stalkers' path along the loch, but there's a high chance you won't meet another soul, having the place all to yourself.

→ On the A894, just N of the Kylesku bridge (IV27 4HW, see 16), turn E at Kylestrome and immediately R into car park. Walk E along the path to shoreline, then continue, avoiding the path going NE, all the way along the loch to the bothy. 5 hours walk.
58.2584, -4.9265 🅱️💬🚶

24 CLACHTOLL BEACH CAMPSITE

Situated directly behind the white sands of Clachtoll beach (see 2) is an extensive grassy area largely given over to this family-run campsite. Mostly tents, popular and renowned for its access to an outstandingly beautiful beach . Closed in winter.

→ 134 Clachtoll, Lochinver, IV27 4JD, 01571 855377.
58.1921, -5.3343 🔺

25 THE SHORE CARAVAN SITE

Tucked away in Achmelvich Bay, this site is a stone's throw away from one of the finest beaches in the country (see 1). A popular family site, especially in the school summer holidays. Plenty of grassy space for tents, despite the name.

→ 106 Achmelvich, Lochinver, Sutherland, IV27 4JB, 01571844393
58.1683, -5.3081 🔺🔔🦀🔥🏠

26 STOER LIGHTHOUSE

En-route to the famous Old Man of Stoer (see 4). Since the lighthouse was automated, some of the unused buildings have been renovated and are available as a self-catering let, with an outbuilding converted to a tiny bookable bothy. Ideal for an unusual get away.

→ Raffin, Lochinver, Lairig, IV27 4JH.
Keeper@stoerlighthouse.co.uk
58.2400, -5.4026 🦀

27 SUMMER ISLES HOTEL

Located 12 miles down a single-track road, with a reputation that says it's worth every mile. Fine dining, a bar with food in a former crofters' pub, sweeping sea views, rooms and a self-catering cottage. Mostly closed in winter, bar open some days with food.

→ Achiltibuie, Ross-shire, IV26 2YG, 01854 622282. Summerisleshotel.com
58.0214, -5.3463 ℹ️🍴🦀

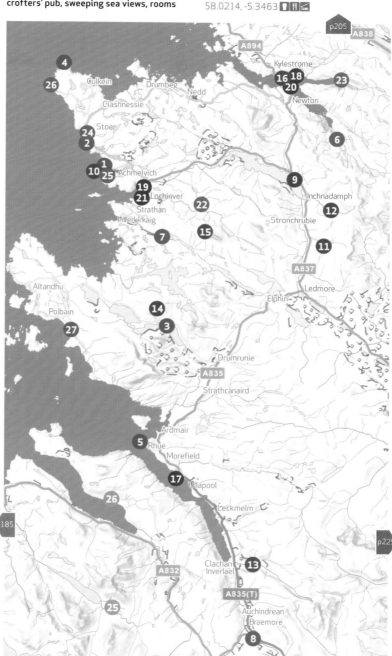

CAPE WRATH & NORTH WEST SUTHERLAND

Our perfect weekend

→ **Visit** thousands of puffins, great skuas and razorbills on Handa Island.

→ **Devour** freshly caught shellfish at The Shorehouse Restauraunt in Tarbet.

→ **Watch** the sun set from your tent near the shore at Scourie Campsite.

→ **Enjoy** a peaceful swim in the turquoise sea at Oldshoremore or Phòllain, and wander through the flower-filled machair.

→ **Camp** amongst the giant dunes at beautiful Sandwood Bay.

→ **View** the staggering cliff scenery at the north west point Cape Wrath, truly the most remote of Britain's four corners.

→ **Spend** a night in one of Scotland's loneliest and loveliest bothies, right by the shore at Kearvaig.

The far north-west of Scotland is a dramatic and sparsely populated land and, like neighbouring Assynt, an area of outstanding geological spectacle and natural, unspoilt beauty.

Tiny hamlets and crofting townships are dispersed along a coast that is studded with beautiful beaches and small islands. Heading north from the Kylesku bridge you will discover picturesque bays at Badcall and Scourie to the west and not far from here, a scenic loop road takes you towards Tarbet. Here you can catch the little ferry to the remarkable Handa island, where tens of thousands of seabirds, including razorbills and great skuas, fill the sky and nest amongst dramatic Torridonian sandstone cliffs.

Further north, two long sea lochs indent the west coast. Lying above them is the intimate harbour village of Kinlochbervie and a series of secluded and tranquil beaches at Oldshoremore, offering bright turquoise water to swim in and intriguing rock formations to explore. If it's beaches you're after, not much further north is the legendary Sandwood Bay, reached only by a 4-mile walk from Blairmore. One of the wildest and most unspoilt beaches in Britain, it is washed clean by Atlantic storms and flanked by dramatic cliffs, undulating dunes and a striking sea stack. The beach is popular with surfers, great for wild camping and the wider Sandwood estate, owned by the John Muir Trust, is also home to the best-preserved area of machair on the mainland, with over 200 species of plant growing behind the dunes.

At the most north-westerly tip of the British mainland sits the isolated headland of Cape Wrath. There are hidden gems to be discovered in this largely bleak and boggy area of moorland, much of it owned by the Ministry of Defence. One of the most remote lighthouses in the country is reached either by a day's walk from Sandwood Bay or a bumpy minibus ride through the military training area. There is staggering cliff scenery and a tiny café inside the lighthouse run by its sole inhabitant. A couple of miles east lies the exquisite Kearvaig Bay; for a true sense of isolation, spend a night in its lonely bothy, looking out on spume-covered sands and an unusual sea stack.

Other highlights of the north coast here include the spectacular Smoo Cave, the abandoned township of Ceannabeinne and wild and wonderful beaches including Balnakeil and Coldbackie. Don't miss stopping at the pretty villages of Durness, Tongue and Bettyhill. Their cosy B&B's, warming cafés and close-knit village life provide a contrast to the vast wildernesses around Ben Hope, Scotland's most northerly Munro, and the endless bog-cotton and lochans of the Flow Country.

BEACHES & BAYS

1 OLDSHOREMORE & PHÒLLAIN

Two connected white sand bays, Am Meallan and Bagh a' Phòllain, with a small island, and rock pools between. The large outcrop between them is known as Eilean na h-Aiteig (either 'isle of the shy girl' or 'juniper isle'). These beaches are some of the best places to swim in the north, and around 200 species of flowering plant grow in the Sheigra-Oldshoremore machair, including mountain avens, not found on other Scottish machair.

→ Leave B801 at Kinlochbervie, dir Oldshoremore (IV27 4RS). After 2 miles turn L signed Oldshoremore/WC/parking. Follow to road end for beach car park. Quieter Phòllain beach is L after Oldshoremore, signed Polin. 5 mins, 58.4773, -5.0872 🐚🚗

2 SANDWOOD BAY

One of Scotland's most remote but iconic wild beaches. A magnificent long stretch of pink-hued sand bounded by cliffs and the Am Buachaille sea stack and backed by a broad belt of rolling dunes. Occasionally the waves uncover a Spitfire engine in the sands, the last relic of a 1941 crash landing. Rip currents can develop here.

→ From turning for Oldshoremore (see 1) follow road ½ mile beyond turning to Polin, to Blairmore and John Muir Trust car park on L. Well-marked 3-mile track to Sandwood across moorland begins over gate opposite. Turn L at end of second loch. Johnmuirtrust.org 1½ hrs, 58.5384, -5.0650 🚻♿👣🚶📷🚗

3 KEARVAIG BAY & BOTHY

On the edge of miles of bleak moorland used for military target practice, and just west of the mainland's highest cliffs. A single track leads down to one of the country's loneliest places. Kearvaig Bay is surrounded by dark rocks, including 40m tall Stack Clò Kearvaig, known as 'the cathedral' due to its pair of spire-like sandstone pinnacles and natural window created by the sea. Standing alone in the bay is one of Scotland's most beautiful bothies. Wood is scarce, so carry some with you and you'll find that a roaring fire makes for one of the best bothy experiences on offer.

→ From Cape Wrath lighthouse (see 16) follow the only road on foot, heading E through the moorland for almost 4½ miles. Shortly after crossing a bridge over the river, turn L onto the track and continue for just over ½ mile until it descends to the bay. 2–2½ hrs, 58.6101, -4.9443 🚐❓👣🚶📷🏕

4 SCOURIE BEACH & BAY

A welcome haven amid beautiful, rugged coastal scenery. Pretty sand-and-rock bay stretching towards Handa Island (see 14; you can spot many seabirds here too). Sheltered and beautiful clear blue water for swimming. Stay at Scourie Campsite (see 24).

→ Heading W on A894 at Scourie (IV27 4TE) turn R on minor road after hotel and campsite, signed Scourie Beach / Burial Ground. Car park. 5 mins, 58.3516, -5.1621 🏕👣🏞🚗

5 COLDBACKIE BEACH

Bàgh Challbacaidh in Gaelic is a gorgeous white sand bay dominated by a sheer cliff of red sandstone. Very peaceful beach offering wonderful views of the Rabbit Islands.

→ On the A836 2½ miles E from the A838 junction. Layby parking on L just before Coldbackie (IV27 4XP). Dune path to beach. 5 mins, 58.5092, -4.3868 🏖👣

6 BADCALL BAY

Tiny, working fishing quay with spectacular sunsets over an archipelago of little islets.

→ 15 miles N of A837 on A894, signed L turn (IV27 4TH). 3 mins, 58.3237, -5.1377 🚗

7 TRÀIGH ALLT CHÀILGEAG

Quiet northern beach surrounded by pink granite and sea caves, and sitting below the ruined lost village Ceannabeinne, meaning head or end of the mountains in Gaelic.

➔ Layby parking 3 miles SE of Durness (IV27 4PY) on the A838, past Sangobeg and Ceannabeinne lost village.

60 mins, 58.5513, -4.6778

8 SANGO BAY

Attractive beach with northern coastal cliffs, golden sands and interesting rock formations to explore. Popular with surfers; rip currents can develop.

➔ Heading E on the A838 in Durness (IV27 4PY). Park by the Durness Visitor Information Centre after the Sango Sands (see 26).

5 mins, 58.5691, -4.7397

9 BALNAKEIL BAY

Spectacular beach dune system, known for its beautiful sunsets set against the backdrop of Cape Wrath. The sandy, crescent-shaped beach faces west and is the perfect sheltered spot for a swim.

➔ From A838 at Durness head for Balnakeil (IV27 4PX) to park in beach car park next to graveyard at end of road. Check out nearby Balnakeil Craft Village on the way, especially the chocolate treats at Cocoa Mountain (see 22).

5 mins, 58.5769, -4.7671

CAVES, RUINS & SHELTERS

10 SMOO CAVE

Dramatic combined sea- and freshwater limestone cavern boasting one of the largest entrances to any sea cave in Britain. Its outer chambers can be explored by following a path from the cliffs. Boat tours heading further into the cave are available in summer (01971 511704, Smoocavetours.weebly.com).

➔ Car park on A838 just E of IV27 4QA between Sangomore and Sangobeg. Follow clearly marked short, steep footpath from car park, or for a less steep path cross the river on the other side of the inlet. Both have steps.

60 mins, 58.5635, -4.7198

11 CASTLE VARRICH

Little is known about the origins of this enigmatic tower (Caisteal Bhearraich on some maps), but follow the short walk from Tongue village to explore the ruins. You'll also be rewarded with fine views of the Kyle of Tongue and of the dramatic peaks of Ben Loyal and Ben Hope.

➔ Park opposite Ben Loyal Hotel in Tongue (IV27 4XE), walk back towards main A838, turn L onto signed footpath for Castle Varrich before the main road and follow to end.

60 mins, 58.4759, -4.4354

12 DÙN DORNAIGIL BROCH

Substantial remains of Iron Age broch, with galleries in the double walls. It sits by the Strathmore river and right at the side of the scenic, winding single-track road between Hope and Altnaharra along Loch Hope.

➔ In the tiny settlement of Hope, 9 miles W of Tongue on the A838, turn L onto single-track road signposted for the broch, past IV27 4UJ. After 10 miles, broch is on R after Altnacaillich.

1 min, 58.3663, -4.6392

COAST & WILDLIFE

13 ARD NEAKIE, LOCH ERIBOLL

Crescent shaped promontory extending out into Loch Eriboll, against a panoramic hinterland dominated by Ben Hope. Once a limestone quarry, it is connected to the shore by two identical sandy beaches, at the end of which stands a ferry house built in 1891. Further along the are old lime kilns.

→ Head N from Eriboll (IV27 4UL) on A838 for 3 miles, and pull off onto end of minor road on L. Good view from further N on the A838 looking down at the Loch.
10 mins, 58.4982, -4.6673 ▲➤▣

14 HANDA ISLAND
Nature reserve on an uninhabited island where 120m tall cliffs rise from the Atlantic. During summer these swarm with over 100,000 seabirds including razorbills, guillemots and puffins. The island had a population of 65 in 1841, before the potato famine drove them to the mainland, and the oldest widow on the island was titled its Queen.
→ From Scourie (IV27 4TE) head NE on A894 for 3 miles, turn L and follow minor road to Tarbet. Small ferry (10 mins) operates Mon–Sat 9am–2pm. (07780 967800, Handa-ferry.com).
30 mins, 58.3832, -5.1869 ➤▾▾▣▣

15 FARAID HEAD
Sandy beaches and marram-backed sand dunes (some of the highest in Scotland) lie before rocky An Fharaid ('lookout point'). Great views of Cape Wrath and seabirds.
→ Start at Balnakeil Bay (see 9). Walk to end of beach and follow road through dunes, which goes through a gate and passes another beach

on L and continues to MOD station. Before MOD gate take R towards the cairn. Return on E side for best chance of seeing puffins in summer.
50 mins, 58.5991, -4.7719 ▣▲▣

16 CAPE WRATH POINT
The most remote lighthouse on the Scottish mainland is situated at the country's most north-westerly point – and one of its most inaccessible, with just one minibus west of the Kyle of Durness. Atop dramatic pink-hued cliffs, the Cape Wrath lighthouse is also home to the Ozone café, which is open 365 days a year, 24 hours a day.
→ Cape Wrath ferry runs from Keodale Pier May–Sept (no advance booking, Capewrathferry.wordpress.com). Cape Wrath minibus runs Easter–Oct, (01971 511284, Visitcapewrath.com). Walkers can take the Cape Wrath Trail from Sandwood Bay (see 2) through very rough terrain, taking 1 day (Capewrathtrailguide.org).
3 hrs, 58.6258, -4.9994 ▣▾▣▣

17 CLÒ-MÒR CLIFFS
Dramatically rising 280m from the Atlantic, these are the highest sheer cliffs on the British mainland. There is a huge seabird colony including terns and puffins and some interesting sea stacks lying further west.

→ No path, easiest route is from Kearvaig Bay (see 3) Follow coast E as it climbs higher for 1¼ miles. There is a trig point at the summit.
60 mins, 58.6135, -4.9181 ▣▾▾▣

18 KYLE OF TONGUE
Deep sea-loch surrounded by magnificent mountain scenery. At the head stands the majestic Ben Loyal and Ben Hope, and in Tongue bay are the three small Rabbit Islands, noted for their fine diving, canoeing and picnic spots.
→ Parking on the S of Kyle of Tongue causeway (A838 W from IV27 4XH), alternatively turn R immediately W of the causeway dir Melness, to gravel area on R.
1 min, 58.4911, -4.4367

LOCAL FOOD

19 SHOREHOUSE SEAFOOD RESTAURANT
Delightful family-run restaurant specialising in shellfish, freshly caught using their own boat in the waters you see as you eat your meal. Wonderful hidden gem in the tiny hamlet of Tarbet and just above the Handa Ferry jetty.
→ Tigh Na Mara, Tarbet, IV27 4SS, 01971 502251. Shorehousetarbet.co.uk
58.3897, -5.1427 ▣

3

20 SMOO CAVE HOTEL

Quality, hearty bar food and a roaring fire. Try the seafood specials and enjoy the friendly, relaxed atmosphere. B&B available.

→ Durness, Sutherland IV27 4QB, 01971 511227. New.smoocavehotel.co.uk
58.5631, -4.7153 🍴🛏

21 WEAVERS CRAFTSHOP & CAFÉ

Small timber-clad café serving up great toasties, soups, tea, coffee and the rest. After you have eaten, shop for locally made Scottish gifts in the craft shop. Closed winter.

→ Weavers Craftshop, Tongue, IV27 4XW, 01847 611332. Weaversbedandbreakfast.co.uk
58.4987, -4.4044 🍴

22 COCOA MOUNTAIN

Café and delicious luxury chocolates at the most remote chocolatier in Europe. Make sure you try the famous hot chocolate!

→ Balnakeil, IV27 4PT, 01971 511233. Cocoamountain.co.uk
58.5701, -4.7640 🍴

23 THE OLD SCHOOL

Former primary school now a B&B and licensed restaurant and café, serving a wide range of dishes prepared in-house using locally sourced produce.

→ Inshegra, Kinlochbervie IV27 4RH, 01971 521383. Oldschoolklb.co.uk
58.4500, -5.0025 🍴🛏

CAMPING & HOSTELS

24 SCOURIE CAMPING & CARAVAN SITE

Family-run campsite beautifully situated at Scourie Bay (see 4). Great sunsets and onsite bar and café The Anchorage.

→ Scourie, IV27 4TG, 01971 502060. Scouriecampsitesutherland.com
58.3518, -5.1561 🏕🍴🛏

25 LAZY CROFTER BUNKHOUSE

Small and welcoming hostel sits amid some great coastal scenery. Cosy, informal atmosphere and high-quality self-catering facilities. Owned by neighbouring Mackay's Hotel, which also has two self-contained lets.

→ Mackay's, Durness, IV27 4PN, 01971 511202. Visitdurness.com
58.5680, -4.7467 🛏

26 SANGO SANDS CAMPSITE

Picturesque pitches by steep cliffs, overlooking some beautiful north coast beaches (see 8). Wonderful sea views and nearby restaurant and bar. Free off-season pitching Nov–March.

→ Durness, IV27 4PZ, 01971 511726/ 07838 381065. Sangosands.com
58.5686, -4.7419 ▲ ▮ ❙❙

27 CROFT 103

Two award-winning luxury lets built using a combination of traditional craftsmanship and contemporary design. One built into the hillside and one by the shore, both with glass fronts to sea views. Eco-friendly, running off renewable energy generated on-site.

→ Port na Con, Laid, Durness, IV27 4UN, 01971 511202. Croft103.com
58.4914, -4.7216 ☁

28 EDDRACHILLIS COTTAGES

Two self-catering cottages with their own two acres of land, just a few minutes walk away from Badcall Bay: the newly refurbished Byre and more traditional Cottage. Can be booked together or individually. Next to Eddrachilles Hotel for quality food, drink and views.

→ Lower Badcall, Scourie, IV27 4TH, 01854 613077. Visitscourie.co.uk
58.3283, -5.1364 ☁

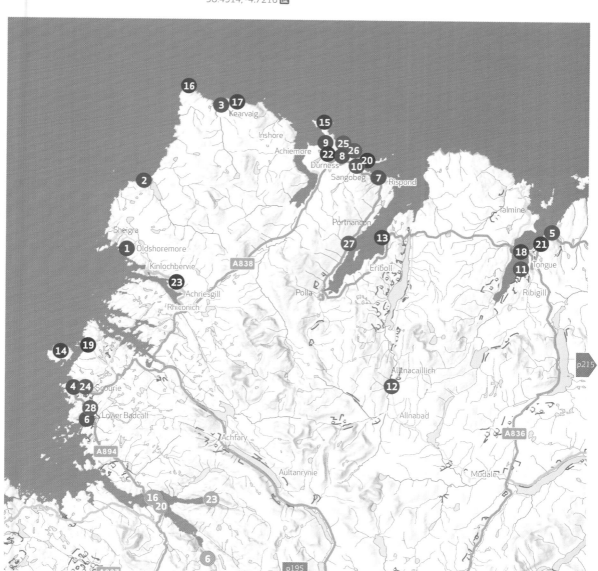

CAITHNESS & EAST SUTHERLAND

Our perfect weekend

→ **Paddle** your kayak along the beautiful northern coastline around Melvich Beach.

→ **Discover** an array of birdlife and flora living on the dramatic high cliffs at Dunnet Head, Britain's most northerly point.

→ **Head** all the way out to the extreme north-eastern tip of the mainland to see the spectacular Duncansby sea stacks and natural arch of Thirle's Door.

→ **Descend** the 330 stone Whaligoe Steps in the cliffs to reach a dramatic old harbour.

→ **Explore** the chambers inside the remarkably well-preserved Grey Cairns of Camster.

→ **Visit** the ruined Castle Sinclair Giringoe, spectacularly situated on the north-east coast.

→ **Watch** the sun go down over the sea and sleep in the shelter of the dunes at the campsite by Dunnet Bay.

Find yourself amongst dramatic coastal scenes, desolate moorlands and hidden ancient sites in the most northeasterly part of the British mainland. Caithness and east Sutherland may be less Highland in character than the north-west, but the largely unspoilt landscapes here offer a powerful sense of isolation.

A vast amount of the area inland is covered by rolling expanses of wildlife-rich peat bogs and moorlands, known as the Flow Country. Here you can discover rare flora, birds and insects living in the blanket bog at the RSPB Forsinard Flows.

The most popular way to enter Caithness is via the North Coast 500 route, a 500-mile scenic route from Inverness. It travels through Easter Ross and then north-east along a mostly low-lying coastline peppered with castles, including the remarkable ruins of Castle Sinclair Girnigoe. You might also make a stop in the windy fishing port of Helmsdale, a cultural hub in Caithness with a heritage centre, art gallery, youth hostel and places to eat and drink. Further north an entirely different old harbour lies at the foot of sheer cliffs and the 330 Whaligoe Steps. After the long climb back up relax inside the café at the top, which serves great food and drinks by windows overlooking the cliffs.

Close to the famous end-to-end destination of John o' Groats lies the true north-eastern tip of the British mainland, Duncansby Head. Known locally as 'Seabird City', the high angular red sandstone cliffs are home to some of Britain's best seabird colonies. A short walk from the lighthouse brings you to the magnificent Duncansby Stacks, which point dramatically out from the sea and are circled by hundreds of kittiwakes and fulmars.

Between here and the surfing hotspot at Thurso you can visit the extreme northern peninsula of Dunnet Head to watch puffins gather on the spectacular high cliffs and seabirds glide above the curling waves of the intensely blue North Sea.

BEACHES & WATERFALLS

1 STRATHY BAY
Delightful, wide sandy beach bounded by the River Strathy on the west and sea-carved cliffs and caverns on the east. Visit in May and June, when cowslips and northern marsh orchids flower behind the sheltered beach. Outstanding views over the Pentland Firth.

→ On the A836, turn R onto minor road by the church at E of Strathy, 200m E from turning to KW14 7RZ. Continue for ½ mile, bearing R at fork, to park behind the cemetery on R.
5 mins, 58.5667, -3.9990 ⚅🚻🏕

2 SINCLAIR'S BAY
Known locally as Reiss Beach, Sinclair's Bay is a wonderful crescent of white sand split in half by a stream. The beach is often quiet and a good place for surfing.

→ 3 miles N of Wick on the A99 (N of turning to KW1 4RL) turn onto minor road signed for Golf Course and Reiss Sands. Continue straight to park at the road end.
5 mins, 58.4842, -3.1251 ⬜⚅🚻

3 MELVICH BEACH
Golden north-coast beach at the mouth of the River Halladale. Popular with surfers

and swimmers, also good for sea kayaking, particularly around the west of the bay and rocky outcrops by Portskerra.

→ Turn NE off A836 in Melvich (KW14 7YJ) signed for Melvich Beach / parking. Car park at road end. Short walk through dunes to beach.
5 mins, 58.5586, -3.9134 ⚅🚻

4 BIG BURN WATERFALL
Hidden gorge with tumbling waterfalls through woodland rich in flora and fauna – spring bluebells, campions and wild garlic grow in abundance here.

→ On A9 just NE of Golspie Inn (KW10 6RS), take slight L fork at the Sutherland Stonework building to park in car park behind their yard, signposted for walk. Clear path begins here and loops through the glen, crossing the burn on small bridges; falls are after about ½ mile.
60 mins, 57.9862, -3.9715 🚶🍂⚅

5 LOCH MIGDALE
Classic Scottish loch that served as the site of a Canadian forestry camp during the Second World War. The woods were owned by Scottish-born philanthropist Andrew Carnegie, who opened Fairy Glen to the public and built a log cabin there. A great camp spot and beach lies at the east end of the loch.

→ Turn off A949 at Bonar Bridge (IV24 3EG) onto A836 and then immediately R signed Migdale. After 1 mile go R through Migdale and then R signed Loch Migdale. Park in a rough layby where road reaches the shore and head SE along the shore. Soon a path forks R off the road to continue along the shore, signed for Ledmore and Migdale. Follow this path with no diversions for 1½ miles to the head of the loch. Take a R to reach the beach.
35 mins, 57.8834, -4.2735 🌲🧍⚅

NORTHERN SCENERY

6 HOLBORN HEAD
North-coast headland with impressive scenery including high cliffs, the angular block of Clett sea stack, a blow hole, stacked red rocks and many seabirds. On a clear day there are great views to the Orkneys.

→ Park at Scrabster Harbour KW14 7UJ. Walk NE past ferry, towards lighthouse. Just before the lighthouse turn L at a gate signed for Holborn Head and go uphill, bearing R slightly on a faint path for about ½ mile. Follow path over a stile, a series of small bridges, another 2 stiles and through an open gateway to a small cairn at the headland. From the cairn return to fork and follow path R along the N

cliff edge, passing a natural arch and sea stack. Return the same way or follow the coast W for just under 2 miles before picking up a straight track from an old quarry that heads SE across the moorland and back to Scrabster.
60–120 mins, 58.6223, -3.5371 🏊▼

7 DUNCANSBY HEAD

Overshadowed by its neighbour John o' Groats (the most north-easterly inhabited place), Duncansby Head is the true north-eastern tip. Great views over to Orkney from the lighthouse. The huge Geo of Sclaites lies a 5-min walk to the south. From here you can continue to the Duncansby Stacks (see below).

→ Turn R off the A99 at John o' Groats at the post office and sign for Duncansby Head. Continue just under 2 miles (past KW1 4YS) to the road end and car park at the lighthouse.
5 mins, 58.6440, -3.0251 🏊

8 DUNCANSBY STACKS & THIRLE DOOR

Magnificent isolated rock pinnacles emerge from the sea at the north-eastern extremity of the mainland. A truly wild and majestic place with an impressive natural archway, high cliffs, wild flowers and kittiwakes and fulmars circling in the sky. No photographer will want to miss this piece of coast.

→ From Duncansby Head car park (see 7) follow signed path from the S of the lighthouse and continue on path for 1 mile.
30 mins, 58.6316, -3.0385 🏊🏊🚶

9 MORVEN

Prominent and unusual cone-shaped mountain that offers extensive views of an otherwise low-lying area. A real overlooked gem of a hill, and the highest in Caithness.

→ From the A9 at Dunbeath take the minor road to Braemore (past KW6 6ET). Park at end of public road, cross bridge, head R and pass the sign for Braemore Lodge. At the estate buildings beyond, head through gate at far side of the compound and follow excellent track, with ever-improving views of Morven. After Corrichoich take a L and head up the steep slopes of Morven. No real paths at this point, and the climb is short but relentless.
2½ hours, 58.2329, -3.6956 ▼🏊🏊❓🏊🏊

HISTORIC REMAINS

10 WHALIGOE STEPS

Whaligoe Haven is a remarkable natural harbour surrounded by 76m cliffs, with 24 boats working out of it in the early 19th century. When boats came in, crews of women would gut the fish at the harbour and carry them in baskets up 365 stone steps to be taken on foot to Wick, over 7 miles away. Today 330 steps remain. Oystercatchers, terns and other seabirds nest in the cliffs.

→ On A99 at Whaligoe, 7 miles S of Wick, take the unsigned fork E at phone box (KW2 6AB) and park in the area R beyond the houses. From here follow the track past a garden to a large stone building with walled yard, the Whaligoe Steps café (see 19). Head R around the building where the steps begin. Take great care, sheer drops and steps can be slippery.
20 mins, 58.3455, -3.1609 ▼🏊🏊

11 BADBEA CLEARANCE VILLAGE

Sad and lonely remains of a village on the cliffs that was something like a refugee camp for families evicted from their homes inland to make way for sheep in the 18th century. Life was hard here, and stories say even children had to be tethered to posts to stop them being blown over the precipitous cliffs; by 1911 the village was empty. Excellent views.

→ On A9 2½ miles S from Berriedale (KW7 6HF) is Badbea car park, on coastal side of the road. Take only path out of the carpark, which leads to the ruined village and monument.
5 mins, 58.1603, -3.5503 🏊🏊✝🏊

15

12 CASTLE SINCLAIR GIRNIGOE

Spectacular ruined medieval castle, destroyed in 1680 in a dispute over the family title. Dramatically situated on the cliffs projecting into Sinclair Bay, it is surrounded by small sea stacks, geos and intricate coastal scenery.

→ From A96 in Wick, turn R onto Henrietta St at KW1 4DG, following sign for Staxigoe. Take 4th R onto Girnigoe St, then L onto Willowbank. At Staxigoe turn L along minor road at crossroads, signed Noss Head, and follow past KW1 4QT to car park by lighthouse gates, where the path to the castle begins.

10 mins, 58.4781, -3.0677 🚫🚲🚶

13 GREY CAIRNS OF CAMSTER

Two extremely well-preserved and restored Neolithic chambered cairns, one long and one round, situated amidst the Flow Country. Excavations in 1865 revealed pottery, flint tools, bones and skeletons. Now a Historic Scotland site, the cairns are open to the public; there are skylights in the chambers, but a torch is still useful and be prepared to crawl and squeeze a bit in the passages.

→ On A99 1 mile E of Lybster, turn L at sign for Camster Cairns onto minor road (dir KW3 6BD). 5 miles to parking layby with info board.

5 mins, 58.3791, -3.2653 ❌🚗🚲🚶

14 CAIRN OF GET

Explore a roofless but well-preserved Neolithic burial cairn situated in a landscape rich in prehistoric monuments.

→ Signed W from A9 at Whaligoe (KW2 6AB) 1½ miles SW of Ulbster. Signposted trail from the last bend in the lane before the car park at road end, follow the black and white poles.

10 mins, 58.3532, -3.1751 🚶

WILDLIFE WONDERS

15 ALLADALE WILDERNESS RESERVE

Forward-thinking rewilding and enlightened land management policies are the driving force behind this 10,000 hectare estate in central Sutherland. Numerous walks and estate-run activities where you can learn about the efforts Alladale are making to bring back native species – including predators – to the Scottish Highlands. Walking in the estate is allowed (leave cars at 57.8652, -4.5903) but ensure all gates are closed behind you. You can stay in lodges on the reserve (see 25).

→ Leave A836 at Ardgay signed Croick, and follow road over and along N side of River Carron for IV24 3BS, turning L at red telephone box 1 mile before Croick church (signed).

1 min, 57.8695, -4.6333 🚗🐦📷🏠🚲🚶📍🚻

16 RSBP DUNNET HEAD

The most northerly point of the mainland, Dunnet Head has dramatic sheer standstone cliffs, a lighthouse and diverse coastal grasslands, where special plants like roseroot and spring squill grow. An RSPB reserve, it is home to an impressive array of birds including puffins, guillemots, razorbills and kittiwakes.

→ Turn W off the A836 at Dunnet (KW14 8XD) and follow the B855 for 4½ miles (taking signed L at Brough) to the car park at road end.

5 mins, 58.6706, -3.3768 🚗🚻

17 RSPB FORSINARD FLOWS

Discover fascinating flora and an abundance of insects and birdlife on the vast peatland landscape of the Flow Country. Look out for greenshanks and dippers searching for food, and carnivorous sundews and butterwort growing on the blanket bog.

→ From A836 N-coast road at Melvich, 1¼ miles E of KW14 7YJ, turn S onto A897 for 14 miles to reserve / visitor centre at the railway station.

30–180 mins, 58.3569, -3.8972 🚆🚗🚻

LOCAL FOOD

18 THE PIER CAFÉ

Popular licensed café/restaurant with wonderful views over Loch Shin. Enjoy drinks and seasonal home cooking with good-quality, local produce by the loch in summer or by the woodburner in winter.

→ Lochside, IV27 4EG, 01549 402971. Pier-cafe.co.uk
58.0275, -4.4045

19 WHALIGOE STEPS CAFÉ

Small and welcoming café/restaurant above the famous Whaligoe harbour steps (see 10). Eclectic and regularly changing Mediterranean menu by owner and chef Karen. Limited opening in winter.

→ The Square, Whaligoe, Ulbster, KW2 6AA, 01955 651702. Whaligoesteps.co.uk
58.3455, -3.1618

20 THYME AND PLAICE, HELMSDALE

Wonderful small coffee house and restaurant serving home-made dishes using fresh, locally sourced produce, home-baked cakes and quality coffee.

→ 10 Dunrobin Street, Helmsdale, KW8 6JA, 07826 929200. Facebook/Thyme.n.plaice
58.1167, -3.6529

21 STACKS BISTRO, JOHN O' GROATS

Family-run coffee house and bistro serving good comfort food made with local produce.

→ Unit 3, Craft Centre, John o' Groats, 01955 611582. Facebook/Stacksbistro
58.6431, -3.0701

22 LA MIRAGE, HELMSDALE

Quirky restaurant created by Nancy Sinclair in the style of her good friend Dame Barbara Cartland. Big portions and good fish & chips for hungry travellers.

→ 7-9 Dunrobin St, Helmsdale, KW8 6JA, 01431 821615. Lamirage.org
58.1168, -3.6528

SLEEP WILD

23 NATURAL RETREATS JOHN O' GROATS

Contemporary, open-plan self-catering lodges with sea views and woodburners, which are part of a welcome rejuvenation of the hamlet. An offshoot of the renovated Inn next door.

→ John o' Groats, Wick, KW1 4YR,
01625 416430. Naturalretreats.com
58.6421, -3.0697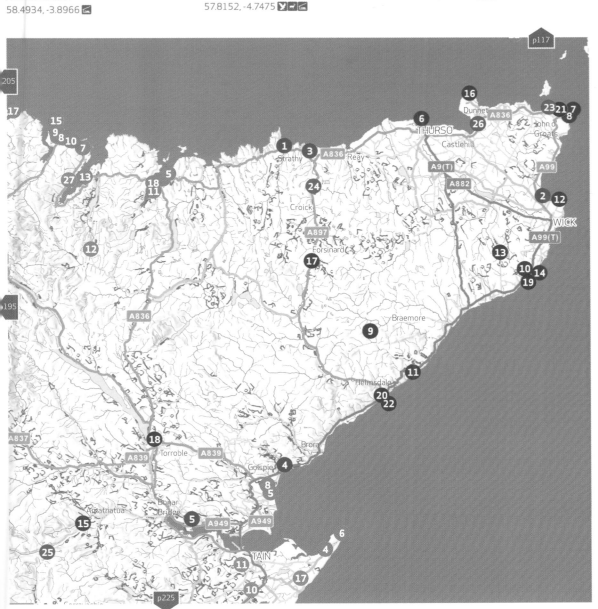

24 CORN MILL BUNKHOUSE
Experience a unique crofting lifestyle in this
small bunkhouse in Strath Halladale.
→ Achiemore, KW13 6YT, 01641 571219.
Achumore.co.uk
58.4934, -3.8966

25 DEANICH LODGE & GHILLIE'S REST
The Alladale Wilderness Reserve (see 15) has
a range of beautifully furnished and secluded
places to stay. Deanich Lodge offers full-
board upmarket bunkhouse accommodation
in a wild situation next to a crashing river or
stay in the rustic-chic Ghillie's Rest.
→ Ardgay, Sutherland, IV24 3BS,
07770 419671. Alladale.com
57.8152, -4.7475

26 DUNNET BAY CARAVAN CLUB
Non-members are also welcome at this
CC site, and can pitch their tents among
grassy dunes by the sweeping stretch of
sand at Dunnet Bay. Ideal location for those
exploring the extreme north.
→ Dunnet, Thurso, KW14 8XD, 01847 821319.
Caravanclub.co.uk
58.6148, -3.3451

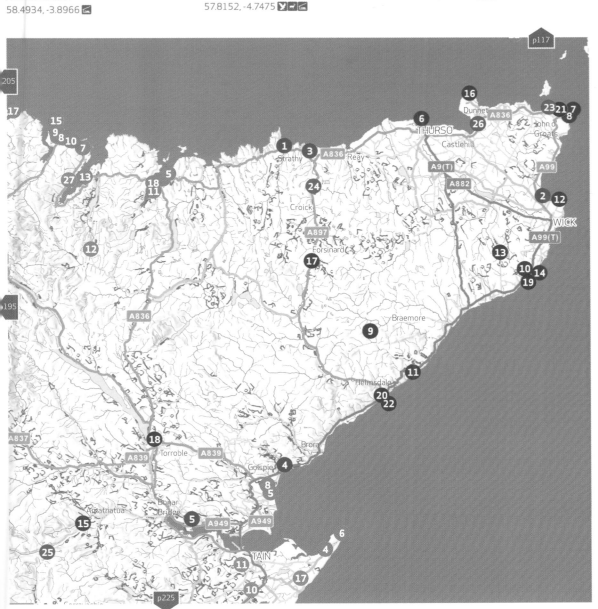

EASTER ROSS &
THE BLACK ISLE

Our perfect weekend

→ **Gaze** over the Moray Firth as the sun rises on Littleferry beach.

→ **Explore** the caves and beautifully circular rock arches at McFarquhar's Bed.

→ **Delve** deep into the magical wooded Fairy Glen and watch the tumbling waterfalls.

→ **Taste** the seasons and go fruit picking at Black Isle Berries.

→ **Stroll** from Rosemarkie beach at low-tide to explore a series of sea caves and stacks lying along the coastline.

→ **Descend** through the woodland to Eathie Haven and visit a charming old salmon bothy.

→ **Look** out for dolphins and porpoises swimming near the lighthouse at Chanonry Point.

→ **Retreat** to the comfort of one of the eco-friendly Black Isle Yurts after your day exploring.

The east coast of Scotland is often shunned in favour of the west, so Easter Ross and the Black Isle tend to be overlooked by popular lists of places to visit. But these two distinct and quietly dignified areas have much to offer the visitor in many varied ways. Like much of the north-east coast, they have an interesting coastline, stunning sea life and an abundance of good places to eat and drink.

The misleadingly named Black Isle is neither particularly black nor an island, but an arable isthmus surrounded on three sides by bodies of water – the Moray, Beauly and Cromarty Firths. Easter Ross is a loosely defined region that mixes wilder landscape to the west with the commanding bulk of Ben Wyvis and a lower-lying promontory to the east, its coast horizontally aligned with that of the Black Isle. All that separates them is a small stretch of water between Nigg and Cromarty.

Food and drink are hugely important to life in the Black Isle, and there is a great deal to see and do in this regard. Farming is extensive here and may be the reason why it is named the Black Isle; traditionally black cattle for beef are raised here, as opposed to white dairy-cattle breeds. There is an abundance of farm shops, farmers' markets, plenty of whisky and beer production and a thriving fishing heritage. Easter Ross is a great area for bird enthusiasts, with several nature reserves and wetland estuaries – the nature reserve at Loch Fleet is a brilliant example.

Because they are peninsulas, the Black Isle and Easter Ross are not so much areas to travel through as places to be visited for their own sake. They require a bit more effort than the honeypots elsewhere but are easily reached, mainly via the A9 and Inverness, the lifeline road of the north east of Scotland. Closer familiarity reveals a manageable area absolutely packed with everything that makes Scotland so great – scenery, culture and a welcoming sense of community.

COASTAL SCENERY

1 ROSEMARKIE COAST

Pleasant beach and a series of sea stacks and caves to explore during low tide. The southernmost, Caird's Cave, is accessible at all tides; despite its small size, this was used as a rock shelter and inhabited as late as the beginning of the 20th century. Pieces of worked bone, stone and deer horn recovered from here in 1912, including a pin inset with amber, are in the National Museum of Scotland.

→ Park at Marine Terrace on the seafront in Rosemarkie (IV10 8UL). From the road end head L along the shore past the Rosemarkie beach café and continue for around 2½ miles on the beach or the coast path. On approaching the blocky stacks keep a lookout for a small path leading L towards Caird's Cave. Return to the beach and explore the stacks and caves further along the coast before returning the same way.

60 mins, 57.6077, -4.1025 🏖️🏊

2 EATHIE HAVEN & SALMON BOTHY

Descend on a path through pine and spruce trees to reach Eathie beach, where Scottish geologist Hugh Miller found his first fossils. The haven was originally a salmon fishing station, where fishermen would often live isolated for months. The former fishermen's bothy is now open to the public and provides good shelter during bad weather, and inside you will find more information on Miller's discoveries and the natural history of the woodland and shore. The area is also a great place to spot dolphins.

→ From the A832 just NE of Rosemarkie take R fork onto single-track road signed Eathie. Park at end of woods ¼ mile before Eathie Mains (IV11 8XY). Follow path into woodland which then makes a steep descent to the shore. At the beach, head R for a short distance to reach the bothy.

35 mins, 57.6459, -4.0492 🚶🚗🏊

3 MCFARQUHAR'S BED

A series of caves and sea arches, best visited when tide is low. Legend says McFarquhar was a local smuggler who hid his contraband in the nearby caves.

→ On the A832 to Cromarty, W of Newton (IV11 8XT), head SE for Navity / Eathie, and then turn L along a rough road. Go past the farm (IV11 8XS) then turn immediately R just after and park at the road end. Continue on foot down the path SE through an avenue of trees and then down to McFarquhar's Bed. The route can be muddy.

60 mins, 57.6622, -4.0131 🏖️

4 PORTMAHOMACK BEACH

Lovely little beach and a quaint seaside fishing village on a spit of land that separates the Dornoch and Moray Firths. Interesting rock pools at low tide.

→ From Tain, or from the B9165 leaving A9 S of Tain, follow signs E to Portmahomack. There is a car park above the beach (opp IV20 1YP).

2 mins, 57.8352, -3.8299 🏖️🍴🏊🚗🍴🚻

5 LITTLEFERRY BEACH

Quiet and pleasant sandy beach backed by an expanse of dunes. These are dotted with gnarled Scots pine; look out for the picturesque one that has a swing hanging from it. Can easily be combined with Loch Fleet (see 8).

→ There is a car park before the small hamlet of Littleferry (opp KW10 6TD) and the beach lies a short walk S over some attractive dunes.

5 mins, 57.9345, -4.0159 🚶🏖️🐚🚗🏊

6 TARBAT NESS

Rugged headland with prominent lighthouse
standing proud overlooking the Moray and
Dornich Firths. Great place to look for sea
life, from seabirds to dolphins.

→ From Portmahomack (see 4) continue E
up the coast. Ample parking at the end of the
road. There are several short trails around the
lighthouse; the buildings around the tower are
private.

5 mins, 57.8650, -3.7766 🐦🐚🔷↗

WILDLIFE WONDERS

7 BEN WYVIS NATIONAL NATURE RESERVE

An unusual mix of plants and wildlife
are found on and around the spectacular
whaleback ridge of this isolated mountain.
The walk begins through birch, aspen and
rowan before opening onto a landscape
of heather and bog plants. The mountain
itself is carpeted with woolly hair moss, and
flocks of dotterel breed here in summer. In
autumn you might hear the roaring of red
stags rutting, and in winter perhaps catch a
glimpse of a white ptarmigan.

→ 4 miles NE from Garve (IV23 2PR) on A835
there is a large signed Forestry Commission
car park on the R. From here a well-made

path leads N into reserve following the Allt
a' Bhealaich Mhòir. After just over 1 mile,
path reaches open country. To climb the
mountain, follow the path, zig-zagging steeply
up boulders towards An Cabar (946m). It is
possible to walk along the ridge to the trig
point at the summit of Ben Wyvis.

2–6 hours, 57.6632, -4.6228 🌿🌼↗🚶

8 LOCH FLEET NATIONAL NATURE RESERVE

Varied and interesting nature reserve; below
the woods, vast sands are uncovered at each
low tide. Amazing place to watch masses
of curlew, shelduck and wigeon wading
and feeding. Can easily be combined with
Littleferry Beach (see 5).

→ From Golspie take minor road past KW10
6ST to forestry commission car park and head
into the forest behind the information boards.
Take a L at a fork to pass a house at Balblair on
the wood edge, and take the path that leads
to the shoreline, ignoring the red marked
woodland path.

25 mins, 57.9486, -4.0263 🚶🌼🐚🔷↗

9 CHANONRY POINT

One of the best places in Scotland to spot
dolphins. Chanonry Point lies at the end of
the mile-long spit of land, Chanonry Ness.

There is a lighthouse, and both seals and
porpoises are seen here regularly.

→ Turn E off the A832 between Fortrose and
Rosemarkie onto Ness Rd, dir IV10 8SD, and
drive to end; car park at the end of the point is
often busy. Alternatively park in Rosemarkie
on the seafront (IV10 8UL) and walk along the
path that runs along the shore from here.

1–20 mins, 57.5738, -4.0940 ↗

10 KILDARY LOCH

Beautiful little loch, popular with local
anglers. Great for a relaxing stroll and a good
opportunity to spot wildfowl.

→ Start from Kildary, and take the lane that
begins next to Kens Garage (IV18 0NX).
Continue straight ahead past the sign for
'Kildary Loch'. Continue straight ahead through
a gate, then across a metal footbridge before
ascending steps to Kildary Loch. The path
then circumnavigates the loch and returns the
same way. 30 mins.

30 mins, 57.7580, -4.0714 🚶🔷↗

11 TAIN HILL

Excellent short walk that passes through
lovely Scots Pine and has great views over
the Dornoch Firth.

→ Starting from the Tain Hill forest car park

(IV19 1PX), follow the red marker posts. When a large Pulpit Rock is reached (the highest point of the walk), go back on yourself, turn R and continue following the red marker posts back round to the car park again.
20 mins, 57.8035, -4.1061 🅥🄰🖼

ANCIENT FORESTS & GLENS

12 BLACK ROCK GORGE
At the edge of Evanton Wood, the Allt Graad rushes through this hidden box canyon. Deep and narrow, it was the setting for a scene in the fourth Harry Potter film.
→ Park in centre of Evanton. On Chapel St, facing N to the chapel at end, turn R onto Camden St (IV16 9XX) and follow to end where a track bends L uphill along tree line. Continue on the track through the woods following signs for Black Rock Gorge. Ignore the first bridge and continue along the path to the second bridge for the best views of the gorge.
35 mins, 57.6672, -4.3684 🄰🖼🚲

13 ROGIE FALLS
Series of waterfalls along the Blackwater River, the largest of which is a good place to watch salmon leaping in autumn, when the area is particularly picturesque.

→ On the A835 E of Garve (IV23 2PR) there is a signed car park 1 mile N of IV14 9EQ. There are waymarked footpaths from the car park.
20 mins, 57.5892, -4.6023 🖼🄰🚲🅿🚻🚲

14 THE FAIRY GLEN
Magical wooded glen with two delightful waterfalls. Well-dressing ceremonies used to take place here; local children would dress the springs with flowers to encourage the fairies to keep the water clean.
→ Car park on N Bridge St in Rosemarkie (IV10 8UP). Follow path from car park upstream passing under a bridge. Soon after small path forks R; stay close to stream. Continue over wooden bridge following steps up to waterfalls. Path can be muddy. Return same way.
30 mins, 57.5937, -4.1242 🚲🧍🅿🚻🚲🖼

LOCAL FOOD

15 BLACK ISLE BERRIES
Family-run farm shop selling a selection of quality home-grown, seasonal fruit and vegetables and a range of local products. In summer you can also pick your own fruit.
→ Ryefield Farm, Tore, IV6 7SB, 01463 811276. Blackisleberries.co.uk
57.5423, -4.3206 🍴

16 STOREHOUSE OF FOULIS
Wonderful farm shop and restaurant serving a variety of fine food and local produce. Housed inside a restored 18th century storehouse by the shore of the Cromarty Firth.
→ Foulis Ferry, Evanton, IV16 9UX, 01349 830038. Thestorehouseathome.com
57.6402, -4.3484 🍴

17 EGG BOX SHOP
Two small sheds with a vending-machine service selling award-winning eggs and Rooster potatoes.
→ 2 in Cromarty; Balmuchy Farm, 57.7815, -3.9095 and Rosefarm, 57.6610, -4.0717
57.7815, -3.9095 🍴

18 ALLANGRANGE ARMS
Serving local real ales and pub food in the bar and fine wines and quality local produce in a dark-wood panelled dining room.
→ 54 Millbank Rd, Munlochy, IV8 8NL, 01463 819862. Allangrangearms.com
57.5484, -4.2638 🍴🛏

19 SUTOR CREEK CAFE
Popular small family-run cafe offering local seafood, wood-fired pizzas and local beers.

→ 21 Bank Street, Cromarty IV11 8YN,
01381 600855. Sutorcreek.co.uk
57.6822, -4.0372

20 THE ANDERSON

A charming and welcoming place to eat, drink
and stay. The award-winning restaurant
gives an international twist to local
ingredients, while the delightfully quirky pub
has a jukebox and an extensive selection of
quality beers, whiskies and wines.
→ Union Street, Fortrose, IV10 8TD,
01381 620236. Theanderson.co.uk
57.5815, -4.1308

21 FORTROSE CAFÉ

Friendly café serving breakfast, lunch and
home baking inside and in the garden area.
→ 67 High Street, Fortrose, IV10 8SU,
01381 620638
57.5820, -4.1302

22 THE CHEESE HOUSE

Luxury Dutch and local cheese shop housed
in an old police station.
→ Old Police Station, Bank St, Cromarty, IV11
8UY, 01381 600724. Cromartycheese.com
57.6812, -4.0350

CAMPING & GLAMPING

23 BLACK ISLE YURTS

Hand-crafted yurts of various sizes
scattered through attractive woodland for
privacy, with wonderful coastal scenery.
Great base for those looking for explore the
surrounding area's secluded sandy beaches,
caves and wooded ravines.
→ Easter Hillockhead Farm, by Eathie,
Rosemarkie, IV10 8SL, 01381 620634.
Blackisleyurts.co.uk
57.6148, -4.1009

24 FORTROSE BAY CAMPSITE

Small and very welcoming seaside campsite
in the historic seaside village of Fortrose.
Pitches are overlooking the Moray Firth.
Light your campfire on the pebble beach.
→ Wester Greengates, Fortrose, IV10 8RX,
01381 621927. Fortrosebaycampsite.co.uk
57.5786, -4.1164

25 BLACK ISLE BERRIES BUNKHOUSE

Bunkhouse situated on a working fruit farm.
Sleeping 19 in a range of rooms, including a
wheelchair-friendly ensuite, it can be booked
for both groups and individuals.

→ Ryefield Farm, Tore, IV6 7SB, 07891 578998. Blackislebunkhouse.co.uk 57.5430, -4.3206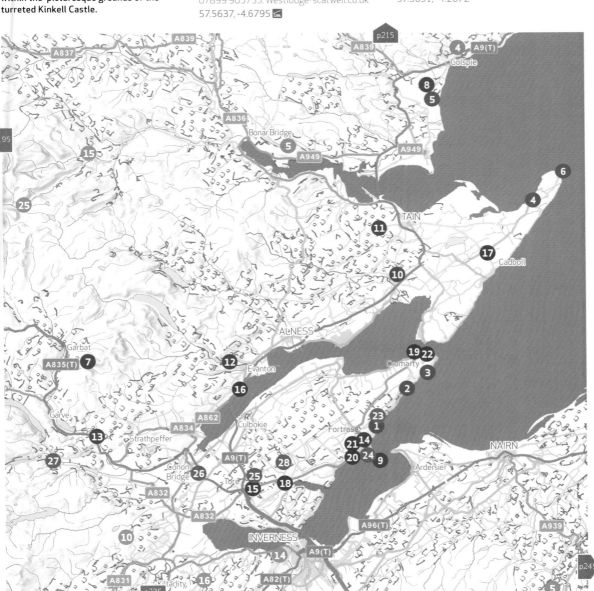

COSY HIGHLAND HOMES

26 KINKELL CASTLE COTTAGE

Formerly an artist's studio, this cosy self-catering cottage for two people is hidden within the picturesque grounds of the turreted Kinkell Castle.

→ Unique-cottages.co.uk 57.5558, -4.4185

27 WEST LODGE STRATHCONAN

Modernised traditional house half way up one of Scotland's longest glens. Sleeps up to six; ideal for relaxing by a wood burner after a day exploring the highlands.

→ Scatwell, Strathconon, IV6 7QG, 07899 905735. Westlodge-scatwell.co.uk 57.5637, -4.6795

28 BLACK ISLE LODGE

A spacious modern Scandinavian lodge with a wood burner and balcony, located in the heart of the Black Isle. The ideal woodland get-away with the family. The town of Munlochy is nearby, and the owners run a B&B with restaurant a short walk away.

→ Balnakyle, Munlochy, IV8 8PF, 01463 811134. Blackislelodge.co.uk 57.5691, -4.2672

LOCH NESS & GLEN AFFRIC

Our perfect weekend

→ **Observe** the lie of the land from the foresters' memorial viewpoint in Glen Affric.

→ **Find** peace wandering along the picturesque River Affric.

→ **Camp** amidst the tree stumps on the beach at Loch Beinn A' Mheadhoin, and take a bracing dip in the loch in the morning.

→ **Reflect** on 1,000 years of history at famous Castle Urquhart on the shore of Loch Ness.

→ **Dine** at the excellent Boathouse restaurant, set in an abbey in Fort Augustus.

→ **Explore** up the quieter south side of Loch Ness to find peaceful Loch Tarff.

→ **Peer** over the breathtaking Falls of Foyers, one of the best waterfalls in Scotland.

→ **Take** a well-deserved rest at the brilliant Cameron's Tea Rooms and Farm Shop.

→ **Stop** for a peaceful picnic at Coire Loch.

Ask someone from another country what comes to mind when they think of Scotland and chances are the Loch Ness Monster will be in the top five responses. The Nessie phenomenon is a good example of the prevailing moods of mystery, myth and legend that linger like mist in the Highland glens, an image that has been promoted and marketed a great deal in television, film and books. It is also clearly good business; the abundance of hotels and shops on the shores of long Loch Ness trading on the monster story attest to this. This is an area busy with tourists and tour buses, all drawn to follow a well-worn trail up and down the A82 by a thing that they can never see. As is often the case in Scotland, however, it doesn't take long to lose the crowds and find your own peace away from the throng; there are numerous spots in the area that are naturally magical, free from shops selling monster key chains and hats.

Loch Ness is part of the Great Glen, the visible geological line of the Highland Boundary Fault that runs from Fort William in the south to Inverness in the north, slicing the country in half. The loch itself is a huge body of fresh water, the largest in the UK by volume, and extremely deep and mysterious. The north side is developed and busy, the south less so and all the better for it. There are numerous lovely smaller lochs in the hills to the south, and incredible waterfalls crashing through chaotic scenery – Falls of Foyers is easily one of the best in the country. To the west of Loch Ness lies beautiful Glen Affric, often described as the loveliest of all Scottish glens, and with good reason. Unbelievably picturesque Scots pines soar over sparkling water, hemmed in by rugged mountains, with the whole scene sett off by a few small cottages.

The quintessential wild activities are found in abundance here. There are numerous lochs of all sizes to swim in, woods of all kinds to explore, and exhilarating, easily accessed walks to suite all abilities. Wild camping is best enjoyed in Glens Affric and Cannich; their long, winding rivers and quiet lochsides make great places to pitch up and rest, with the opportunity of a swim in the morning. The region is best reached via the famous A82 trunk road, giving you the opportunity to travel the distance of the Great Glen and see first-hand the impact this unique geological fault has on the landscape. It is also easy to head south to here from Inverness after driving north up the A9 from Perth.

RIVERS & WATERFALLS

1 FALLS OF FOYERS

Superlative waterfall, one of the best in Scotland. Set amid scenery that would not look out of place in the Canadian Rockies, this crashing mass of water has inspired much poetry and writing. Combine with a visit to Cameron's Tea Room (see 22).

➔ From the centre of Foyers (450m S of IV2 6XU), cross the road in front of the shop and café and follow good path down to the falls viewpoint, passing several information boards.
5 mins, 57.2489, -4.4913

2 DOG FALLS

Atmospheric little waterfall tumbling through a narrow gorge. Combine with Coire Loch (see 11) and the surrounding Scots pines to make an interesting short excursion. Find pools for wild swimming spots along the river, especially below the narrow wooden bridge just beyond the falls.

➔ From Cannich on A381 take road signed Glen Affric past IV4 7NB. After 4½ miles park in the Dog Falls car park. Head E past WCs following river downstream. Waymarked path doesn't lead to the falls; when it crosses the road, instead of following the path L continue on road for a short distance until the falls viewpoint on R. about 500m from the car park.
10 mins, 57.3134, -4.8440

3 INVERMORISTON FALLS

Great short walk through forestry to a viewpoint overlooking a waterfall underneath a beautiful double-arched Thomas Telford bridge. Good for stretching the legs; can be muddy.

➔ From the large parking area in the centre of Invermoriston (IV63 7WE), follow the path from the S end of the car park through the trees to the small summer-house overlooking the falls and bridge.
5 mins, 57.2115, -4.6159

4 PLODDA FALLS

40m waterfall, the highest in an area well known for its waterfalls. Set amongst huge Douglas fir trees, with a platform giving a spectacular view over the edge.

➔ From the A831 on the S side of the river in Cannich take minor road to tiny village of Tomich. Continue on rough 5 mile forest road (past IV4 7LY) signed Plodda Falls, to car park. Follow short Plodda Falls trail for 300m to the top of the falls; longer walks here too.
5 mins, 57.2725, -4.8545

5 RIVER AFFRIC

Scenic and simple short loop walk that follows the sublime River Affric on a small promontory between two lochs.

➔ Park as for Loch Affric memorial (see 21). Follow the blue waymarked River Affric route downhill, R along the river and back up steps.
30 mins, 57.2629, -4.9858

6 RIVER OICH

Serene river set amongst Scots pine. Good chance to see red squirrels.

➔ From Fort Augustus take minor road signed Auchteraw to the Forestry Commission car park (just past PH32 4BW). Follow the yellow River Oich trail, well waymarked from car park.
60 mins, 57.1413, -4.6992

LOCHS & RIVERS

7 LOCH BEINN A' MHEADHOIN

Stunning freshwater loch with promontories and islands just east of Loch Affric. There are plenty of great spots on the foreshore to camp and swim, including a beautiful and romantic sandy beach dotted with ancient tree stumps, which make great seats for sitting on around a campfire.

→ From Cannich on the A381 take the road signed Glen Affric past IV4 7NB. At about 8½ miles, roughly a quarter of the way up the loch, there is a large layby. Head down the bank towards the island linked to the shore by a sandy beach with tree stumps.

5 mins, 57.2832, -4.9280

8 LOCH TARFF

Lonely and little-visited loch with several islands lying 960m above the south side of Loch Ness. A great place to stop and spend the night in a campervan.

→ From Fort Augustus take the B862 past PH32 4BZ to the loch. Access the loch on a small promontory with a new carpark over half way up the loch as you head W.

5 mins, 57.1513, -4.5993

9 LOCH RUTHVEN

RSPB reserve at a broad, tranquil loch that is home to half the UK's population of Slavonian grebe – at their golden-tufted best in spring. Easy to reach and enjoy.

→ The loch lies on the S side of Loch Ness, just under 1 mile off the B851 (dir IV2 6UA). From the reserve entrance follow a short path up the S side of the loch to a bird hide.

10 mins, 57.3226, -4.2630

10 LOCH NAM BONNACH

Remote and peaceful loch, great for a swim in a wilder setting.

→ Start from the end of the public road (no parking here, limited space to pull the car off the road beforehand) at Drumindorsair (N from IV4 7AQ) and take the track through the gate on the L, which then turns R. Head uphill to a gate, pass through. Stay on the main track, ignoring turn offs.

45 mins, 57.4905, -4.5445

11 COIRE LOCH

Peaceful and secluded little lochan with water lilies floating on the surface – a good sign of the water's purity. A great picnic spot.

→ Park as for Dog Falls (see 2) and start the waymarked path. This crosses the road at one point, and then bends back to cross the road again and pass over the river on a thin wooden bridge. Stay on this as it rises and winds up to a perfect viewpoint overlooking the och, and then follow as the path drops down to the loch shore after nearly 1 mile in all.

25 mins, 57.3128, -4.8335

12 TORR WOOD CIRCUIT, LOCH NESS

Pleasant amble along the shores of Loch Ness, with a circuit through peaceful woods past an attractive castle.

→ Start from the Dores Inn carpark (IV2 6TR) (see 27) and take the path that goes behind the Nessie spotter's caravan. The path runs behind a beach and through a gate. Stay on the main path at a fork and follows the E side of the loch heading N. The path heads back R near a house and jetty, take a L on the path that heads uphill past the house. The path reaches a gate on the edge of some woodland, take a R here then a L at a T junction further ahead. Take a L on to a rough path and then the next L to retrace your steps back to the start.

2 hrs, 57.3858, -4.3396

CASTLES & RUINS

13 CHANGE HOUSE

Good viewpoint on the south side of Loch Ness, and the remains of an old 18th-century travellers rest visited by Boswell and Johnson. Good access for swimming in Loch Ness.

→ From Inverfarigaig head NE along the side of Loch Ness past IV2 6XS for approx 3½ miles, until roughly opposite Urquhart Castle on the N shore, to a layby with a few picnic tables (IV2 6TY). Follow the Change House path sign back along loch shore to the ruin.

5 mins, 57.3237, -4.4082

15

14 CRAIG PHADRIG

Impressive vitrified Pictish hill-fort hidden in a forest, dated to the mid-4th century BC. Good views over to the Munro of Ben Wyvis.

→ Start from the parking area on Leachkin Brae (about 100 W of the turning to IV3 8RX). Follow the path at the far end of the car park taking 3 forks R, then bear L following the main path. The path levels off and reaches a big grassy clearing, the site of the fort.
15 mins, 57.4772, -4.2697 🏔️🐕🖼️🌀

FORESTS & GLENS

15 URQUHART WOODS

Interesting example of an ancient 'wet wood', given its character by sustained flooding. The woods lie in the bay to the N of Urquhart Castle, and access to Loch Ness at the far end is possible in very dry spells, since the bridge washed away in 2007.

→ Start from the cemetery car park to the E of Drumnadrochit (100m E of IV63 6UF, around the corner) and cross the stile by the bend as R end of cemetery. Follow path past cemetery and sewage works to enter the woodland.
5 mins, 57.3326, -4.4651 🚻❓

16 REELIG GLEN

Short walk through a lovely forest with a stand of huge Douglas fir. This includes two that have been Britain's tallest tree, the affectionately named Dughall Mor and a more recent 64m usurper that was the tallest conifer in Europe in 2014.

→ At Easter Moniack SW of Inverness, off the A862 park in the Forestry Commission Reelig Glen car park (400m SE of IV5 7PR). Walk south on a path that follows the Moniack Burn upstream, and follow the easy loop path with no turn-offs for 1 mile, crossing the Moniack Burn by bridge along the way.
60 mins, 57.4498, -4.4033 🔄🚶🏔️🚻🏞️

17 DAVIOT WOODS

Relatively young woodland with plenty of wildlife and level, family-friendly paths. Good walk to break a journey on the A9.

→ Leave the A9 at Daviot West, dir IV2 5XL. Park to the R of the quarry beyond this. There are several short waymarked paths that head into the forest behind the information board.
60 mins, 57.4299, -4.1402 🏔️🚻❓🚶

18 ALLT NA CRICHE

A mix of birch and pine forests, with a fine little waterfall. Good views over Loch Ness from a lofty viewpoint that obscures the crowds.

→ Start from the Forestry Commission car park NE of Fort Augustus on the A82 (½ mile beyond Inch Hotel, PH32 4BL) Follow the white waymarked walk that climbs steeply up the Allt na Criche burn to a super viewpoint.
30 mins, 57.1595, -4.6630 🚶🏔️🏞️

19 TREES FOR LIFE, DUNDREGGAN

Pioneering estate that is the flagship for a charity aiming to bring back Scotland's natural flora and fauna through tree planting and conservation. Original forest here is extended by new native planting, so the walks allow you to sample both ancient wonders and the work of this forward-thinking estate.

→ Dundreggan Estate is on the A887 2 miles E of IV63 7YJ. From the car park, follow the track signed Trees for Life. There are three waymarked walks.
2 hrs, 57.1935, -4.7660 🚻

20 LITTLEMILL

Step back in time at Littlemill, to see a landscape from the last Ice Age. Pools, ridges and lochans shaped by glaciers dot the landscape.

→ From the A9 take the B851 signed Fort Augustus, dir IV2 6XH. After 1 mile park in Forestry Commission car park on L. Follow the blue waymarked path to the kettle lochans.
10 mins, 57.4023, -4.1591 🚩🍴

21 LOCH AFFRIC MEMORIAL VIEWPOINT
Often described as the most beautiful glen in Scotland. Loch, trees, mountains, glens – Glen Affric has it all, with picture postcard scenery in every direction. This memorial was constructed to honour the foresters who worked in the glen.
→ From Cannich on the A381 take the road signed Glen Affric past IV4 7NB. Follow 11 miles to the extensive car park at the end of the public road into the glen. Follow the white waymarkers that start where the road turned into the carpark. The path is a loop that climbs uphill to a stunning viewpoint and back to the carpark.
10 mins, 57.2664, -4.9860 🚶🏞️✝️🍴🚩

22 CAMERONS TEA ROOM
Cosy and friendly café with great food and peaceful ambience, popular with local cyclists. They keep a pair of tame roe deer who love to be petted. Not to be missed if you are in the area.
→ Foyers, IV2 6YA, 01456 486572.
57.2455, -4.4860 🚩🏞️🛏️🍴

23 FOYERS STORES & WATERFALL CAFÉ
Lovely local café and shop. A great place to spot red squirrels in the woods opposite.
→ Foyers, IV2 6XU, 01456 486233.
Foyersstoresandwaterfallcafe.co.uk
57.2502, -4.4902 🍴🍽️

24 THE BOATHOUSE
Excellent restaurant set in the grounds of St Benedict's Abbey, right on the shores of Loch Ness.
→ Fort Augustus, PH32 4BD, 01320 366682.
Lochnessboathouse.co.uk
57.1458, -4.6746 🏞️🍴

25 THE STRUY INN

Beautiful old inn, traditional in character, with open fires. The small restaurant serves great food. Rooms available.

➜ Struy, IV4 7JS, 01463 761308.
Thestruy.co.uk
57.4220, -4.6651

26 CNOC HOTEL

Traditional hotel with a beautiful garden, offering a restaurant serving local produce, a bar and a popular afternoon tea.

➜ Struy, IV4 7JU, 01463 761264.
Thecnochotel.co.uk
57.4284, -4.6597

27 THE DORES INN

Highly rated local Inn with excellent views over Loch Ness.

➜ Dores, Inverness, IV2 6TR 01463 751203.
Thedoresinn.co.uk
57.3820, -4.3332

28 CANNICH CAMPSITE

Situated on the Affric–Kintail way, this peaceful campsite sheltered by trees is a great budget base to explore the area.

➜ Strathglass, IV4 7LN, 01456 415364.
Highlandcamping.co.uk
57.3441, -4.7594

29 CRASKIE ESTATE CAMPING PODS

Comfortable and well-located camping pods. They come with USB charging points and speakers for your music.

➜ Glencannich, Cannich, IV4 7LX,
01456 415398. Craskieestate.com
57.3633, -4.8227

30 INVER COILLE CAMPSITE

Small, family-run campsite perfectly situated for the Great Glen Way. On-site shop, communal areas and fire pits, plus geodomes with woodburners.

➜ Invermoriston, IV63 7YE, 01320 351224.
Inver-coille.co.uk
57.1896, -4.6196

31 MORAG'S LODGE HOSTEL

Cheerful, award-winning hostel with a range of rooms. Enjoy meals, bike hire and an amazing rustic bar. They have pub quizzes and their own beer, brewed by Loch Ness Brewery.

➜ Bunoich Brae, Fort Augustus, PH32 4DG,
01320 366289. Moragslodge.com
57.1475, -4.6829

32 LOCH NESS BACKPACKERS LODGE

Comfortable and friendly little hostel with relaxed vibe and no curfew. Well situated in Lewiston minutes from Loch Ness.

➜ Coiltie Farmhouse, Drumnadrochit,
IV63 6UJ, 01456 450807.
Lochness-backpackers.com
57.3292, -4.4717

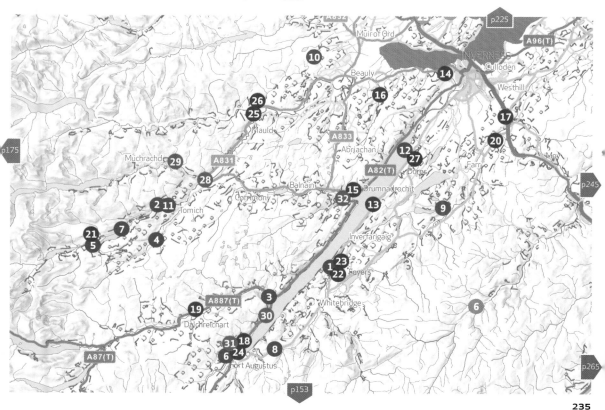

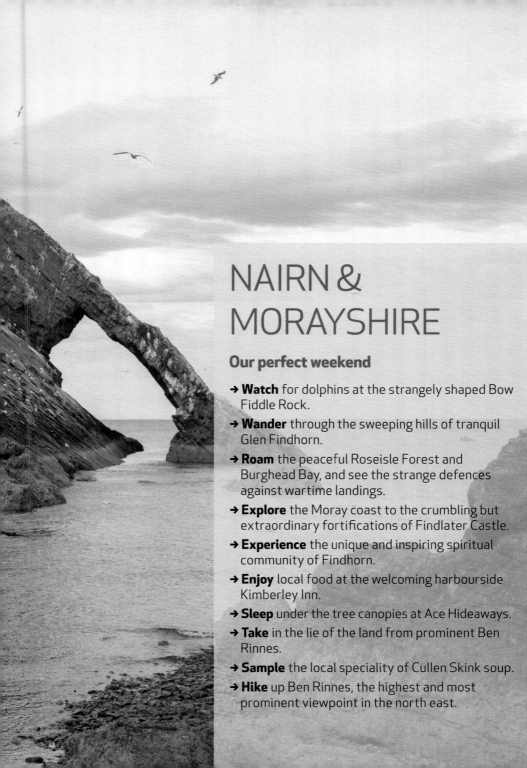

NAIRN & MORAYSHIRE

Our perfect weekend

→ **Watch** for dolphins at the strangely shaped Bow Fiddle Rock.

→ **Wander** through the sweeping hills of tranquil Glen Findhorn.

→ **Roam** the peaceful Roseisle Forest and Burghead Bay, and see the strange defences against wartime landings.

→ **Explore** the Moray coast to the crumbling but extraordinary fortifications of Findlater Castle.

→ **Experience** the unique and inspiring spiritual community of Findhorn.

→ **Enjoy** local food at the welcoming harbourside Kimberley Inn.

→ **Sleep** under the tree canopies at Ace Hideaways.

→ **Take** in the lie of the land from prominent Ben Rinnes.

→ **Sample** the local speciality of Cullen Skink soup.

→ **Hike** up Ben Rinnes, the highest and most prominent viewpoint in the north east.

Sea life, smooth whisky and small fishing villages are the defining features of this busy, populous region, which stretches from the north-east Cairngorms down to the Moray Firth. Crossed by the rivers Findhorn and Spey, the inland area is famous for Speyside single malts, one of the whisky distilling regions whose name is legally protected. The coastal scenery is teeming with seals, dolphins and porpoises – we saw porpoises playing in front of Portknockie sea stacks within roughly five minutes of arriving!

The area begins in the Corrieyairack Forest, at Loch Spey, a small freshwater loch. From this comes the Spey, a powerful river that flows eastward and gathers pace before it reaches the sea at Spey Bay. The boundaries of the protected whisky area, which is home to about half of all Scotland's distilleries, approximately follow the profile of the river, and this culture of flowing water seems to inform the mindset of the area in general.

Picturesque villages dot the coastline from Nairn in the west to Cullen in the east, on the border with Aberdeenshire. They are extremely beautiful, nestled in coves and linked by a long-distance cliff-top path from Forres to Cullen. Several large RAF bases are located around Lossiemouth, and interesting military bunkers and defence fortifications are to be found in the dense forests that grow right down on to the dunes.

Food and drink are the mainstays of business in the area, and there are many welcoming cafés and pubs in places like Findhorn, with its lively, eco-inspired artistic atmosphere. Obviously whisky is a massive draw, and the long-distance walking route the Spey Way visits many of the attractive villages and distilleries, so you can sample along the way to discern what gives the whisky here its unique personality. The closer you get to the coast, the less wild the area becomes, and the vast expanses of farmland and densely populated towns and busier villages, such as Elgin and Forres, make opportunities for wild camping less frequent than in the quieter hinterlands of the Cairngorms.

The best approach to the area is from the west, coming down from the hills and through an ever-changing landscape. Travelling the coastal trail is also very straightforward, dipping into and sampling the delights of the small granite towns on your way.

BEACHES & BAYS

1 LOGIE HEAD

A picturesque stretch of coastline with a beautiful beach and dramatic cliff faces – famous for their climbing opportunities – only a mile from Cullen. A fine coastal walk with a great opportunity to spot dolphins in the Moray Firth.

→ In Cullen (AB56 4WB), park in the town centre car park and walk down towards the harbour then head R past a hostel and onto the coastal path.

60 mins, 57.7008, -2.7919

SEA STACKS & CAVES

2 BOW FIDDLE ROCK

Extraordinary and unique rock formations on the coast of Moray Firth. One of the most unusual sea stacks in all of Scotland, resembling a bow and fiddle – hence the name – or the tail of a whale, depending on the viewpoint.

→ On the A98 just before Cullen, take the A942 signed Portnockie. Head to the most north-easterly point in the town, Addison Street (AB56 4NN), where there is usually plenty of room to park on the roads. Walk R

down the winding seafront road and path that head to the shore.

15 mins, 57.7061, -2.8528

3 CLASHACH COVE

Gorgeous sand and pebble beach with a sea arch, sometimes also called Cove Bay. The strata of the golden sandstone cliffs tilt opposite ways around a dramatic faultline here, and there are two caves, the smaller one with a Pictish crescent and V symbol carved high on the east wall.

→ From the B9040 between Burghead and Lossiemouth take the turning for Hopeman. Head towards the harbour then turn R along Beach Terrace (IV30 5RX) and L to park above the East Beach. Begin from here, walking E along the coastal path that soon climbs. As the path comes to a fork, take the L to the cove.

25 mins, 57.7137, -3.4128

RIVERS

4 RANDOLPH'S LEAP

A wooded gorge on the River Findhorn, named after the point where the river banks are closest together. The story goes that a Randolph clan chief chased a Comyn clansman who managed to escape via this

point. The Comyns were defeated soon after, and over time the name changed from Comyn's Leap to Randolph's Leap as the lands were turned over to the Randolphs.

→ Leave the A940 6 miles S of Forres on the B9007 signed Carrbridge. Turn R to park at the Logie Steading visitor centre (IV36 2QN) and walk SW along the road to paths R into woods towards. Visit the Olive Tree Café (see 18) after your walk.

15 mins, 57.5250, -3.6716

5 DULSIE BRIDGE

The Dulsie military bridge was built in 1755, crossing a deep, winding gorge on the peaceful River Findhorn. There is a waterfall, a sandy beach, and deep pools below.

→ Leave the B9007 signed for Dulsie Bridge, following the single-track road for 1½ miles. Park at the signed layby on L (past IV12 5UR) and follow the path upstream to good views of the gorge.

10 mins, 57.4508, -3.7813

GLENS & HILLS

6 GLEN FINDHORN

In a lonely corner of the Highlands and somewhat overshadowed, this softly contoured gem of a glen is up there with the prettiest and most charming.

➔ Leave the A9 for Findhorn Bridge and take the road signed Coignafearn just N of the bridge. Follow past IV13 7YB to the car park at the road end near Coignafearn Old Lodge. Walk along the River Findhorn until it eventually reaches Coignafearn Lodge.

60 mins, 57.2097, -4.1856 ✈✚🏃

7 BEN RINNES

Being the most prominent hill in the area, this is arguably the finest – and most popular – viewpoint in the north-east, boasting extensive views over the land to Aberdeenshire in the east and the Cairngorm mountains in the south.

➔ On the B9009 heading SW from Dufftown, take the turning signed Edinvillie, past AB55 4DA and park at the car park L after 620m, which is next to the path. Pass through the gate and follow the path to the summit.

90 mins, 57.4031, -3.2400 📷🏔

8 BIN OF CULLEN

A short leg-stretcher through pretty scenery. Bin of Cullen is not particularly high, but its prominence offers outstanding views all along the coastline and out to sea.

➔ The walk begins at a forestry track 3km SW of Cullen on the B9018. Turn R off the B9018 at a sign for 'Hill of Maud' and follow the track for 2km. The walk starts here (AB56 5YX). There is space for cars but do not block access. Follow the main track, take a L at a junction after a bridge and head through Pine trees. L again after the track levels off. Stay on this to the summit and retrace your steps back to the start.

50 mins, 57.6652, -2.8734 🚗🏕🔍🏔🌳🚻

RUINS & CASTLES

9 FINDLATER CASTLE

Situated on a rocky promontory projecting into the sea are the remains of Findlater Castle, dating back at least to the 15th century. It is a dramatic site, with sheer drops from the fortifications to the sea 15m below, and takes a head for heights and careful footing to explore inside. Take care here; nobody maintains the paths or masonry, so be sensible about risks.

➔ Continue around coastal path from Logie Head (see 1) for 1½ miles SE past West Sands. At this small bay begin the ascent at the rear of the beach towards the castle, which will soon come into view. There is a much shorter walk N, from a car park at the end of a lane signed Sunnyside Beach, Findlater Castle and Doocot off a minor road E of Cullen (just W of AB45 2UD), but the coastal walk is worth it if you have time.

90 mins, 57.6924, -2.7704 🏰🅿🚻🔀🚻

10 LOCHINDORB CASTLE

The ruined 13th-century castle of Lochindorb was the stronghold of the colourful Comyn clan, and sits on a man-made island in a loch once strategic for the river route north. It is now a quiet place and home to an array of birdlife, including black-throated divers and greylag geese. Especially beautiful when the surrounding moors are full of purple heather in summer.

➔ From the A939 7½ miles N Grantown-on-Spey take the junction signed Lochindorb. The loch and then the castle shortly come into view. There is some space to pull off before PH26 3PY.

2 mins, 57.4060, -3.7085 🏰🏔🛶🚣

11 DUFFUS CASTLE

Sitting in the open countryside of Moray is one of the finest remaining examples of a Norman motte and bailey in Scotland. Some of the masonry has collapsed, but the majority of the fortress remains well preserved and you can explore the inner tower.

→ On the B9012 NW of Elgin follow signs for Duffus Castle and park at the car park (turning ½ mile W of IV30 5RH).

1 min, 57.6877, -3.3613

FORESTS

12 SLUIE WALK

A magical walk through the Darnaway forest. Between the trees there are impressive views overlooking the River Findhorn as the waters rapidly rush through the gorge below.

→ On the A940 S of Forres look for a small sign for Sluie Walk just under 2 miles S of IV36 2SQ and park down this road. Start on the clear footpath and turn right going downhill, which soon follows parallel to the gorge. The path eventually loops around back to the starting point.

25 mins, 57.5503, -3.6649

13 ROSEISLE FOREST & BURGHEAD BAY

Lining the sandy Bay of Burghead is Roseisle Forest, a peaceful woodland made up of conifers. Beyond this enchantment is the beach, lined from end to end with Second World War anti-tank blocks and pillboxes – some of which can be entered – that are sinking into the sand.

→ From the B9013 E of Kinloss, turn N at FC signs for Roseisle opp turning to IV30 8XA. Follow just under 1 mile to car park (pay) at end.

30 mins, 57.6722, -3.5031

14 CULBIN SANDS & FOREST

Extraordinary sandy forest scenery, receiving international recognition for its diverse landscape and quantity of plant, lichen and fungi breeds. There are raised walkways and towers. Follow paths through the forest and onto the shoreline to experience the natural diversity of the area.

→ Leave the A96 at Brodie Castle sign and follow to a T junction; take R signed Culbin. Follow road dir IV36 2TG but turn L for Cloddymoss after 1½ miles to the car park L just before the houses at the end. Walk N through the forest towards the shoreline.

30 mins, 57.6347, -3.6995

15 LOCH NA BO

Lovely little man-made loch hidden in a forest and ringed by foliage. Good for a short walk and picnic.

→ Loch Na Bo is served by a carpark 2km SE of Lhanbryde. Turn off the B9103 immediately after a small bridge, and head up a rough unsigned track to the carpark (IV30 8QY). Several waymarked routes all lead to the loch and surrounding forest. To circumnavigate the loch, follow the white marker posts with yellow bands. Take a L as you face the notice board and follow the path clockwise around the loch.

60 mins, 57.6217, -3.2047

LOCAL FOOD

16 THE BAKEHOUSE CAFÉ, FINDHORN

With a menu based on seasonal, local ingredients, the Bakehouse Café offers healthy and sustainable food, prepared freshly that day. Opened by the Findhorn Foundation (see 26) as part of the 'slow food' movement, it emphasises fairly traded and artisan-quality foods. Open every day in the heart of Findhorn; shorter hours in winter.

→ 91-92 Findhorn, IV36 3YG, 01309 691826. Bakehousecafe.co.uk

57.6597, -3.6105

17 PHOENIX COMMUNITY STORE & CAFÈ

At the entrance of the Universal Hall in the Findhorn Foundation (see 26) is the Phoenix Cafè, serving a range of light lunches, snacks and hot drinks using local and organic sources wherever possible. The works of local artists decorate the walls.

→ The Park, Findhorn, IV36 3TZ, 01309 690110. Phoenixshop.co.uk
57.6523, -3.5934 🍴

18 THE OLIVE TREE CAFÉ, FORRES

Beautifully situated above the River Findhorn, this café serves freshly made food from local and seasonal ingredients and bakes on the premises every day. Lovely mezzanine to relax, outside courtyard to enjoy lunch and even racks for your bikes.

→ Logie Steading, Dunphail, IV36 2QN, 01309 611733. The-olive-tree-cafe.co.uk
57.5350, -3.6606 🍴

19 THE KIMBERLEY INN, FINDHORN

Great inn serving quality meals and great selection of wines, beers and spirits. In summer take a seat at one of the outdoor tables overlooking the lovely Findhorn Bay, and when it's a little colder enjoy a drink next to the open fire.

→ Findhorn, IV36 3YG, 01309 690492. Kimberleyinn.com
57.6592, -3.6116 🍴

20 ROCKPOOL CAFÉ

Modern café-bistro with a fresh and friendly atmosphere in the heart of Cullen, a romantic harbour settlement. Serving everything from hearty Scottish breakfasts and fresh seafood to children's menus, ideal for winding down with friends or family.

→ 10 The Square, Cullen, Buckie AB56 4RR, 01542 841397. Rockpool-cullen.co.uk
57.6913, -2.8200 🚲 🍴

21 CULLEN BAY HOTEL

Cullen is famous for Cullen Skink, its unique and delicious haddock soup. The best is to be found at the Cullen Bay Hotel, which also has sweeping views over the Moray Firth.

→ Cullen, AB56 4XA, 01542 840432. Cullenbayhotel.com
57.6925, -2.8400 🍴

COTTAGES & CAMPING

22 CULLEN HARBOUR HOLIDAYS

Lovely spacious cottage with traditional beams and stone walls located in Cullen harbour. Magnificent views of the Moray Firth, a great opportunity to watch the sunset or see dolphins from the doorstep. There is also a cosy hostel around the corner.

→ Port Long Road, Cullen, AB56 4AG, 01542 841997. Cullenharbourholidays.com
57.6939, -2.8216

23 2 STATION ROAD COTTAGE, BUCKIE

Cosy renovated and modernised fisherman's cottage for two, in a little coastal village. Views out over the harbour – ideal for spotting dolphins – and a short walk to local shops and a welcoming harbourside pub.

→ Findochty, Buckie AB56 4PN, 019755 62871. Moraycoastalcottages.co.uk
57.6976, -2.9032

24 CLUNY BANK HOTEL, FORRES

Family-run hotel with luxurious en suite rooms in a stately Victorian mansion. Relax in the lounge bar and indulge in a dram from the collection of over 40 whiskies. Small, well-regarded fine-dining restaurant where the table is yours all evening.

→ 69 St Leonard's Road, Forres, IV36 1DW, 01309 67430. Clunybankhotel.co.uk
57.6072, -3.6012

25 ACE HIDEAWAYS, FORRES

Woodland camping and glamping in the Findhorn valley. Set a tent up under the canopy or enjoy one of the shepherd's huts (for two) or bell tents (for up to ten), each in their own little clearing. On the doorstep experience white-water rafting run by a sister company, or just unwind with a walk through the woodland. Small site, closed in winter.

→ Auchnagairn, Dunphail, Forres, IV36 2QL, 01309 611729. Acehideaways.co.uk
57.5152, -3.6844

26 FINDHORN ECOVILLAGE

This experimental community is one of the largest and longest-established 'intentional communities' in the country, where 40 small businesses and people from 40 countries have found a home. Owned by the Findhorn Foundation charitable trust, it promotes sustainable living and has an eco-footprint half of the UK average. There are educational programmes, along with public performances in the Universal Hall; go along for a workshop or an experience week that might change your whole outlook. Visit wesbite for B&Bs.

→ The Park, Findhorn, IV36 3TZ, 01309 690311. Findhorn.org
57.6531, -3.5938

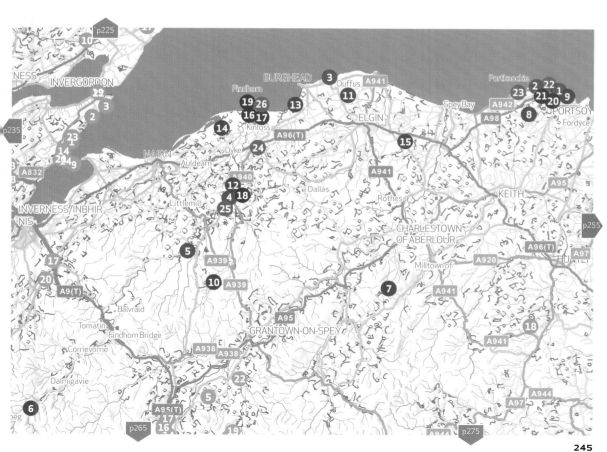

ABERDEENSHIRE

Our perfect weekend

→ **Follow** the winding River Dee on its snaking journey to the sea at Aberdeen.

→ **Ascend** Clachnaben and picnic below its giant granite tor.

→ **Explore** the ruins of dramatic Dunnottar Castle, one of the most extensive and interesting in Scotland.

→ **Savour** some of the best fish and chips in the country at The Bay in Stonehaven.

→ **Wander** slowly along St Cyrus beach and nature reserve, soaking up the sea air.

→ **Visit** the Troup Head gannet colony to see thousands of these wonderful diving seabirds.

→ **Stroll** amongst the spectacular Sands of Forvie, one of the most unusual landscapes in the area.

→ **Prop** up the bar at the Pennan Inn, scene of the film *Local Hero*.

→ **Take** in the crashing waves at the incredible Bullers of Buchan

→ **Investigate** the mysterious Tomnaverie Stone Circles.

Aberdeen, translating roughly as 'the confluence of the Rivers Dee and Don' is the commercial heart of the north-east coast and this is perhaps not an area one traditionally associates with wilderness. However, upon further investigation it encompasses a huge variety of landscapes and geology and, like much of Scotland, perfectly reflects the dynamics of the Highland-Lowland divide. This region is of course critically important because of North Sea oil, the black gold that has sustained the economy of the north-east for decades. But it also includes parts of the alpine semi-tundra environment of the Cairngorms and the busy, maritime communities of Banff and Buchan. All these characteristics make Aberdeenshire incredibly hard to put in a tidy pigeonhole, but one thing is certain: it offers you perhaps the greatest variety of landscapes and experiences in the entire country.

When considering the geography of Scotland, it is often enlightening to start with its rivers. The Rivers Dee, Don and Deveron, snaking eastward like veins towards the sea from their lofty sources in the wild and remote Cairngorms, provide the structure for the many prosperous communities of Aberdeenshire, culminating in the grey granite city of Aberdeen itself. The North Sea is important too, bracketing the area physically in the east but opening it up economically and providing wealth, stability and many generations of jobs. Even today, it is not uncommon for more than one generation of a family to be working in the oil industry.

With all this variety, it follows logically that there is an abundance of choice in Aberdeenshire. The traditional outdoor activities of hill-walking, mountaineering, camping and wild swimming are best enjoyed in the less populated, more rugged landscapes in the west of the region. The coastline is perfect for indulging in the history and social environment of the area, with enough rainy-day activities to entertain any younger members of the party. There are also plenty of castles and forts in the area, pointing to its strategic importance as a vital part of Scotland's economy for centuries.

As you'd expect from such a populous economic area, getting into and around Aberdeenshire is straightforward. It is most scenically approached on the A93 that heads north from Perth and through Glen Shee and down through Deeside. It is best to enter Aberdeenshire as the rivers flow downstream – the geography takes on a greater significance this way. For the time-conscious or those already on the east coast, excellent motorway links serve Aberdeen north from Dundee, or south from Inverness.

BEACHES & COASTLINE

1 BULLERS OF BUCHAN

Amazing sea arch you can walk around and view from several angles, very dramatic in rough weather – take care along the precipitous cliffs. It also gives its name to the picturesque little hamlet nearby, once a fishing village.

→ Off the A975 S of Peterhead there is signed space to park just before the village (AB42 0NS). From here head E on a path to the houses and follow the cliff top path in a loop.

10 mins, 57.4331, -1.8183 🔽🔁

2 SANDS OF FORVIE

Forvie is a lonely place where the shifting sands reveal lost ruins – a church is all that remains of a village long reclaimed by an ever-changing lunar landscape. Now a nature reserve, this is a starkly beautiful location to watch seals and birdlife.

→ Begin at the Forvie visitor centre on B9003 towards Collieston (AB41 8RU). Follow red waymarked route which passes the N side of Sand Loch, head R along the clifftop path and R at red marker to reach a ruined church. Alternatively follow path leading S from car park along Ythan River to the sand dunes.

40 mins, 57.3174, -1.9857 🔽🌸🔁🐾🔺

3 TROUP HEAD

Troup Head is an RSPB home to a range of seabirds, including Scotland's only mainland colony of 1,500 gannets nesting on steep cliffs. This short walk also has elevated views over the Moray Firth, a popular area for dolphins, porpoise and whales.

→ Turn off the B9031 1 mile SW of AB45 3JL, signed Troup Head / Northfield Farm, and follow to end. Park at RSPB car park just beyond the farm. Head N on track out of the car park and R at junction just beyond, then pass through a field. Take R fork at field end, then L at clifftop. Path follows the clifftop.

10 mins, 57.6946, -2.2960 🔽🌸🔁 ✖️

4 ST COMBS BAY

Huge expanse of pristine sand, backed by extensive dunes. A great place for wading birds, best at low tide.

→ Park in St Combs. On Church St, just S of cemetery (AB43 8ZY). Take grassy track which joins with another track and leads downhill to the dunes. Head S along the beach.

5 mins, 57.6285, -1.8729 🔁🔆🍴🔁🔺

5 WHITELINKS BAY

Crescent of sand with several sinking Second World War pillboxes.

→ Park in Inverallochy and from the end of Shore St (AB43 8WA) walk SE on a grassy path between the golf course and the sea.

10 mins, 57.6686, -1.9184 🔺🌸🔁

6 ABERDOUR BEACH

Red sandstone cliffs and arches – which look like caves until you get close enough – form a colourful rugged backdrop to this beach.

→ Signed from B9031 W of New Aberdour. Follow minor roads past AB43 6HR to beachside car park. Head down to shoreline and R for the cliffs. Take care at high tide.

5 mins, 57.6719, -2.1879 🔽❓🔁

7 WATERS OF PHILORTH

The River Philorth is a great place to see wading birds – oystercatchers, herons and sanderling. Reached over Fraserburgh Bay, there is a wide sweep of sand good for swimming and walking.

→ Starting from the esplanade at the E of Fraserburgh (AB43 9TA), head down on to the dunes and follow the beach S to the River Philorth after just over 2 miles.

40 mins, 57.6735, -1.9648 🔺🔁🔺✖️

8 BALMEDIE BEACH

Huge expanse of sandy beach with extensive and beautiful dunes. There is a scattering of Second World War anti-tank blocks and some well-preserved pillboxes. Good for seabirds.

→ In Balmedie take North Beach Rd past AB23 8WU to the Balmedie Country Park visitor centre. Head further E out of the car park to reach the beach, and S to find the pillboxes.

5 mins, 57.2543, -2.0364 🏖🚶🐕🏕🏊🏄

9 CULLYKHAN BAY

Delightful little cove with several sites of interest. Fort Fiddes (see 19) is above, and beyond it to the N is Hell's Lum, a collapsed sea cave, which is particularly atmospheric when the waves can be heard through it.

→ Park as for Fort Fiddes (see 19) and head down the wooden steps to the beach.

5 mins, 57.6844, -2.2742 🏖🥾🐚🏊

10 ST CYRUS NATURE RESERVE

Wonderful Nature Reserve for spotting birdlife and butterflies, not to mention a stroll along the wide expanse of pristine sand backed by impressive dunes.

→ Signed from the A92 N of Montrose (DD10 0AQ) with a large car park and visitor centre.

Walk N along the road next to some cottages, turn R and cross a bridge, and the path heads up and over the dunes on to the beach.

10 mins, 56.7642, -2.4183 🏖🚶🏄🏊🏕

RIVERS & LOCHS

11 RIVER DEVERON

Wide and beautiful river. This gentle walk starts at the Adams mansion Duff House, now a gallery for art and furnishings, which is wonderful in itself. Popular with fishermen, the River Deveron is also a great place to spot kingfishers and other birdlife.

→ Starting from Duff House (AB45 3SX), head SW for ½ mile to the river. Follow it upstream for a further 2¼ miles to reach Bridge of Alvah.

15 mins, 57.6527, -2.5308 🚶🏊🏄

HILLS & FORESTS

12 CLACHNABEN

This hill would be unremarkable if it were not for the giant granite tor that sits atop it. An extremely prominent landmark that can be seen for miles around, it offers extensive views in all directions.

→ From the Forestry Commission car park ½ mile N of Bridge of Dye (AB31 6LT) head out on

the path in the R corner through forest then downhill with a wall on your L. Cross a stile, take a R after a bridge, then R again at the next fork. The path skirts the beautiful Black Hillocks Forest (see 14) before ascending up to Clachnaben, which is prominent ahead.

90 mins, 56.9680, -2.6339 🏞🏕🌲

13 MITHER TAP, BENNACHIE

There is an old couplet for guiding sailors 'Clachnaben and Bennachie, twa landmarks fae the sea', and like its poetic partner to the south (see 12) Bennachie is a prominent hill with a huge amount of character. Its highest point is Oxen Crag, but Mither Tap is the distinctive one, with a fort on its summit and old farming settlements and standing stones on its slopes.

→ Follow the signs for Back o' Bennachie Forest Walks from the B9002 at Ryehill, past AB52 6RH to a Forestry Commission car park. Walk out on the brown Quarry Trail path but take a R it when you reach a track, then soon after a L. Ignoring any turn offs, stay on this path, which ascends Mither Tap.

90 mins, 57.2911, -2.5289 🏔🏞🏕🏰🏕🌲

14 BLACK HILLOCKS FOREST

En route to Clachnaben (see 12) is a lovely

plantation of Scots pine. A tranquil destination to wander amongst beautiful trees.

➔ Start as for Clachnaben (see 12), but detour R into the woods.

30 mins, 56.9641, -2.6077 🎋🏕️💧🔺

15 SCOLTY HILL

Prominent local landmark near Banchory. This easily accessible hill has a large tower, General Burnett's Monument, on top, with a viewing platform giving excellent views over the surrounding landscape. The woodlands themselves are a lovely place to wander.

➔ In Auchaltie, just S of Banchory on the B974, take the fork into Scolty Woods 300m N of AB31 6PT and follow to the car park. Leave the car park following the white waymarkers, ignoring any turn offs. Go through a gate, bear L and then take the next R and begin the ascent. The tower is soon reached.

40 mins, 57.0355, -2.5309 🚶💧🔶🔭

FORTS & CASTLES

16 TOMNAVERIE STONE CIRCLE

Mysterious stone circle atop a hill near Tarland, consisting of a central cairn with cremated remains (now grassed over), and a later circle of monoliths including a recumbent one with two upright 'flankers', a characteristic of circles in this part of Scotland.

➔ Leaving Tarland on the B9119 heading S, take a L immediately after AB34 4YP. After ½ mile find a signed car park R with path to circle.

20 mins, 57.1194, -2.8497 🔶✝️🔶

17 DUNNOTTAR CASTLE

Without a doubt, this extensive medieval fortress is one of the greatest castles in Scotland. Perched on a flat-topped promontory facing out to sea, which may have been fortified for over 1,400 years, Dunnottar Castle is an awe-inspiring and justifiably popular place.

➔ Start from the dedicated car park beside the A90 S of Stonehaven (AB39 2TL). Follow the obvious path the short distance out towards the sea and castle.

5 mins, 56.9459, -2.1985 🌊🏰🔶🔶

18 TAP O' NOTH HILLFORT

This partly vitrified Iron Age fort is somewhere between 2,000 and 3,000 years old, and was once surrounded by more than 100 houses. It is easy to see why this location, atop a prominent hill, was chosen, and the views are superb.

➔ There is a signed car park for the fort approx 1 mile W of Rhynie on the A941 (AB54 4HH). The Tap lies directly N up a path from the car park entrance, through a gate up the field, through the next gate and on a path L heading around the hill, and finally another gate and a R to the top of the hill.

60 mins, 57.3511, -2.8584 🔶🏰🔶🔶

19 FORT FIDDES

The promontory of Castle Point is appropriately named – the remains of a 20th-century look-out, the 18th-century battery of Fort Fiddes, a medieval castle, and an Iron Age vitrified fort are all crammed onto this one bit of land. Can be combined with Cullykhan Bay (see 9).

➔ 500m W of Nethermill (AB43 6JA) on the B9031, take signed turn for Cullykhan Bay and Fort Fiddes to car park. Descend steps to N of the car park to reach grassy ridge that juts out and connects the headland to the mainland.

5 mins, 57.6854, -2.2719 🐚🔶🔶🔶

20 DUNNIDEER CASTLE

Interesting hill with the picturesque remains of one of the oldest castles in Scotland on top of it – potentially dating back to 1260. It stands within the wider remains of a

17

vitrified hillfort. The ascent is quick and straightforward, and the views extensive.

➜ Start from a small layby L on the minor road W out of Insch (just after AB52 6LW). From here go through kissing gate and R to walk up beside a fence. Go through gate at the top of the field and bear R up to the castle.

15 mins, 57.3422, -2.6458

21 NEW SLAINS CASTLE

One of a select group of atmospheric buildings that are claimed to be an inspiration for Bram Stoker's Dracula, New Slains Castle is a now-roofless ruin perched atop a cliff overlooking the sea. Called 'new' to distinguish it from nearby (and nearly gone) Old Slains Castle, it was built and reworked over several centuries.

➜ Start from the car park signed Slains Castle by the church at the end of the main street (AB42 0NA), take a path through the trees heading SE. At a fork take a L and continue to the coast. The path heads L and north up the coast. Beyond the castle the coastline is also attractive. Old Slains Castle is near Collieston to the S (57.3606, -1.9141).

20 mins, 57.4153, -1.8319

LOCAL FOOD

22 THE BAY FISH & CHIPS, STONEHAVEN

Award-winning fish and chips with Marine Stewardship Council approval – they don't get much better than this.

→ Beach Rd, Stonehaven, AB39 2RD, 01569 762000. Thebayfishandchips.co.uk
56.9685, -2.2055 ▯▯

23 BIRDHOUSE CAFÉ, BANCHORY

Well-regarded local café serving excellent coffee and cake.

→ 74 High St, Banchory, AB31 5SS, 01330 822072. Birdhousecafe.co.uk
57.0512, -2.5029 ▯▯

24 THE HARBOUR RESTAURANT

Booking ahead is essential at this tiny restaurant, serving excellent seafood and local meat. Right on the harbour, great views.

→ Harbour Road, Gardenstown, AB45 3YT, 01261 851663.
57.6731, -2.3372 ▯▯ ▯▯

25 PORTSOY ICE CREAM

Award-winning local producer of ice cream, with an ever-changing range and the option to take a tub home. Perfect after a day strolling on the Moray Firth coastline.

→ 24 Seafield Street, Portsoy, AB45 2QT, 01261 842279. Portsoyicecream.co.uk
57.6814, -2.6902 ▯▯ ▯▯

HOTELS & COTTAGES

26 PENNAN INN

Friendly seafront hotel and restaurant with a small but excellent menu. Located in the ridiculously picturesque little fishing village made famous as 'Ferness' in the well-loved film *Local Hero*. The huge beach in the film was actually on the west coast: here there is a little stone harbour instead.

→ Pennan, Fraserburgh AB43 6JB, 01346 561201. Thepennaninn.co.uk
57.6788, -2.2596 ▯▯ ▯▯

27 WEAVERS COTTAGE, CROVIE

This beautiful little cottage sits yards from the sea in the picturesque fishing village of Crovie. Furnished with a strong Indian influence, it is an unusual base from which to explore the coast.

→ Crovie, Banff, AB45 3JQ. Cottages.com
57.6797, -2.3241 ▯▯ ▯▯ ▯▯

CAMPSITES & CABINS

28 GREENPARK LEISURE, GLASSEL

Cosy insulated wigwams and pods, well spaced on a site with good amenities, ideal for exploring Deeside.

→ Glassel, Banchory, Aberdeenshire, AB31 4DB, 01330 825544. Greenparkleisure.co.uk
57.0777, -2.5569 ▯▯

29 HIGH SEAS HOBBITS, ROSEHEARTY

Interesting cylindrical cabins set on a peaceful farm, with sea views, their own firepits and a loo in an old whisky barrel.

→ Milestone House, Rosehearty, Fraserburgh, AB43 6JY, 07964 989737. Highseashobbit.com
57.6817, -2.1325 ▯▯ ▯▯ ▯▯ ▯▯ ▯▯

30 YTHAN VALLEY CAMPSITE, NR ELLON

Surrounded by trees and big skies, this quirky and welcoming little campsite with bunkhouse is located in a quiet and less-visited part of Aberdeenshire. A nice touch is the fresh bread and a cooked breakfast which can be delivered to your tent every morning. Eat it in your sleeping bag!

→ Smithfield, Ythanbank, nr Ellon, AB41 7TH, 01358 761400.
Smithfield.ythanvalley@googlemail.com
57.4006, -2.1578 ▯▯ ▯▯ ▯▯ ▯▯

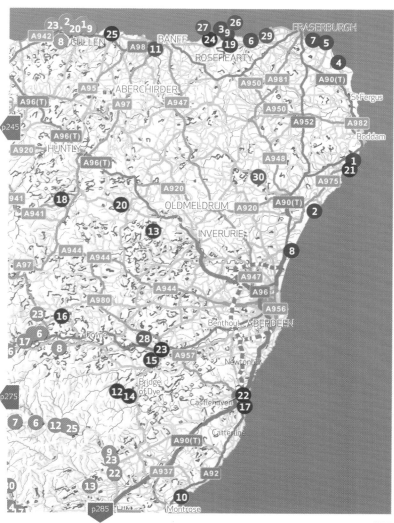

NORTHERN CAIRNGORMS

Our perfect weekend

→ **Climb** over the Cairn Gorm plateau to sparkling Loch Avon.

→ **Dare** to crawl under the extraordinary roof of the legendary Shelter Stone.

→ **Watch** red squirrels whilst eating cake at the Potting Shed Tearoom at Inshriach Nursery.

→ **Wander** through ancient Scots pines in Inschriach forest and listen for the distinctive 'lekking' call of the capercaillie.

→ **Look** for ospreys at the RSPB reserve of Loch Garten and Loch Mallachie.

→ **Camp** and wake up next to the tranquil turquoise waters of Lochan Uaine.

→ **Soak** up the atmosphere in remote, windswept Ryvoan Bothy.

→ **Follow** in the footsteps of history by following an ancient track through the awe-inspiring Lairig Ghru.

The story of the Cairngorms is the story of time. At roughly 40 million years old, the lumbering red hills of the northern Cairngorm plateau form one of the last truly wild and desolate areas in the Highlands, and to explore them fully is to discover an area uniquely shaped by natural forces and largely untouched by humans. So vast are the mountains that throughout history they have presented a serious barrier to movement, and this shaped the character and remote atmosphere of the Highlands. The great Caledonian Forest that clad most of the Highlands in ancient times has all but disappeared, except in the Cairngorms. It is one of the few places to experience the swathes of Scots pine that were largely lost centuries ago.

Many of the attractions in the Cairngorms require effort to reach, because even today these peaks shoulder aside the roads. Lochs are hidden a day's walk from the car, to drive around the massif takes hours, and the distances involved make it unlikely you will see everything in one visit. And of course the blunt, scoured and rolling nature of the mountains is a consequence of millions of years of exposure to harsh conditions and savage weather.

The northern Cairngorms are bordered by the river Spey to the north, with the Feshie and the Avon to the west. They are primarily reached from Aviemore in the north, which lies just off the A9 trunk road. As a result of their emptiness they have been somewhat neglected in favour of more accessible and instantly appealing places. Those who can see past this underdog status will find enjoyment that is hard won, but worth every ounce of effort. Follow in the footsteps of generations of adventurers by navigating over the windswept plateau of Cairn Gorm to spend a night under the giant Shelter Stone by the pristine perfection of Loch Avon. This is a truly wild experience that requires planning and consideration, but which will be repaid in unparalleled feelings of solitude and wilderness.

If too much wilderness leaves you feeling lonely, the northern Cairngorms have much to see and do in towns and villages. An absolute must is to finish off your visit with a welcoming pint in the Old Bridge Inn on your return to Aviemore. First impressions are worth nothing in the Cairngorms, but with effort and patience they are an area of Scotland that seep in and stay for good in the mind of the explorer.

LOCHS & WILD SWIMMING

1 LOCH AVON

This secluded loch, also called Loch A'an, draws you in from the moment you glimpse it shining far below the mountains. Set between steep mountain slopes, the effort to find it is repaid by the unique experience of enjoying isolated and pristine sandy beaches in such rugged and dramatic scenery.

→ From the car park at the Cairn Gorm ski centre (PH22 1RB), head up the path to the W side of Coire Cas to the Fiacaill a' Coire Chais ridge. Descend straight ahead into Coire Raibert, and Loch Avon should be visible far below. Follow the steep, rocky path on the E bank of the stream to reach the water. Return by the same route. Serious undertaking in bad weather.

2–4 hrs, 57.0997, -3.6352 🚶♀️❓🐚⛰️🏕️

2 LOCHAN UAINE

Set amid an ancient Scots pine forest, this tranquil lochan gets its beautiful turquoise clarity from the abundance of iron in the rock, concentrated in the water by the restricted inflow and outflow to give it the appearance of a miniature Canadian glacial lake. More fancifully, it is called the Fairy Loch, with the colour attributed to fairies washing their clothes in it. Ringed with sandy beaches, it is unique and easily accessed, but there can be leeches here. Ryvoan bothy (see 19) lies beyond.

→ Starting from Glenmore Forest visitor centre (PH22 1QY) follow the path that runs E to Glenmore Lodge. Continue past a sign for Nethy Bridge, and follow the good path as it winds through forests and over several small bridges to Lochan Uaine.

60 mins, 57.1751, -3.6549 🚶🏕️❓🐕

3 LOCH AN EILEIN

This extremely picturesque loch is the destination for justifiably one of the most popular short walks in the Cairngorms. Fringed with pine trees and adorned with a ruined castle, it provides a good excursion and easily accessible swimming spot.

→ From the B970 1 mile S of Inverdruie (dir PH22 1QT) take the signed Loch an Eilein turn and follow to end for the car park (pay per person). The loch is a short walk beyond, and is well signed. Good paths ring the loch and the surrounding area is well worth exploring.

10 mins, 57.1524, -3.8225 🐕🚶🏕️🐚🐕

4 LOCHAN MOR

This peaceful and little-frequented lochan is also called the Lily Loch for the waterlilies that float in abundance on the surface. Much quieter than its more popular neighbour of Loch an Eilein (see 3), it is the perfect place to unwind in beautiful surroundings.

→ Park as for Loch an Eilean (see 3) and walk back ½ mile to Milton Cottage – there is limited space to pull off in one layby between cottage and car park. Take the turning N by cottage and walk through forest to the N shore.

20 mins, 57.1635, -3.8209 🚶⛱️🐕

5 LOCH MALLACHIE

A beautiful forest loch, a unique and serene place that juxtaposes ancient Scots pine forests with calm, lucid waters. Part of an RSPB reserve, together with nearby Loch Garten, which is a brilliant place to spot ospreys in the spring and early summer.

→ To walk through forest to loch, park in Garten Woods car park opp Boat of Garten turning from the B970, ½ mile S of PH24 3BY. Follow Red Trail through trees to Loch. For ospreys and Loch Garten, take Loch Garten turning from B970 at PH24 3BY and follow 1½ miles for RSPB osprey centre (PH25 3HA).

60 mins, 57.2351, -3.7139 🐕🚶⛱️🐕

6 UATH LOCHANS

Four small, sparkling lochans amid magical wild woodland scenery. You can either follow the easy boardwalk path around the water, great for wildlife spotting with children, or climb upwards to Farleitter Crag, which has fantastic views down over the lochans.

→ Take the Glenfeshie turning from the B970 (dir PH21 1NX) 7 miles S of Inverdruie. After 1 mile take R to park at Uath Lochans car park after 400m. Follow the boardwalk path or red marker posts to turn L onto trail that curves around the lochans and continues up to Farleitter Crag.

90 mins, 57.0960, -3.9194 🚶🏃⛱♀

7 FESHIEBRIDGE

Fabulous clear water flows down rapids into huge river pool with white shingle beach opposite. Interesting rock shapes and patterns. Rest under the large Scots pine on the bank. A great, fun location and one of the few with clear, non-peaty water.

→ As for Loch an Eilein but continue on B970 to Feshiebridge. 3 miles beyond Eilein turn off. Park close to bridge to find pool downstream.

2 mins, 57.1156, -3.8982 ♀🏊

8 THE SHELTER STONE

This giant fallen boulder in front of the cliffs at the west end of Loch Avon rests on smaller rocks to leave space for about five people beneath it. It has been used as a dark but comfortable refuge or a 'howff' for centuries and is immortalised in many climbers' and travellers' accounts of the Cairngorms. It is a welcome sanctuary in one of the wildest spots in Scotland.

→ Park and start as for Loch Avon (see 1). Follow path to the SW end of the loch, continuing into the boulder field beyond. The shelter is conspicuous as the largest boulder in the field, with a cairn on top. Return by the same route.

3 hrs, 57.0944, -3.6489 🚶📷⛰❓♿

9 INSHRIACH FOREST

On the edge of the Cairngorm mountains, this 32 sq km area of land contains small but pristine remnants of ancient Caledonian forest. Waymarked walking trails and cycling routes offer plenty of opportunities to explore the area. Look out for capercaillies.

→ Take minor road as for Uath Lochans (see 6), but continue to car park L after 2 miles.

5 mins, 57.0960, -3.9153 ♀🚴🏊

10 GLEN FESHIE

Landseer's famous stag was monarch of this glen, and overgrazing by deer very nearly destroyed the ancient forest here. Now it is one of the most successful 'rewilding' projects in the country, where careful culling has led to a host of young trees and a hugely increased variety of wildlife. Look out for the majestic waterfalls in spring and early summer, when the snow is melting off the mountains and the rivers are in full spate. For an overnight stay there is Ruigh Aiteachain Bothy (see 20).

→ From the B970 at Feshiebridge take the road dir PH21 1NH signed Auchlean to car park L after 4 miles. Walk ½ mile along the tarmac road ending at Achlean farm, pick up the main path through a gate and over a stream and walk into the glen, crossing Allt Gharbhlach. Crossings could be difficult after heavy rains.

1–3 hrs, 57.0353, -3.8963 🚶🅱♀❄🏊

11 THE NORTHERN CORRIES

Easily reached via the ski centre car park, these ragged and dramatic amphitheatres give the visitor a taste of mountaineering atmosphere without putting in too much effort. The high cliffs are a playground for climbers in both summer and winter, but

even a walk into either corrie is a brilliant experience. Coire an t-Sneachda is the first and most easily accessible corrie, Coire an Lochain lying further to the west.

→ Park as for Loch Avon (see 1) but head SW on an excellent path that leads away from the main ski developments. This contours the hill and leads S into the corrie.

90 mins, 57.1143, -3.6663

12 LAIRIG GHRU

This 19-mile walk is an established route through the Cairngorms, used for centuries as a drovers' road to the southern half of Scotland. The remains of a glacial trench, the Lairig Ghru is hemmed in on both sides by four of the five highest mountains in the UK. Wild, desolate and surrounded by stunning scenery, it demands care, as the pass reaches 835m and is very susceptible to bad weather. The Lairig Ghru can be walked in either direction, but the classic route is to walk N to S, from Rothiemurchus in Speyside to the Linn of Dee in Deeside. Many people split the walk into a two-day trip, stopping off at Corrour Bothy (see 18) or camping halfway through. Mostly clear paths, but bring a map.

→ Start by Rothiemurchus Camp and Caravan Park (500m E of PH22 1QN, layby parking).

Head down the path next to the caravan park and follow all signs for Lairig Ghru through the Rothiemurchus Forest. There are clear paths, and the way should be obvious, eventually bearing E down Glen Laoigh Bheag to Derry Lodge and the Linn of Dee. You will need to arrange transport if you wish to return to the start, as there are no practical public transport options.

8-10 hours, 57.0692, -3.6931

LOCAL FOOD

13 POTTING SHED TEAROOM

Idyllic family-run nursery. Alongside the interesting hardy plants, the potting shed has been converted into a rustic tea room with excellent views of red squirrels and birdlife in the surrounding forest, serving highly regarded home-made Norwegian-style cakes. Open Wed–Sun.

→ Inshriach Nursery, Aviemore, PH22 1QS, 01540 651287. Inshriachnursery.co.uk
57.1432, -3.8591

14 ROTHIEMURCHUS FARM SHOP

Estate shop with a superb selection of homegrown and local produce and foodstuffs, from Highland beef to heather honey.

→ Inverdruie, Aviemore PH22 1QH, 01479 812345. Rothiemurchus.net
57.1762, -3.8177

15 MOUNTAIN CAFÉ

Laid back café run by a New Zealand ex-pat who fell in love with the Cairngorms. A real community feel, with local artworks adorning the walls and local produce in abundance on the menu. Especially good for children's food.

→ 111 Grampian Road, Aviemore, PH22 1RH, 01479 812473. Mountaincafe-aviemore.co.uk
57.1912, -3.8290

PUBS & BREWERIES

16 THE OLD BRIDGE INN

Cosy highland pub with log fire and welcoming atmosphere. Amazing steaks and very dog friendly. There is even a bunkhouse next door.

→ Dalfaber Road, Aviemore, PH22 1PU, 01479 811137. Oldbridgeinn.co.uk
57.1836, -3.8304

17 CAIRNGORM BREWERY

Don't let the humdrum exterior fool you – this independent brewery produces award-winning craft beers with strong local connections,

18

including one that supports Scottish wildcat conservation. Tours and tastings.

➜ Dalfaber Industrial Estate, Aviemore, PH22 1ST, 01479 812222. Cairngormbrewery.com
57.2009, -3.8203

BOTHIES & OFF GRID

18 CORROUR BOTHY

Deep in the Cairngorms, Corrour Bothy stands as a cosy outpost of shelter at the wildest heart of the Highlands. Much photographed and frequented, it lies directly below the shapely peak of the Devil's Point.

➜ Follow directions as for Lairig Ghru walk (see 12). 2½ miles S from Pools of Dee you reach Clach nan Taillear (Stone of the Tailors). Cross the Dee shortly beyond this at an obvious path to the bothy, below Devil's Point. 8 hours walk.
57.0420, -3.6809 B V Y 🏔

19 RYVOAN BOTHY

This windswept refuge sits defiantly on the heathery hills above the treeline in magnificent and desolate scenery. In an RSPB reserve on the ancient pass between Glen More and Nethy Bridge, it is not far from Lochan Uaine (see 2); combine the two for a varied excursion. Bothy is small but full of character and often busy.

➜ Start as for Lochan Uaine (see 2). Continue on path past the lochan, getting rougher as it winds uphill. At fork take L signed Nethy Bridge and continue on, and emerge from forest. From here the landscape becomes bleaker. Bothy soon reached on your L. 1½ hours walk.
57.1836, -3.6458 Y 🏔 B

20 RUIGH AITEACHAIN BOTHY

This popular, well-kept stone bothy is situated deep in Glen Feshie (see 10) amongst an impressive display of mature trees. Sir Edwin Landseer studied red deer here for his famous painting *Monarch of the Glen*; the lone chimney stack of the cottage he stayed in still stands near the bothy.

➜ Start as for Glen Feshie (see 10). After crossing Allt Gharbhlach, follow path into Scots pine woods. Take a R then L and continue on good path to bear R along a track. Stay straight ahead at the next crossroads and continue on this path to Ruigh Aiteachain, approx 3½ miles, 1½–2 hours (stream crossings can be difficult after heavy rains).
57.0117, -3.9004 B

21 FORDS OF AVON REFUGE

Extremely basic but atmospheric shelter set in the wilds of the River Avon. Don't expect comfort. A handy stopping place for those who want to explore the wilder hills or take a more ambitious hike S through Glen Derry to the S Cairngorms, ending at the Linn of Dee and Derry Lodge (see p272, listing 14).

➜ From the N end of Loch Avon (see 1) follow paths along the N side of the River Avon approx 1½ miles to the shelter. 2 hours walk.
57.1093, -3.5833 B Y ? 🏔

22 LAZY DUCK, NETHY BRIDGE

Hostel, off-grid huts and a tiny four-pitch semi-wild campsite. The waterside Duck's Nest is a wonderfully peaceful experience.

➜ Nethy Bridge, PH25 3ED, 01479 821092. Lazyduck.co.uk
57.2634, -3.6318 🖼

HIGHLAND HOMES

23 INSHRIACH HOUSE

A charming and eclectic collection of holiday options in the grounds of an Edwardian country house. Stay in the artist's bothy, yurt, converted truck or shepherd's hut. The house can be booked for larger groups, and the estate features everything from white-water rafting to the annual Insider music festival.

➜ Inshriach, PH22 1QP, 01540 651341. Inshriachhouse.com
57.1423, -3.8649 🖼

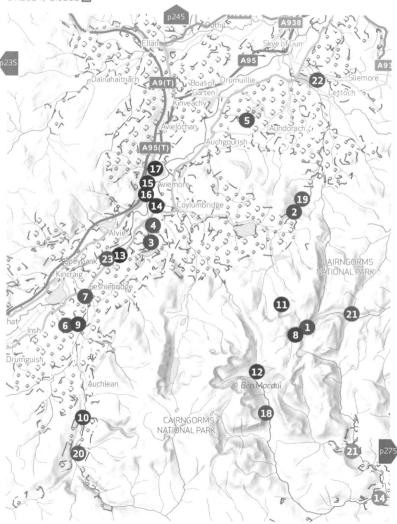

SOUTHERN CAIRNGORMS

Our perfect weekend

→ **Marvel** at the barren wastelands of Glen Shee.

→ **Soak** up the slow pace of life in beautiful Braemar and stay in a former hunting lodge.

→ **Plunge** into the refreshing pools of Dee beneath a gothic bridge.

→ **Wander** amongst venerable Scots pine at atmospheric Derry Lodge.

→ **Watch** deer shifting through the forest at Glen Tanar, and watch for golden eagles overhead.

→ **Scramble** up dark Lochnagar to see one of the most spectacular corries imaginable.

→ **Refuel** after your exploits at the excellent Bothy Café in Braemar.

→ **Unwind** with a smooth glass of Royal Lochnagar whisky at the distillery.

The landscape of the southern Cairngorms differs in many ways from its neighbour to the north. Whilst beautiful, the northern reaches have been to some extent infiltrated by tourism. By contrast, the southern Cairngorms feature little in the way of development, and the villages that nestle into the rounded, heathery hills are lovely in their own right. Whatever your views on royalty, the association with 'Royal Deeside' since Queen Victoria fell in love with the area has brought the benefit of protecting and preserving much of Scotland's traditional landscape here. This remains one of the best places in the country to see wonders such as abundant Scots pine, while in Balmoral, there is a romantic castle and any development has been carried out sensitively.

The southern Cairngorms hide their jewels well, and it is easy to pass through the barren lands of Glen Shee and follow the Dee to the east coast and wonder what all the fuss is about. However, just as in the northern Cairngorms, the bulky, rounded hills hide beautiful secrets, and even the hairpin bends of Glen Shee make for excellent cycle touring, with many places to pull off and camp by a river. There are towering corries – the cliffs of Lochnagar and Dubh Loch are as impressive as anywhere in Scotland – and the lonely lochs are a wild-swimming paradise if you are prepared to brave the waters at a higher altitude. The lifeblood of the area is the Dee, the fast-flowing river that crashes its way from barren Braeriach through the southern Cairngorms and out into the North Sea at Aberdeen.

The towns of the southern Cairngorms are wonderful in their own right, and considerable effort has gone into preserving their heritage and traditional character. Food, drink and accommodation are similarly traditional, with emphasis placed on local produce and royal charters, in which the holders take great pride.

The distances to travel are vast (walking between glens is almost quicker), and the few roads that cut the glens and provide access to the wonders of the area are often snow-bound and inaccessible in winter. The area is best reached via Perth and Blairgowrie on the A93 and through stark and desolate Glen Shee, itself a veritable Arctic landscape in winter. Decent roads also lead in from Aberdeen at the other end of the A93, and over the high pass of the Lecht from Grantown-on-Spey on the A939 in the north.

LOCHS & WILD SWIMMING

1 LOCH CALLATER

Easily reached on a track but with a wild feel to it, Loch Callater is hemmed in on all sides by mountains. It has a comfortable bothy at its head and forms part of the ancient Jock's Road, a drovers' route across the mountains to Glen Clova. Loch Callater is particularly lovely in March, when the sun is out but there is still snow on the surrounding peaks. This track is an easy cycle.

→ Park at the large car park off the A93 opp Auchallater Farm (AB35 5XS). From the car park follow the obvious track through the hills to the head of Loch Callater, ignoring any turns and forks along the way. It is possible – and recommended – to walk around the loch, although the inflow river at the far end of the loch may have to be waded.

50 mins, 56.9431, -3.3535 🦅🏞🐚🏔🏕🅱🏊

2 LINN OF QUOICH

The Quoich is a tributary of the River Dee, and the beautiful Linn of Quoich was a favourite spot of Queen Victoria. The river narrows to a bottleneck with the water-sculpted Earl of Mar's Punch Bowl. Legend says he mixed spirits and toasted the Jacobite uprising here, but even if it was a bowl then, it is a hole you can fit a person through now. A lovely cottage, wonderful Scots pine and an abundance of wildlife complete the scene.

→ From Braemar follow the Linn of Dee road W out of town. Cross the river at the Linn of Dee and double back along the N side for 3½ miles to Quoich car park at the end of the public road (past AB35 5YJ). Follow path to the river. The bridges washed away in the 2016 storms, so the only access may be on the W side path, which initially leads away from the Quoich but then takes a R fork back to near the Punch Bowl.

30 mins, 57.0029, -3.4544 🦅🐚🏞

3 LOCH MUICK

This grand, 2-mile loch is an excellent and easily reached introduction to the landscape of the southern Cairngorms. Sitting within the boundary of the Balmoral estate, the loch is enclosed by steep mountains, including the famous and atmospheric Lochnagar (see 7). On the north shore sits Glas-allt-Shiel, once Queen Victoria's summerhouse, now an open and popular bothy.

→ Leave the B976 S of Ballater on minor road by the bridge, signed Glen Muick. Park at the large Spittal of Glen Muick car park at the road end, past AB35 5SU. Loch Muick is a short distance beyond, and a good path rings the entire body of water. 2–4 hours circuit

10 mins, 56.9437, -3.1526 🦅🏔🏞📖🅱

4 DUBH LOCH

Those who put in the extra effort to continue on beyond Loch Muick (see 3) are rewarded with the black Dubh Loch – about as lonely and unspoiled as it gets for a wild-swimming location. Set below Creag an Dubh Loch, one of the UK's largest and finest mountain cliffs, this is the epitome of wild Scotland.

→ Park as for Loch Muick and walk down the W shore. Take a R fork after Glas-allt-Shiel Bothy and follow this path up and over to Dubh Loch.

2½ hrs, 56.9266, -3.2432 🦅❓🔺🏞🏊

5 PATTACK FALLS

This impressive river crashes its way through a turbulent gorge into a broad pool, and is easily accessible from the road.

→ Park at Druim an Aird car park on A86 W of Laggan approx 1¼ miles E of PH20 1BY. Head SE from the car park on a good path, till you reach a fork. The falls are to your R from here.

5 mins, 56.9814, -4.3606 📖🚶🏊

6 LOCH KINORD

Lovely loch that forms part of a nature reserve, excellent for swimming. Can be combined with Burn o' Vat pothole (see 11) for an interesting day out. You may see adders in the woods.

→ Park at the Burn o' Vat visitor centre on the B9119 (AB34 5NB). Cross main road and go L, following waymarked trail around N side of loch. 30 mins, 57.0854, -2.9261 🏊🐕🚗🏕️🌊

MOUNTAINS & GLENS

7 LOCHNAGAR

One of the grandest mountains in Scotland, Byron's 'dark Lochnagar' has inspired countless climbers to visit its towering slopes, and many songs and poems have been written about it. A giant corrie of gullies, ridges and cliffs encircling a dark body of water, Lochnagar is a fabulous viewpoint and a great day out. This is a serious mountain walk, so take both care and proper equipment.

→ Park as for Loch Muick (see 3). After crossing the river S, take R signed Lochnagar following good paths through forest, past the shooting lodge and up into the hills beyond. Take path L, heading for the distinctive cone of Miekle Pap, which rises to a bealach and reveals the corrie. For the summit, follow rim of the corrie to a giant cairn atop a tor on the NW side. Return the same way; those adept at scrambles might take the steeper SE path following the Glas Allt down to Loch Muick. Upto 8 hours round-trip.

5–8 hrs, 56.9554, -3.2410 🏊🐕🥾❓🏕️⛰️🌊

8 GLEN TANAR

Glen Tanar is an idyllic place to spend time amongst great swathes of Scots pine. The forests and rivers are full of wildlife, and a good path leads through the glen to the most easterly Munro, Mount Keen.

→ Leave the B976 SW of Aboyne at Bridge o' Ess on single-track road through the Glen Tanar Estate (dir AB34 5EU). Park at Braeloine car park on R after 1½ miles (pay). Various walks are listed on boards at the car park.

Time varies, 57.0571, -2.8585 🅿️🚶🚴🏕️🛖🦌🌊

9 CARN AN T-SAGAIRT MOR

The remains of a fatal RAF Canberra crash in 1956 lie scattered on the barren summit plateau of this Munro. A large section of wing with the RAF roundel still preserved is particularly striking, as are the views back to lonely Loch Callater (see 1). This is a serious mountain walk and proper care and equipment should be taken.

→ Park as for Loch Callater and head up the track to the loch. Follow the decent stalkers' path behind Lochcallater Lodge up into the hills beyond. At a line of metal fence posts with aircraft wreckage, the paths turns S and traverses Carn an t-Sagairt Mor. Leave the path near the top and make your way to the summit at 1047m. The aircraft wreckage is in several locations on the plateau.

3 hours, 56.9431, -3.3025 🏊🐕🥾❓⛰️🌊

10 CREAG CHOINNICH

Excellent short walk up Creag Choinnich, which overlooks Braemar and is prominent from the village. Great views out over Braemar, Glen Shee, the Linn of Dee and into the high Cairngorms.

→ From the car park in the village centre (on Balnellan Rd AB35 5YE) dir opp St Margaret's church. Walk up L side of the church and where this lane bends to the R there is a gate into the forestry. Head through this and follow the signed path through the forest and up the hill. 30 mins, 57.0103, -3.3833 🚶🏕️🌊⛰️

11 BURN O' VAT

This immense pothole, 13m deep, was sculpted by glacial meltwater spiralling

21

around a rock over thousands of years. It can be entered via a narrow gorge if the water is not running too high, and to stand in its vast gloom gives an impressive feeling of the power of water to form the landscape. The cave behind the waterfall has served as a hiding place for outlaws over the years. Wear sound shoes.

→ Park at the Burn o' Vat visitor centre on the B9119 (AB34 5NB), where you will find information on the Vat and taxidermy examples of local wildlife. A well-marked path follows the river upstream to the entrance to the Vat, a squeeze through cracks in the rock. Take care: high water levels are a hazard.

30 mins, 57.0839, -2.9503 ⛅❄️📷

SACRED & ANCIENT

12 BALMORAL MEMORIAL CAIRNS

These gems are hidden deep in the Balmoral Forest. Erected to commemorate events in the lives of royals past and present, they appear almost like cult objects in their construction and some command fantastic views over the southern Cairngorms. Prince Albert's cairn is the largest and most impressive. There is little in the way of signage, which makes their discovery even more special.

→ You could start at the car park at the B976 junction off the A93 in Crathie, but a closer option is to cross the bridge, turn L along the B976, then R at Easter Balmoral dir AB35 5TE and the distillery. There is a small parking area about 100m up this road at the start of a gravel track L. Walk up the road opposite, passing some beautiful cottages, to a gate on the L, beyond the cottage with the hedges trimmed into pyramids. Follow this path uphill through forestry to the largest cairn, passing smaller cairns along the way.

60 mins, 57.0260, -3.2213 🚶📷⛪🍴⛰️❄️

13 BLACK WOOD & DUN DA-LAMH FORT

This large Pictish defensive structure is an incredible viewpoint over the moody and atmospheric Black Wood. Of uncertain age, it also contains a dugout thought to have been made by the Home Guard in the Second World War.

→ Park as for Pattack Falls (see 5) and head NE. The path isn't waymarked at first, so a map is helpful, but can be found by bearing R, then L and through a gap in a fence. Thereafter follow the blue hilltop fort signs.

2 hrs, 57.0058, -4.3364 🚴📷📷⛰️

14 LINN OF DEE & DERRY LODGE

From its source in the high Cairngorms the Dee is funnelled through a rocky gorge at the Linn of Dee, before continuing on to the sea on the East coast. The Linn of Dee is a justifiably popular place, with a gothic bridge set off by wild and imposing scenery. For those walking the Lairig Ghru route through the Cairngorms from north to south (see 12, Northern Cairngorms, p262), this will feel like a welcoming place, with the challenging mountains behind them. For those walking it the other way, it will feel like the last outpost of comfort, with the brooding valley ahead. Beyond the Linn of Dee is Derry Lodge, an abandoned but spectacular shooting house that may come back into use as a hostel. Bob Scott's bothy is nearby.

→ From Braemar follow the Linn of Dee road W out of town, past AB35 5YB, to signed car park after crossing the river. Walk back to view the Linn of Dee bridge. Heading N from the car park follow the path marked Glen Lui through forestry. It becomes a substantial track that follows the Lui Water up Glen Lui to Derry Lodge (57.0215, -3.5806), set amidst a ring of pines. 5 mins walk to bridge.

2 hrs, 56.9883, -3.5451 🚶🐕🅱️

LOCAL FOOD & DRINK

15 THE BOTHY

Excellent cafe, behind well-stocked Braemar Mountain Sports and a great place to refuel following an excursion to the hills. Browse the many old climbing and mountaineering magazines or enjoy a coffee looking out over the river gorge from the balcony.

→ Invercauld Road, Braemar, AB35 5YP, 01339 741242. Braemarmountainsports.com
57.0063, -3.3982 ⏹

16 DEESIDE DELI & GARDEN SHOP

Family-run deli and sandwich shop providing high-quality produce and local beers.

→ 47 Bridge Street, Ballater, AB35 5QD, 01339 755741. Gowsdeli.co.uk
57.0494, -3.0403 ⏹

17 CAMBUS O' MAY CHEESE COMPANY

Hand-made cheese from family recipes in the heart of Deeside, including some from raw milk. Book in advance for a tour.

→ Ballater, AB35 5SD, 01339 753113. Cambusomay.com
57.0690, -2.9813 ⏹

18 ROYAL LOCHNAGAR DISTILLERY

One of the smallest distilleries in Scotland, Lochnagar became Royal after Queen Victoria visited in 1848, as maybe the first distillery tourist in Scotland. Its water source is high in the corries of brooding Lochnagar, and it retains a rustic, old-world charm.

→ Crathie, Ballater, AB35 5TB, 01339 742700.
57.0299, -3.2088 ⏹

BOTHIES & REFUGES

19 CALLATER STABLES BOTHY

This simple but well-located bothy next to Callater Lodge is perfect for exploring the hills of Lochnagar and the White Mounth. Easily accessed via a vehicle track. No fire.

→ At the head of Loch Callater (see 1). Approx 1 hour walk-in.
56.9436, -3.3526 ⏹⏹

20 GELDER SHIEL STABLES

One of the 'royal' bothies of the southern Cairngorms, it sits at the back of an estate cottage still used by the royal family. Refurbished in 2015 and given the additional name of Ernie's Bothy, this comfortable doss is a brilliant spot to stop on the way to Lochnagar from Royal Deeside.

→ Good track S from Balmoral Memorial Cairns (see 12) to Loch Muick (see 3). Fork R after 1½ miles, then L to bothy. Possible restrictions Sept–Oct call 01339 742 534. 2 hours walk-in.
56.9950, -3.2243 ⏹

21 BOB SCOTT'S

Beautiful bothy set amidst Scots pine by the lovely Lui Water. It is popular, and having a tent in case it is really full is a good idea.

→ Park as for Linn of Dee and walk towards Derry Lodge (see 14). Bothy is before the Lodge, in trees down a smaller path on L after nearly 3 miles. 1 hour walk.
57.0186, -3.5784 ⏹⏹⏹⏹

HOSTELS & LODGES

22 BRAEMAR YOUTH HOSTEL

Well-equipped and comfortable hostel situated in a grand former hunting lodge.

→ Corrie Faragie, 21 Glenshee Road, AB35 5YQ, 01339 741659. Syha.org.uk
57.0029, -3.3923 ⏹

23 ROYAL DEESIDE CAIRNGORM LODGES

These wooden lodges scattered in a beautiful Scots pine forest are an eco-friendly base from which to explore Deeside. Red squirrels in abundance.

→ Logie Coldstone, Aboyne, AB34 5PQ, 07583 436040. Cairngormlodges.com
57.1233, -2.9368 ⏹

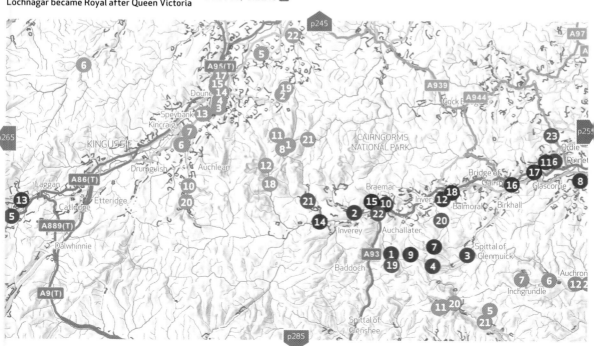

ANGUS

Our perfect weekend

→ **Gaze** upon the sweeping drama of Corrie Fee National Nature Reserve.

→ **Wash** away your worries in brilliant Loch Brandy.

→ **Stay** a while in the paddocks of Greenhillock, and rediscover your den-building skills.

→ **Adventure** to the remote Falls of Unich, nestled in the hills miles from anywhere.

→ **Re-energise** at Sinclairs Larder in Edzell.

→ **Breathe** in the fresh sea air on a long walk up Montrose Beach.

→ **Visit** unique Elephant Rock for a cliff walk and a glimpse of sea life.

→ **Sample** Arbroath Smokies and take some home as a souvenir.

→ **Walk** up Kinpurney Hill, where nothing seems to get finished – maybe the views are just too distracting.

→ **Dream** the afternoon away at the peaceful Rocks of Solitude.

→ **Shelter** from bad weather by the fire at the cosy Glen Clova Inn.

Angus is one of those areas of Scotland where you can clearly see the stark contrasts between Highland and Lowland. Though it is not thought of as particularly wild, it has rugged mountain scenery and glens as atmospheric as anywhere in Scotland, rising up out of flat, fertile farmland and green rolling hills. The variations in landscape make this an interesting place to visit, because you could easily spend the morning on a traditional seafront beach and the afternoon up a Munro in Glen Clova.

Angus stretches from the eastern fringes of the Highlands in the Cairngorms to the North Sea coast, and is split down the middle by the change in landscape. The western half is mountainous and lonely, and certainly shares more with the Cairngorms than is often considered. In contrast, the eastern, seaward half is well connected and developed.

For those seeking mountain experiences away from the crowds of the honeypot areas on the west coast, the five Angus Glens make an excellent choice and cede nothing in majesty to their western neighbours. The coastline of Angus, where the rivers that began life in those mountain glens flow into the sea, is also lovely. There are expansive beaches with unique rock formations and superb views. Food is an important part of the culture of Angus, which shares its famous cattle with nearby Aberdeen, and of course the Arbroath Smokie, a hot-smoked haddock protected by law, is not to be missed!

The main road into Angus is the A90 motorway, which links Dundee to Aberdeen on the north-east coast. Little roads head off west into the five main glens like crooked fingers, and navigating your way between each glen can be time consuming and confusing. Angus is a good example of one of those areas that is closer to other areas than you might think, just not by conventional transport; it is probably quicker to walk from Angus into Deeside than it is to drive or cycle.

BAYS & SHORELINE

1 LUNAN BAY
Beautiful sandy beach with caves, a river, the ruined **Red Castle** and a great café.

→ S of Montrose take minor roads to Lunan and beach car park (DD11 5ST). There are boardwalk paths over the dunes to the beach, and the castle is to the R as you approach the beach, above the river.

2 mins, 56.6553, -2.5053 ⛰🏊🍴📷

2 SEATON CLIFFS
Windswept cliff-top walk to **Needle E'e**, a large hole in the cliffs that gives an unusual frame for looking out to sea. Further along the coast there is an impressive sea stack, the **Deil's Head**, caves, and a blowhole.

→ Start from the Victoria car park at the E end of the King's Drive along the Arbroath seafront (starts at DD11 1BP) and head L along the coast away from town, on a good path that follows the top of the cliffs.

30 mins, 56.5633, -2.5467 ⛰🐾📷

3 MONTROSE BEACH
Montrose is blessed with an absolutely enormous sandy beach – it extends all the way up to St Cyrus Beach in Aberdeenshire (see

p251), and the two would blend seamlessly if not for the River North Esk dividing them.

→ From the Seafront Splash area (DD10 8EL) on the promenade just outside Montrose head L up the beach as far as you want.

5 mins, 56.7217, -2.4459 ⛰🏊⛰🎪

4 ELEPHANT ROCK
This unusual natural arch does actually resemble an elephant. It is located on a pretty stretch of cliff between Boddin and Ferryden and lies below a graveyard – look for the headstone of George James Ramsay, which states the poor man died 19 years before he was born.

→ Start from a white gate on the minor road between Boddin and Usan (E from DD10 9TD). Very limited space to pull off. A straight path leads from the roadside to the cliff top, passing under a railway bridge.

5 mins, 56.6765, -2.4666 ⛰🔽📷🏊✝

WILD LOCHS

5 LOCH BRANDY
Loch Brandy lies high above Glen Clova, and is hemmed in on three sides by precipitous cliffs. A circuit above the loch gives amazing views both over Angus and across to Deeside

and Lochnagar – far away in the terms of road travel but a short distance as the crow flies. A great viewpoint to get a true feel for the geography of the area.

→ From the car park by Glen Clova hotel (DD8 4RA), a good path passes the bunkhouses at the top of the car park and continues onto the open hill, passing through a gate. Stay on path to the loch. To make a complete circuit, walk clockwise, L up and around rim of the corrie.

60 mins, 56.8621, -3.0909 ⛰🏊⛰

6 LOCH LEE
Attractive loch set in a rolling glen, which does double duty as a reservoir and has a small hydro scheme on one of the burns flowing into it. The walk in passes the ruins of sandstone **Invermark Castle** and an attractive church, while the good track beside the loch leads to wilder Glen Lee beyond, the setting for the beautiful **Falls of Unich** (see 7) and wonderful wild camping spot.

→ From the B966 at Edzell take minor road for Invermark up Glen Esk to its end at DD9 7YZ. There is a signed car park R before the end. Walk on along the road to the loch, passing the castle with the Water of Lee on your L and the church at the water's edge.

20 mins, 56.9090, -2.9359 ⛰🐾⛰🎪📷

11

WATERFALLS & RIVERS

7 FALLS OF UNICH

Hidden from view until you are almost upon them, these beautiful falls are a hidden gem, and make both a brilliant wild camping spot and a refreshing place to dip in a wild pool.

→ From Loch Lee (see 6) continue along the track on the N side of the loch past the turn to Inchgrundle House and a boarded-up cottage in a small plantation. Continue up the glen until the falls can be spotted on your L side. Cross a small bridge L and follow the path to the falls.

2 hours, 56.9093, -3.0088 🏊🏕️🥾🔦🎒

8 RIVER NORTH ESK

The River North Esk is an interesting waterway – gentle and peaceful in the wide areas, but turbulent in the narrows and gorges. Flanked by lush woodland, it is an attractive place to wander. There are several decent pools in the wider upstream areas of the river, beyond the red arch of Gannochy Bridge.

→ In Edzell, there is signed access to the river down a track beside the garage (just S of DD9 7TA). Take a L when you reach the river and follow good path on the L bank. At Gannochy Bridge, cross the road and bridge, then take a L through an obvious blue door to continue the walk on the opposite side of the river.

45 mins, 56.8365, -2.6663 🏊🏊🥾🔦🎒

9 ROCKS OF SOLITUDE

The River North Esk (see 8) runs through the Highland Boundary Fault, the geological rift between Highlands and Lowlands, which is most evident at the Rocks of Solitude. As its name suggests, this is a great place to sit and ponder the wonders of Scotland's interesting geography – or watch salmon leap in autumn.

→ Continue upstream from Gannochy Bidge for approx 1½ miles to the rapids, beyond a semi-circular seat. Path can be muddy, sensible footwear recommended.

60 mins, 56.8437, -2.6756 🚶🏊🪑🥾🔦🎒

10 REEKIE LINN FALLS

Giddy, steamy falls that cascade through a deep, narrow gorge in Glen Isla. Their name comes from the spume that fills the air as the water tumbles around.

→ Park at the Bridge of Craigisla (S of PH11 8QG), a few miles N of Alyth on the B954. The gorge and falls are easily reached a path that heads out from the car park at the N end of the bridge downriver along the rim of the gorge.

20 mins, 56.6690, -3.2103 📹🔦🪑🏕️

HILLS & VIEWPOINTS

11 CORRIE FEE

Scenic and fascinating National Nature Reserve and SSSI. It can be a shock to emerge from peaceful Glen Doll Forest (see 18) into this amphitheatre carved by the power of water and ice. As well as being awe-inspiring, this nature reserve is also an important area for fauna and especially flora – extremely rare Arctic and alpine plants grow here. For this reason, camping is not permitted beyond Glen Doll Forest up to the rim of the corrie.

→ Park and start the walk as for Glen Doll but follow well-placed signs for Corrie Fee, ignoring all turn offs. Once in Corrie Fee you can continue on the path up the side of the waterfall at the head of the corrie. The Munros of Mayar and Driesh lie on the plateau beyond.

60 mins, 56.8638, -3.2263 📹🏊🏕️🎒🔄

12 HILL OF ROWAN

This summit above Tarfside village would be just another lovely heather-clad hill, but for the massive 19th-century Maule Monument built atop it. It is a prominent landmark for miles around, and the views from it up into Glen Esk are great.

→ From Tarfside centre car park (DD9 7YU), cross the bridge over the Water of Tarf. The road bends L for Invermark, after the bridge; take the road straight ahead, and then take the track ahead again when this minor road shortly bends R. Pass through a gate and head uphill to the obvious monument.
60 mins, 56.9043, -2.8665 🌾🏔️🚶🐾

13 CATERTHUN FORTS
The 'white' and 'brown' Caterthun Forts – one of stone, the other of earthen embankments – are situated on a ridge of hills near Edzell. These Iron Age forts are amongst the best preserved in Scotland.

→ The Caterthun Forts lie either side of a minor road signed from the B966 S of Edzell (opp DD9 7QR). There is a layby L at the summit of the road after just under 1 mile, with brown Caterthun to the E of the road and white to the W. There are rough tracks to both; white is closer, but neither is very far. 60 mins walk to each fort.
60 mins, 56.7841, -2.7419 🏕️🚶🏔️🐾

14 AIRLIE MEMORIAL TOWER
This prominent local landmark on Tulloch Hill is a monument to a local Earl who was killed in the Boer War. Although it is not possible

to go up the tower, there are excellent views from the summit.

→ From car park opp the Dykehead Hotel on B995 N of Kirriemuir (DD8 4EE), head N along road then take L fork signed for Glen Prosen. After ½ mile take track R into the trees, then L at T junction through Scots pine to another junction. Take R uphill to the monument.
45 mins, 56.7392, -3.0248 🚶🏔️🐾🏕️🏔️

15 KINPURNEY HILL
The ruined 18th-century tower atop this hill was intended as an observatory, but never completed. It sits within a large ancient fort, which also appears to be unfinished. Nowadays it is an excellent objective for a shorter hill walk, and on a clear day the views are extensive.

→ Start from the car park by the WCs in Newtyle (PH12 8TU). Follow this road away from the village and take a R by Denend Farm to go through a kissing gate. Follow the Edderty Burn upstream via a path that crosses a bridge and a pair of double gates. Keep following the path, and after another gate bear left and follow purple waymarkers for the rest of the walk.
60 mins, 56.5626, -3.1038 🚶🏔️🏕️🐾

16 SCURDIE NESS
Scurdie is a Scots word for the basalt found on this promontory jutting out into the North Sea south of Montrose. It is an excellent place to spot seals, dolphins and occasionally whales. The buildings around the lighthouse, erected in 1870, are now a private home.

→ Walk from Ferryden, just over the River South Esk from Montrose. Follow the road E along the shore, at the end of the village take a R (DD10 9RW) by a small car park and follow signs for 'lighthouse' on past the end of the public road, hugging the coastline.
20 mins, 56.7015, -2.4370 🏕️🚶🏔️

FORESTS & WOODLANDS

17 CORTACHY WOODS
Magnificent specimen trees including Douglas fir and wellingtonia, planted in the 1870s, can be seen on the banks of the fast-flowing River South Esk. This riverside amble visits an attractive little island in the middle of the river, which used to be accessible until the floods of 2016 destroyed the bridges.

→ From the car park beside the primary school in Cortachy (DD8 4LX), off the B995 N of Kirriemuir. Head L down the road past the entrance to Cortachy Castle, cross the bridge

10

and head L through a double gate with stone gateposts. Pass through the trees before following the River South Esk upstream.
60 mins, 56.7296, -2.9917 🚶🏕🔍⛺

18 GLEN DOLL FOREST
This diverse and well-managed forest is an excellent place to wander, or shelter in if the weather is beating down Corrie Fee (see 11). The Forestry Commission are working to increasing biodiversity in the area, planting many native species. Information boards and signage explain the ancient landscape. There are peaceful wild-camping sites to be found throughout the forest.
➔ Starting from the Glen Doll forestry car park (pay) at the top of Glen Clova (DD8 4RD), head out on a good path through the forest.
30 mins, 56.8663, -3.2164 ⛺🚶👶⛺

19 CROMBIE COUNTRY PARK
Great for a relaxing walk amongst beautiful woodland and a great place to see red squirrels, roe deer and woodpeckers. Deer hides and a circular walk around the reservoir.
➔ From the country park car park off the B961 N of Carnoustie (turning N ½ mile E of DD5 3QL), follow signs through the woods.
90 mins, 56.5512, -2.7677 🚶🏕🔍🅿🚗🖊

20 WHITE WATER FOREST WALK
The White Water is a turbulent river that winds its way through the leafy Glen Doll Forest (see 18) – an easy short stroll.
➔ Park and start as for Glen Doll, initially following signs for Corrie Fee. White Water is marked with white waymarkers – beyond junction for Jock's Road follow the waymarkers to cross the bridge and along the White Water.
30 mins, 56.8717, -3.1855 🚶🏕🔍🔍

LOCAL FOOD

21 GLEN CLOVA HOTEL
A hearty, warm and welcoming place after a long wet day on the hill, with a bar and restaurant, both with wood burners, serving local produce. The quintessential Highland inn – great whisky, great food and a cheery atmosphere. B&B available.
➔ Glenclova, Angus, DD8 4QS, 01575 550350. Clova.com
56.8443, -3.1044 🍴🛏🔧

22 SINCLAIR'S LARDER, EDZELL
Friendly and relaxing café on Edzell's main street. Their eggs and salmon are unbeatable.
➔ 63 High Street, Edzell, DD9 7TA,

01356 648285. Facebook/Sinclairs Larder
56.8109, -2.6565 🍴

23 BEL'S BUTCHERS, EDZELL
Extremely well-regarded local butcher selling a great variety of local produce.
➔ 25a High Street, Edzell, DD9 7TE, 01356 648409. Belsbutchers.co.uk
56.8092, -2.6555 🍴

24 M&M SPINK, ARBROATH
The world-famous Arbroath smokie – salted haddock hot-smoked in a barrel over beech and oak – is a EU protected food, and deservedly so. M&M Spink sells particularly good ones.
➔ 10 Marketgate, Arbroath, DD11 1AY, 01241 875287. Arbroathsmokies.co.uk
56.5563, -2.5821 🍴

25 THE RETREAT, GLENESK
The Retreat is part of the Glenesk Folk Museum, a focal point for the community in the easternmost Angus glen. Serves hearty local food and bakes on the premises.
➔ Glenesk, Tarfside, DD9 7YT, 01356 648070. Gleneskretreat.scot
56.8989, -2.8086 🍴

CAMPING & GLAMPING

26 CLIMBERS BUNKHOUSE

Situated behind Glen Clova Hotel, these stone bunkhouses offer cheerful communal accommodation. There are also luxury lodges for rent further away.

→ Glenclova, Angus, DD8 4QS, 01575 550350. Clova.com
56.8443, -3.1044 🏕️

27 GLEN PROSEN HOSTEL

18-bed bunkhouse in beautiful Glen Prosen, the hidden gem of the Angus Glens.

→ Glenprosen, Kirriemuir, DD8 4SA, 01575 540238. Prosenhostel.co.uk
56.7799, -3.1018 🏕️

28 TARFSIDE WILD CAMPING

Riverside wild camping is permitted at the village field next to the car park in the small hamlet of Tarfside. There is a toilet block in the car park (cold water only).

→ Tarfside, Brechin, DD9 7YU
56.9046, -2.8320 🔺

29 GREENHILLOCK GLAMPING

This peaceful and eco-friendly campsite has pitches and bell tents with firepits, and allows you plenty of space to unwind amongst wild flowers. With a bug zone, an art shack and a den-building area, excellent for children who love the outdoors.

→ Lower Greenhillock, Kirkbuddo, DD8 2NL, 07967 200893. Greenglamping.co.uk
56.5877, -2.8195 🏕️🏕️🛶

COTTAGES & HOTELS

30 THE BOTHY, GLEN CLOVA

Homely self-catering cottage for two in beautiful Glen Clova. It is an excellent base to explore this most wonderful of Glens.

→ Clach Na Brain, Glen Clova, Kirriemuir, DD8 4QU, 01575 540330. Thebothyglenclova.co.uk
56.7822, -3.0256 🏕️

31 GLEN ISLA HOTEL

Highly rated old country coaching inn situated in close proximity to walking trails in lovely Glen Isla.

→ Kirkton of Glenisla, Blairgowrie, Perthshire, PH11 8PH, 01575 582223 Glenisla-hotel.com
56.7296, -3.2841 🍴🍺

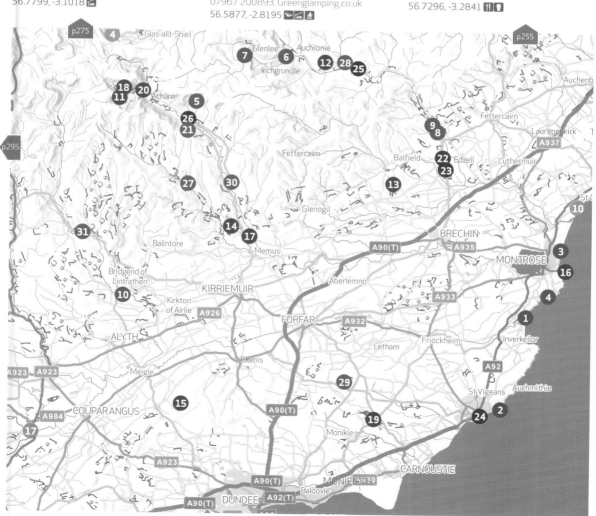

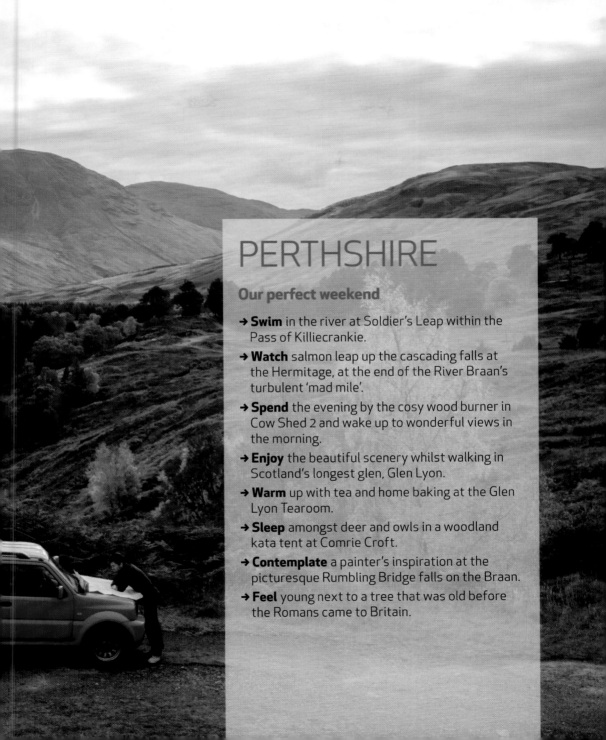

PERTHSHIRE

Our perfect weekend

→ **Swim** in the river at Soldier's Leap within the Pass of Killiecrankie.

→ **Watch** salmon leap up the cascading falls at the Hermitage, at the end of the River Braan's turbulent 'mad mile'.

→ **Spend** the evening by the cosy wood burner in Cow Shed 2 and wake up to wonderful views in the morning.

→ **Enjoy** the beautiful scenery whilst walking in Scotland's longest glen, Glen Lyon.

→ **Warm** up with tea and home baking at the Glen Lyon Tearoom.

→ **Sleep** amongst deer and owls in a woodland kata tent at Comrie Croft.

→ **Contemplate** a painter's inspiration at the picturesque Rumbling Bridge falls on the Braan.

→ **Feel** young next to a tree that was old before the Romans came to Britain.

Perthshire is an area of outstanding scenic beauty lying at the geographical heart of the Scottish mainland. Often referred to as the gateway to the Highlands, it can be reached from both Glasgow and Edinburgh in around an hour's drive and so is the perfect area to visit if you're seeking a quick and simple escape to beautiful countryside.

The region is a joy to explore at any time of year, however autumn is most wonderful –the woodlands and forests are ablaze with colour and the rivers and falls are in full spate after heavy showers. There are picture-postcard scenes in Glen Lyon, described by Sir Walter Scott as the 'longest, loneliest and loveliest glen in Scotland', which stretches on for 35 miles. At its end lies the sleepy village of Fortingall, where the air is feathered with chimney smoke from cottages framing the churchyard in which Britain's oldest tree stands.

In fact, in this 'big tree country' you'll find many remarkable trees, including the Mother Larch planted in 1738 in Dunkeld and the UK's widest conifer within the beautiful Cluny House Gardens. There is also an abundance of wildlife and flora to be discovered within the Highland part of Perthshire and the region's wonderful nature reserves – rare Arctic-alpine flowers grow on the slopes of Ben Lawers, and ospreys soar around the Loch of the Lowes. Wild swimmers can clamber down into hidden river pools set in picturesque woodland gorges like the tumbling Falls of Bruar or Soldier's Leap in the spectacular Pass of Killiecrankie.

Vibrant towns and villages like Pitlochry and Aberfeldy offer plenty of interesting places to eat and shop. Families can enjoy many nature-based activities, sample local cuisine and dance at ceilidhs during lively festivals like the Comrie Fortnight in summer and Aberfeldy's October TayFest. Couples might prefer days out on romantic riverside walks at the Birks of Aberfeldy or the Hermitage, where you can picnic beneath glorious mature trees by cascading waterfalls. Afterwards, retreat to relax by the fire in one of the many cosy cottages in the area.

RIVERS & WATERFALLS

1 LOWER FALLS OF BRUAR
Scenic and popular woodland gorge with waterfalls, stone bridges, a natural arch and caves to explore.

→ Signed Bruar/B8079 off A9 N of Pitlochry (PH18 5TW). Park at House of Bruar and follow signed footpath up through woods to the first bridge and falls. Scramble down to the pool.

10 mins, 56.7739, -3.9341 🄻🖼️🅜🔖🗻

2 SOLDIER'S LEAP
A picturesque gorge opening out to a large, hidden river pool. A railway line passes above and there is a white pebble beach on the far side, where you can enjoy a picnic after a swim. Access is a scramble, but peaceful and private once there.

→ From Soldier's Leap visitor centre (NTS) well signed on B8079 N of Pitlochry (PH16 5LF). Follow paths down to the Soldier's Leap, but bear down L via an informal path through steep woodland to reach flat rocks by large river pool, 100m downstream of the Leap.

5 mins, 56.742, -3.774 🖼️🄴🖼️🅜🏊

3 BIRKS OF ABERFELDY
An area of attractive mixed woodland surrounding the Falls of Moness, named after the Robert Burns poem. A well-defined path takes you through mature birch, ash, oak and elm trees and over the falls. Most delightful after heavy rainfall in late autumn.

→ Car park off B846 Crieff Rd, S of Aberfeldy (just N of turning to PH15 2ER). Information board shows various pathways.

45 mins, 56.6150, -3.8663 🖼️🅟

4 THE HERMITAGE
Beautiful woodland trail and pools along the River Braan leading to Ossian's Hall, a Georgian viewpoint overlooking Black Linn waterfall where you can watch the salmon jump upstream in autumn. Pools for swimming upstream from the bridge and waterfall.

→ Well-signed NTS site, off A9 W of Dunkeld, ¾ mile W of turning to PH8 0DU.

2 mins, 56.5574, -3.6141 🖼️🍼🌲

5 FALLS OF ACHARN
Wonderful wooded gorge with tumbling waterfalls and a small man-made cavern and balcony, known as Hermit's Cave, built in the 18th century to provide picturesque views of falls. Great place to spot red squirrels.

→ Park in Acharn Village (PH15 2HT) on S of Loch Tay. Follow path signed for walk as it ascends into the woods and to the cave before continuing uphill to upper falls.

30 mins, 56.5639, -4.0241 🖼️🔖🚶

6 RUMBLING BRIDGE, RIVER BRAAN
Dramatic falls with many pools and ledges to explore up and downstream, the scene of Millais' painting *The Sound of Many Waters*. Not to be confused with the double Rumbling Bridge on the River Devon (see 22).

→ From the Hermitage (see 4) walk a mile up along the gorge known as the 'mad mile', or park at Rumbling Bridge, signed off the A822 2 miles S of Dunkeld (turning dir PH8 0BP).

10 mins, 56.5510, -3.6352 🆅🔖

7 LINN OF TUMMEL
Impressive pools by these roadside falls. The lane continues along the wild shores of Tummel and Rannoch lochs.

→ Signed Clunie/Foss off A9 between Pitlochry and Killiecrankie (just N of PH16 5NE). Follow road 2 miles to car park. You can also take a longer woodland walk to the other bank from Soldier's Leap visitor centre (see 2).

3 mins, 56.7185, -3.7827 🆅🖼️🄴🖼️🅜🏊🔖

9

8 THE LINN

Sometimes called Linn a' Chullaich, but not named on maps, Comrie's very own pool is a lovely hidden place for a dip. It has a small stony beach where you might find locals warming up with lunch by a campfire.

→ Head W from Comrie and cross humpback bridge off A85 signposted for Ross. Take L fork and after 1 mile, after PH6 2LE, park on L.
2 mins, 56.3561, -4.0036

SCENIC GLENS

9 GLEN TILT

Beautiful and peaceful long glen. Wonderful views of the surrounding hill and mountain scenery, with woodlands and river throughout.

→ N off B8079 through Blair Atholl, follow signs for Old Bridge of Tilt / Glen Tilt car park (over bridge from PH18 5TP). From here follow green waymarked route for 2 miles to viewpoint.
90 mins, 56.7939, -3.8341

10 GLEN LYON

This magnificent glen is the longest in Scotland and particularly beautiful in autumn, when small remnants of ancient Caledonian forest are ablaze with colour and the River Lyon tumbles fast through the gorge.

→ Layby parking near the Bridge of Balgie near Glen Lyon Post Office (PH15 2PP).
2 mins, 56.5910, -4.3196

11 SMA' GLEN

Small scenic glen, only 4 miles long. Drive along the famous old Military Road and stop for a picnic by the River Almond. Towards the upper end you can see Ossian's Stone from the road. The surveyor of the Military Road noted that when this massive boulder was shifted off the route an ancient burial cist was found below it, and the regiment ceremonially re-interred the remains nearby.

→ 5 miles N of Creiff on A822, opening is just N of B8063 to Buchanty (PH1 3SH).
2 mins, 56.4544, -3.7940

12 LITTLE GLENSHEE

Unlike famous Glen Shee further north, Little Glenshee is smaller and quieter, and there is a reasonably straightforward walk through that offers classic views of heathery Scottish hill country.

→ N off the B8063 2½ miles E of Harrietfield above River Almond. Follow minor road for 2½ miles, past PH1 3TN, to a small car park by ford over burn. Cross footbridge and follow the path to hairpin bend in road. At the green right of way sign head N up track past farm. Continue for 2 miles to a gate in wall. Return same way or continue through to Strath Braan.
1½–2½ hours, 56.4908, -3.6587

ANCIENT TREES

13 FORTINGALL YEW

Probably Britain's oldest tree, the Fortingall Yew is estimated to be around 3,000 years old and sits within the churchyard of the charming and peaceful village Fortingall. If visiting in autumn, see if you can spot the branch that recently changed sex to bear fruit. Great local food at nearby Fortingall Hotel.

→ Park by Fortingall churchyard (PH15 2LL). Tree is by the church, surrounded by a wall.
2 mins, 56.5982, -4.0509

14 MOTHER LARCH

This giant larch grows by the ruined cathedral in Dunkeld. It is the sole survivor of a group of five that were brought here from the Tyrol mountains over 250 years ago and provided seed for the larches around the area. From here pick up the waymarked Fiddler's Path, which runs alongside and over the River Tay to return past other mature trees, including Neil Gow's Oak.

➜ Park at Atholl St car park, Dunkeld (PH8 0BB) and follow waymarked path signed for cathedral. Larch is near the cathedral tower. From here continue L at path junction to follow Fiddler's Path; the oak is at 56.5632, -3.6074. 10–90 mins, 56.5650, -3.5910 ▣▣▣

15 BIRNAM OAK

The last surviving oak from Birnam Wood, it was probably here when the ancient forest was celebrated in Macbeth; a neighbouring sycamore is thought to be 300 years old. Reached by a gentle walk along the River Tay.
➜ Park in Dunkeld (PH8 0BB). Cross bridge S over River Tay and immediately L down steps by Toll House. Continue E along bank of river, crossing a small bridge before reaching the sycamore tree then the Birnam Oak shortly after. It's possible to follow this path in a circuit past Beatrix Potter Exhibition and Gardens – her interest in fungi began here. 90–120 mins, 56.5613, -3.5754 ▣▣▣

16 CLUNY HOUSE GARDENS

Secluded woodland gardens with a Himalayan feel, where beautiful, rhododendrons, lilies and blue poppies grow and red squirrels roam. Also home to the widest conifer in the UK, a giant wellingtonia with an 11m girth.

➜ Signed from B846 just N of Aberfeldy, take minor road approx 3 miles to PH15 2JT. Clunyhousegardens.com.
10 mins, 56.6406, -3.8298 ▣▣▣

17 MEIKLEOUR BEECH HEDGE

Drive or walk below the longest in hedge in Britain, and at 30m the highest of its kind in the world. Particularly impressive in autumn when it turns into a tapestry of colours.
➜ 4 miles S of Blairgowrie on A93, S of crossing with A984, either side of PH2 6DY. Parking in layby under hedge towards S end.
1 min, 56.5311, -3.3645 ▣

WILDLIFE WONDERS

18 BEN LAWERS NNR

Discover remarkable rare Artic-alpine flora growing by the slopes of the Ben Lawers mountain range. Look for yellow and purple saxifrage in spring, globeflower and moss campion in early summer. Further up the valley is the monumental hydroelectric dam.
➜ From the A827 NE of Killin along Loch Tay, take the hill road (near FK21 8TY) to Ben Lawers car park after 2 miles. A short nature trail begins from the information boards..
60 mins, 56.5091, -4.2786 ▣▣

19 LOCH OF THE LOWES

Natural reserve with observation hides, currently home to a pair of breeding ospreys, red squirrels, otters, beavers and much more.
➜ Signed from A923 N of Dunkeld, E of PH8 0ES. Follow road to centre after 300m on L.
5 mins, 56.5745, -3.5602 ▣▣▣

RUINED & ANCIENT

20 LOCHLEVEN CASTLE

Substantial and well-preserved ruins of a medieval castle on a small island in Loch Leven, where Mary Queen of Scots was famously imprisoned for a year in 1567.
➜ Via small passenger boat from Kinross Ferry Landing (KY13 8UF) . Closed in winter.
10 mins, 56.2008, -3.3920 ▣▣

21 COMRIE EARTHQUAKE HOUSE

One of the oldest seismic observatories in the world, built in 1874 to the west of Comrie, which lies on the Highland Boundary Fault and is Britain's 'earthquake capital'. No entry, but both original and modern instruments can be seen though windows.
➜ From A85 W of Comrie take bridge over River Earn signed for Ross. House is uphill in

field opposite cottages after 450m (PH6 2JU).
5 mins, 56.3721, -4.0008

22 RUMBLING BRIDGE, CROOK OF DEVON
A double, or even triple, bridge over the River
Devon at a dramatic gorge. At the lowest level,
is an ancient slab for foot traffic. An arched
road bridge was built in 1713 and then a higher
one put on top a century later. Sometimes
confused online with the Rumbling Bridge
waterfalls on the River Braan (see 6).

→ Shortly after the A823 leaves the A997, past
KY13 0QR, is layby parking before the bridge
on R and a path into the woods. Follow path for
views of the bridge and falls downstream.
5 mins, 56.1777, -3.5856

LOCAL FOOD

23 GLEN LYON TEA ROOM
Delightful family-run tea room and shop in
Scotland's longest glen. Enjoy lunch, home
baking or a cup of tea by the fire inside or
on the outdoor benches overlooking the
beautiful surrounding scenery.

→ Bridge of Balgie, Glenlyon, PH15 2PP,
01887 866221. Facebook/Glenlyon-Tearoom
56.5920, -4.3185

24 HABITAT CAFÉ, ABERFELDY
Enjoy an award-winning coffee inside or on
one of the south-facing outdoor benches
at this popular modern café in the central
square of lovely Aberfeldy.

→ 1 The Square, Aberfeldy, PH15 2DD, 01887
822944. Facebook/HabitatCafeAberfeldy
56.6197, -3.8650

25 BLAIR ATHOLL WATERMILL TEA ROOM
Wonderful baking and light lunches served
within the original kiln drying floor or in the
tea garden outside.

→ Ford Road, Blair Atholl, PH18 5SH,
01796 481321. Blairathollwatermill.co.uk
56.7645, -3.8472

26 THE SCOTTISH DELI, DUNKELD
One of two family-run stores selling quality
local produce, gourmet sandwiches, home
baking, teas and coffees.

→ 1 Atholl St, Dunkeld PH8 0AR,
01350 728028. Scottish-deli.com
56.5656, -3.5856

27 GLOAGBURN FARM SHOP, TIBBERMORE
Family run café where everything from the
pastry to the jam is made on the premises.

The farm shop stocks an extensive range of home-made and fine Scottish foodstuffs.

→ Tibbermore, PH1 1QL, 01738 840864. Gloagburnfarmshop.co.uk
56.3960, -3.5482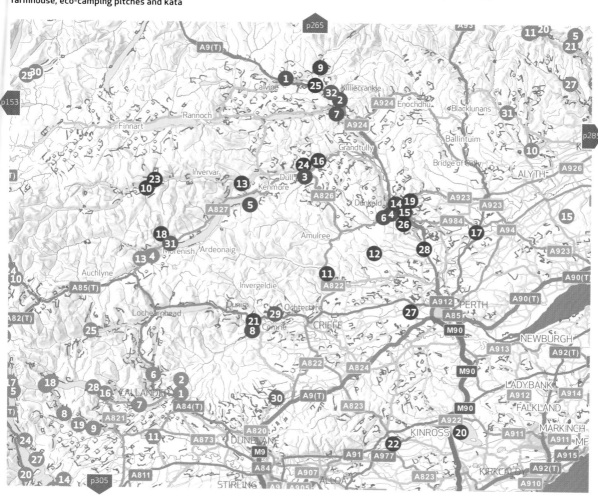

28 BANKFOOT INN

18th-century pub and restaurant serving hearty meals and a huge selection of ales.

→ Main St, Bankfoot, PH1 4AB, 01738 787243. Bankfootinn.co.uk
56.5005, -3.5146

SLEEP WILD

29 COMRIE CROFT

Award-winning accommodation including a self-catering steading bunkhouse and farmhouse, eco-camping pitches and kata tents, all in wonderful surroundings close to the charming village of Comrie. There is also a great on-site shop, event space, mountain bike trails and tea room.

→ Braincroft, by Crieff, PH7 4JZ, 01764 670140. Comriecroft.com
56.3849, -3.9400

30 CRAIGHEAD HOWF

Idyllic self-catering accommodation including a treehouse, garden house and traditional Scottish stone steading, surrounded by natural gardens, lochan and woodland areas.

→ Craighead Farm, Braco, Dunblane, FK15 9LP, 01786 880321. Craigheadhowf.co.uk
56.2470, -3.9260

31 LOCH TAY HIGHLAND LODGES

Scandinavian-style lodges, glamping domes, wigwams and bunkhouse situated by the shores of Loch Tay with views to the hills. Watersports and riding on the doorstep.

→ Milton Morenish Estate, by Killin, FK21 8TY, 01567 820323. Lochtay-vacations.co.uk
56.4941, -4.2508

32 LETTOCH COTTAGES

Beautiful open-plan cottages in Killiecrankie, northern Perthshire. Cow Shed 2 is our favourite; it was skilfully converted using natural and recycled materials and there are excellent views.

→ Killiecrankie, PH16 5LR, 01796 470048. Lettochcottages.com
56.7535, -3.8002

LOCH LOMOND, TROSSACHS & BREADALBANE

Our perfect weekend

→ **Wake** with a morning dip in sparkling Loch Lubnaig, with a coffee at the café to warm up afterwards.

→ **Climb** Ben A'an for stunning views over picturesque Loch Katrine, source of so much inspiration for artists and poets.

→ **Spy** on the beavers building their dams on the shores of the River Tay.

→ **Cycle** around Loch Katrine, camping at Brenachoille Point and stopping for lunch at the friendly Pier Café in Stronachlachar.

→ **Take** the ferry over to Inchcailloch island on Loch Lomond, for panoramic views of the largest loch in Scotland.

→ **Search** for Rob Roy's cave on the bonny banks of Loch Lomond, and imagine how it would have felt hiding out there.

→ **Finish** your weekend with a visit to the rustic Falls of Dochart Inn.

This stunning region, stretching from Balloch in the south to Killin the north, is long revered in poetry, prose, art and song. It was immortalised in Sir Walter Scott's tales of Rob Roy MacGregor and his epic poem 'The Lady of the Lake'. This was Scotland's first National Park, and remains one of only two in the country today, the other being the Cairngorms. Here where the Highland Boundary Fault rears up the landscape changes from Highland to Lowland. Stand atop Conic Hill and look down the spine of islands lined up in Loch Lomond – that is the line of the geological fault responsible for the entire Highland landscape. This is an easily accessible region, and so something of a magnet for tourists and outdoor lovers looking to escape the Central Belt.

The Trossachs, 'the Highlands in miniature', border the park to the east. They form a photogenic area of sparkling lochs and steep-sided valleys, winding to a climax at Loch Katrine, one of the best in the country. Loch Lomond is the heart of the territory, the largest freshwater loch in the UK, long and snaking and dotted with many enticing islands. North-east of Loch Lomond lies the bulky, mountainous land of Breadalbane, 'Land of the Giants'.

Being a national park, the area is bursting with opportunities; just about any outdoor activity can be indulged in here. Wild swimming is particularly good in the Trossachs, where it is not uncommon to see many people out enjoying the lochs on a summer's evening. Walking is excellent here, with the best-known long distance trail in the country, the West Highland Way, passing right through the middle of the region. Boating and canoeing are also extremely popular on Loch Lomond and in the Trossachs, where the leafy little islands are great to pull up on for lunch.

The national park is easily reached from the Central Belt – indeed, the suburbs and outlying areas of Glasgow pretty much end at Balloch, the gateway to the park. For this reason, the park is under a great deal of visitor pressure, and the authorities operate a by-law system that prohibits camping on the east side of Loch Lomond between 1 March and 31st October, except in designated campsites such as Sallochy. These restrictions aim to conserve the stunning ecosystems that are suffering prolonged damage at the hands of many wild campers, so please respect these by-laws and make sure you know the rules before you set out. Contact the National Park Authority 01389 722600.

RIVERS & WATERFALLS

1 BRACKLINN FALLS

Crashing waterfall passing through a chaotic rocky gorge. A beautiful wooden and copper-topped bridge spans the river, and the scene is finished off by pretty woodland.

→ From Callander on the A84 head N on minor road (dir FK17 8LT). There is a signed Bracklinn Falls car park (56.2477, -4.2012) ½ mile beyond the Callender golf club car park. From here follow good path from the entrance all the way to Bracklinn Falls

15 mins, 56.2491, -4.1879

2 SCOUT POOL

Wide and deep plunge pool at the foot of a small waterfall and gorge. Hidden away in the hills above Callander and popular with locals, who on hot days jump from the cliffs and bathe in the pool.

→ Continue beyond the car park for Bracklinn Falls (see 1), going through gates to the end of the public road (FK17 8LT). Head R down a rough track towards a gate. Go through, cross a bridge and take a R to follow the river downstream. Scout Pool is soon reached.

5 mins, 56.2706, -4.2019

3 FALLS OF DOCHART

This wide and unusual waterfall system tumbles through the centre of the pretty village of Killin, giving it a huge amount of character. If the water is not in spate it is possible to clamber over the rocks and boulders, giving lots of angles from which to view the unique waterfall, and making it popular with photographers.

→ In the centre of Killin, on the A827 from Crianlarich to Aberfeldy (FK21 8SL).

2 mins, 56.4625, -4.3199

4 RIVER TAY BEAVERS

One of the best places to spot beavers in Scotland. There is a beaver dam on a small island lying not far off the shore of this peaceful and winding river where it runs into Loch Tay. Approach quietly at dusk around August and September for the best chance to see the beavers and their kits playing and foraging in the surrounding waters.

→ Start from rough parking area R near the end of Pier Road in Killin (dir FK21 8TL). Head S through a gate and follow a straight path along the loch shore, with loch on L and wall on R. Where the loch bends to the river, look over to an island at the rivers mouth for the beavers.

10 mins, 56.4722, -4.3023

LOCHS

5 INVERSNAID, LOCH LOMOND

These small, sandy beaches not far from the Inversnaid Hotel are a great place from which to swim in Loch Lomond and are easily reached on the West Highland Way path, which runs all the way up the east side of Loch Lomond.

→ Park as for Rob Roy's Cave (see 17). Follow the West Highland Way path S down the loch for various little beaches and coves.

15 mins, 56.2391, -4.6844

6 LOCH LUBNAIG

Sparkling loch nestled amidst dark and towering hillsides. There is an excellent swimming spot in front of a café and campsite (see 26).

→ Located on the W side of the A84 3 miles N of FK17 8HD. The beach in front of the car park is a safe and comfortable entry spot.

2 mins, 56.2774, -4.2834

7 LOCH VENACHAR

Long and snaking loch, popular with local campers and fishermen. Numerous spots exist to enjoy the waters.

6

→ There are 2 car parks on the north side where the A821 runs beside the loch. Good swimming and picnic spots exist all along the shoreline between them. Heading W, park at the first (FK17 8HP) and walk W along the shore. The second carpark is several minutes further along the road.

5 mins, 56.2262, -4.3196 ⛰️🅥🏊

8 LOCH CHON

Amazing wild-swimming spots with several leafy islands. Beautiful woodlands throng the crinkled shores.

→ Loch Chon lies on the W side of B829, along the winding road W out of Aberfoyle. As you head N there are two car parks 350m apart on the E side of the loch (past turning to FK8 3TS). From the second car park, head through the green barrier to the loch.

2 mins, 56.2056, -4.5347 ⛰️🌊🏊

9 LOCH ARD

A brilliant swimming spot in the Trossachs, also very popular for canoeing and kayaking. Easily accessed from the roadside, or through forest walks.

→ Loch Ard Forest is signed from the B829 W of Aberfoyle. Cross River Forth (dir FK8 3TF) and L onto forestry road. Follow signs to car

park, 1 mile along the forest road. Echo Rock or the iron cross is a good spot for launching a canoe close to the road, with layby parking.

5 mins, 56.1832, -4.4480 🚗🏊🌊🏊

10 LOCH ARKLET

Viewpoint and camping spot with an excellent panorama over to the Arrochar Alps. Black grouse gather in a 'lek' on the foreshore, so come in the evening in early summer to watch the males strutting their stuff. Great place for a picnic.

→ Near the end of B829 road leading W from Aberfoyle to Inversnaid. Pass Lochs Ard and Chon. Arklet is reached shortly after. There is space to pull a car off the road beside a gate at K8 3TX. Cross road and down path to loch

5 mins, 56.2507, -4.5920 🅥🏔️🏕️

11 LAKE OF MENTEITH

Tranquil loch that is the only natural 'lake' in Scotland – a couple of others so named are man-made. Its islands are home to Inchmahome Priory, a beautiful ruined monastery, and Talla Castle, seemingly built of stone taken from the priory. There is an attractive beach just off the road with a fun rope swing. Popular with local fishermen.

→ Priory/ Lake of Mentieth Fisheries is signed

down the B8034 off the A81 E of Aberfoyle. Go past FK8 3RA and the car park for the Inchmahome ferry. After ½ mile park in layby L and cross road for a short line of steps out to a small hidden beach.

2 mins, 56.1738, -4.2751 🚣🍴🏕️🌊🏊🚤

MOUNTAINS & VIEWPOINTS

12 DUNCRYNE HILL

Also known as the Dumpling, this pudding-shaped lump has incredible views out of all proportion to its size and the effort required to climb it.

→ Layby parking opp the playing field in the centre of Gartocharn (G83 8NW). From here walk SW on minor Duncryne Road. After ½ mile take the path L through the gate at the end of the trees and head through the forest. The path is straightforward, and passes through 3 gates and another patch of woodland before ascending steeply.

20 mins, 56.0407, -4.5125 ⛰️📷🏔️

13 SRÒN A' CLACHAIN

Short ascent up a prominent hill behind Killin, giving amazing views over Loch Tay and Ben Lawers, the tenth highest mountain in Scotland.

→ From Breadalbane Park in Killin (behind FK21 8UJ) take the path that leads out from the SW corner. Go through a gate and head uphill. The path leads over a stile by oakwoods, then doubles back on itself into moorland and on to the summit. You can walk on to the higher peak of Creag Buidhe just behind.
30 mins, 56.4666, -4.3352

14 CONIC HILL
Short but strenuous hill walk giving unrivalled views over Loch Lomond and the highland boundary fault. Very popular.
→ Park at the National Park visitor centre at Balmaha (G63 0JQ). Take the path at the back of the car park and turn R at the immediate junction. Next L, then up and through a gate to follow the good West Highland Way path as it skirts the N side of the hill. When the path is alongside the summit, head R up the slopes to the top.
60 mins, 56.0960, -4.5273

15 INCHCAILLOCH SUMMIT
The summit of the prettiest island on Loch Lomond enjoys views in every direction. Inchcailloch is a varied and interesting little island with a tiny campsite and the remains of a medieval church.

→ Park as for Conic Hill (see 14). Take the short ferry over to Inchcailloch (01360 870214, Balmahaboatyard.co.uk), and follow the path leading off from the jetty R through the woods, then L at the information board. Follow uphill to the summit, marked by a bench.
30 mins, 56.0793, -4.5544

16 BEN A'AN
Giving perhaps the best views-to-effort ratio of any Scottish mountain, this small and simple ascent gives wonderful views over Loch Katrine. Very popular, and deservedly so.
→ From the large forestry commission car park on the A821 by Loch Achray (300m W of FK17 8HY). Cross the road and take the signed path, which is steep but straightforward, with no turn offs. Under the summit block bear L and follow the worn path up through the short bouldering section to the top.
90 mins, 56.2430, -4.4201

CAVES

17 ROB ROY'S CAVE
Adventurous scrambling leads to a surprisingly cavernous hideaway where Scottish folk hero Rob Roy was supposed to

have hidden during his time on the run from the authorities for cattle rustling.
→ From the end of the B829 take minor road L to large car park at the end by Inversnaid Hotel (beyond FK8 3TU). Head N on the West Highland Way skirting the loch shore. After about 1 mile a rocky, bouldery section is reached; the cave is down by the loch shore and marked by graffiti.
30 mins, 56.2532, -4.6942

LOCAL FOOD

18 THE PIER CAFÉ
Friendly local café serving great food and offering unrivalled views of Loch Katrine from a conservatory overlooking the shore.
→ Stronachlachar, FK8 3TY, 01877 386374. Thepiercafe.com
56.2577, -4.5775

19 THE WEE BLETHER TEAROOM
Generous portions of cake at this popular and quirky café.
→ Kinlochard, FK8 3TL. Weeblethertearoom.co.uk
56.1880, -4.4912

20 THE COACH HOUSE

Bustling café serving excellent soup with some of the biggest portions of bread we've ever seen!

→ Church Road, Luss, G83 8NN, 01436 860431. Facebook/Coachhousecoffeeshopluss
56.1011, -4.6372 🍴

INNS & PUBS

21 THE DROVERS INN

Beautiful and friendly Scottish inn with 300 years of history and character. Rob Roy was reputed to have visited.

→ Inverarnan, G83 7DX, 01301 704234. Thedroversinn.co.uk
56.3283, -4.7216 🍴🛏

22 FALLS OF DOCHART INN

One of the best traditional inns in Scotland, an absolute must visit. Drink your whisky by the open fire.

→ Gray St, Killin FK21 8SL, 01567 820270. Fallsofdochartinn.co.uk
56.4623, -4.3192 🍴🛏

HOSTELS & HOTELS

23 INVERSNAID BUNKHOUSE

Friendly little hostel with a licensed restaurant, set in a lovely converted church. Proximity to the West Highland Way gives it a cosmopolitan atmosphere, busy with those walking the hallowed route.

→ Inversnaid, FK8 3TU, 01877 386249. Inversnaid.com
56.2462, -4.6715 🍴🛏

24 ROWARDENNAN YOUTH HOSTEL

Simple hostel set in a lovely old lodge on the eastern shore of Loch Lomond. Very well situated for those walking the West Highland Way from Milngavie to Fort William.

→ Rowardennan, By Drymen G63 0AR, 01360 870259. Syha.org.uk
56.1579, -4.6435 🛏

25 MONACHYLE MHOR

Luxurious and quirky hotel offering quality rooms and excellent food in beautiful Balquhidder. Location of various events and festivals throughout the year. An excellent place for a weekend getaway.

→ Balquhidder, Lochearnhead FK19 8PQ, 01877 384622. Mhor.net
56.3452, -4.4693 🍴🛏

CAMPSITES

26 THE CABIN AT LOCH LUBNAIG

Straightforward clean little campsite stopover with a café on the shores of Loch Lubnaig. (Postcode leads to the wrong side of the loch: stay on A84.)

→ Callander, FK17 8HF, 07803 257645. Thecabinatlochlubnaig.co.uk
56.2777, -4.2834 🍴

27 SALLOCHY CAMPSITE

Welcome tents-only rest spot on the shores of Loch Lomond. Very popular with West Highland Way walkers. Closed in winter.

→ Sallochy Bay, Rowardennan, G63 0AW, 01360 870142. Scotland.forestry.gov.uk
56.1271, -4.6076 🍴⛺

WILD CAMPING

28 BRENACHOILE POINT, LOCH KATRINE

This headland is an excellent place to wild camp and take in this most beautiful of Scottish lochs, immortalised in *The Lady of the Lake* by Sir Walter Scott. The road is extremely quiet, with only residents' cars allowed, and owned by Scottish Water. You can reach Brenachoile Point from the Sir Walter Scott steamship car park (the route here), or better still, cycle around from Stronachlachar (FK8 3TY).

→ Start from the Loch Katrine Experience centre (signed from the A821 N of Aberfoyle, after FK17 8HZ). Head out on the road that leaves the car park at the loch end, through the barriers. Stay on this tarmac road just over 2 miles. Brenachoile Point is on your L and juts out into the water. 60 minutes walk-in.
56.2519, -4.4548 🚶‍♂️🚴⛺🏕🛶

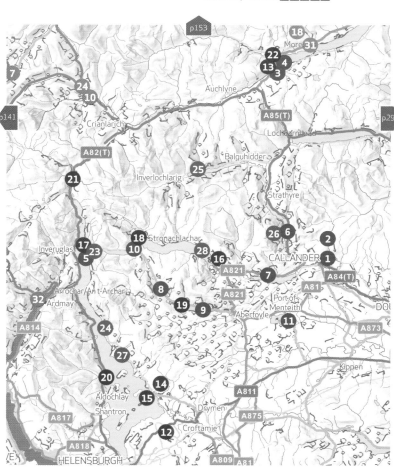

About the authors

Kimberley Grant is a photographer, writer and content producer from Glasgow. A passionate visual story teller, she graduated from the Glasgow School of Art with a degree in Visual Communication in 2012 and has since been producing work predominantly within the travel & lifestyle category.
kimberleygrant.com | @kimberleygrant

David Cooper is a photographer, writer and mountaineer from the Shetland Isles. Currently living in Glasgow he combines these practices into his creative content.
davidboysoncooper.com | @davidboysoncooper

Richard Gaston is a self taught photographer from Ayrshire who honed his skills photographing mountains in the Highlands of Scotland. He works for major fashion labels and travel & life style publications throughout the world.
richardgaston.com | @richardgaston

Wild Guide Scotland online
wildguidescotland.com | @wildguidescotland

Ordnance Survey National Grid References

1 Isle of Arran

1 NS0179545573
2 NR9574220715
3 NS0057221029
4 NS0521530974
5 NS0195123775
6 NR8998145992
7 NS0207522332
8 NS0297425000
9 NR8999626594
10 NR8838230930
11 NR8821528775
12 NS0100145297
13 NR9820539194
14 NS0208222256
15 NR9316750578
16 NS0239833552
17 NR9788450768
18 NS0179335953
19 NR9259950950
20 NR9092532391
21 NS0430824672
22 NR9259950950
23 NR9555721649
24 NS0088335794
25 NS0157636041
26 NS0316920733
27 NR9347850384
28 NS0019437576
29 NR9422649959
30 NR9640021800

2 Islay, Jura & Colonsay

1 NR2062563173
2 NR3999897979
3 NR5212673563
4 NM4278000054
5 NM6851902132
6 NR2378870930
7 NR3462345375
8 NR3458244083
9 NR3199248594
10 NR5422171056
11 NR3812798283
12 NR2934247776
13 NR2708441555
14 NR3491544364
15 NR3620689450
16 NR7050097051
17 NR3690345081
18 NR5267967116
19 NR4312769224
20 NR5272066969
21 NR2166363173
22 NR5301869205
23 NR3893194172
24 NR4018645609
25 NR6442996923
26 NR3204348301

3 Isle of Mull

1 NM3399117245
2 NM3000521470
3 NM3931118847
4 NM3716351181
5 NM4265457739
6 NM4457642275
7 NM3246635480
8 NM4435839086
9 NM2939826063
10 NM2941819465
11 NM4105518740
12 NM4402132287
13 NM4957718442
14 NM3017824004
15 NM4027627906
16 NM3409746238
17 NM4302052069
18 NM2996923348
19 NM4437139810
20 NM4289143594
21 NM4928055016
22 NM4410857192
23 NM3061423642
24 NM4072952354
25 NM3007521309
26 NM3737450911
27 NM7228736896
28 NM3583040704
29 NM4330043413

4 The Small Isles

1 NG3602303854
2 NM3383895620
3 NM4075880179
4 NM2657804770
5 NM4707088296
6 NM4710889923
7 NM4015099540
8 NM2797905537
9 NM4748983426
10 NM4578384323
11 NG3148700540
12 NM4632084703
13 NG2793106098
14 NG3269502080
15 NM4841183817
16 NG2751305478
17 NM4843483804
18 NM4221679519
19 NM4029199764
20 NG3197901368
21 NM4809489383
22 NM4041699222
23 NM4786188861
24 NM4836083898
25 NM4785786585
26 NM4227879527
27 NG2652405343

5 Isle of Skye

1 NG2230855022
2 NG4931919310
3 NG5203960454
4 NG5234157734
5 NG3116429982
6 NG3143136073
7 NG4895119723
8 NG4345825677
9 NG5395412813
10 NG4444320894
11 NG3955664319
12 NG5003353991
13 NG5127618599
14 NG4523569092
15 NG4135663109
16 NG1537543159
17 NG4925728689
18 NG4124576246
19 NG1268647112
20 NG5115741008
21 NG2525047663
22 NG4383674026
23 NG5016965625
24 NG3449250869
25 NG2159648749
26 NG3793531843
27 NG4820043678
28 NG2637056411
29 NG4114920531
30 NG3483034768
31 NG4882829776
32 NG3962162997
33 NG2211946971
34 NG6016711788

6 The Uists, Barra & the Barra Isles

1 NF8733576784
2 NF8234776805
3 NF8140076735
4 NF7862110707
5 NF8917480890
6 NF6945905739
7 NF6917306053
8 NF6090605348
9 NL6335595015
10 NF7022369760
11 NL5648883262
12 NF7579736399
13 NF9234269468
14 NL6651497946
15 NF8376965725
16 NF8987360461
17 NL6780399542
18 NF6947305906
19 NL6658298187
20 NF8050575986
21 NF8076164228
22 NL6640698279
23 NF7651836185
24 NF7496667664
25 NF9322181396
26 NF8385359871
27 NF8727275347
28 NF7066303932
29 NF7490975833

7 Harris, Lewis & St Kilda

1 NB5416648880
2 NB0845936354
3 NB0483533065
4 NB0168413350
5 NG0638999880
6 NF1013299288
7 NB0022531903
8 NG1765793873
9 NF9725492346
10 NG2469994768
11 NB2130033009
12 NB1374440130
13 NB1004208787
14 NB0330731972
15 NF9911789914
16 NF9890890020
17 NG0136386326
18 NB1929144212
19 NB0471332873
20 NG1713394815
21 NG1177792806
22 NF1034199223
23 NB0494607809
24 NG0235788700
25 NG0081792849
26 NB0942936859

8 Orkney

1 HY1763400776
2 HY2188815724
3 HY2189215356
4 HY2505928325
5 ND4107091392
6 ND2030498848
7 HY2384204212
8 HY3775226426
9 HY3794406420
10 ND3110894641
11 HY2348928534
12 ND2908188630
13 HY2313218740
14 HY2395828525
15 HY6767437781
16 HY2433800415
17 HY3517814050
18 HY3268610551
19 ND2927794285
20 HY2194103036
21 ND4734298729
22 HY2413703950
23 HY2478727306
24 HY4212407992
25 HY4494510935
26 HY4441110163
27 ND4663250599
28 ND1997099724
29 ND3470989400

9 Shetland

1 HU3193792621
2 HU2457078585
3 HU3661120879
4 HU4895054727
5 HP5826111398
6 HU4466089013
7 HP6597916423
8 HP6523614515
9 HP5673304010
10 HU2839942603
11 HU2637683465
12 HU2062578493
13 HU5291385281
14 HU3503083475
15 HP6069018490
16 HP6300316469
17 HU4574423676
18 HU2539844786
19 HU3588267852
20 HU3948653097
21 HP6383412284
22 HU4767441377
23 HU4074007890
24 HU2222947751
25 HU2372780595
26 HU3947444888
27 HU2260048666
28 HU2435978940

10 Argyll

1 NM7365117293
2 NR6553654009
3 NS1916388613
4 NR6546626008
5 NR8090337408
6 NR6988874610
7 NR6875407768
8 NN1804100374
9 NS1481884318
10 NN0197227263
11 NS0996596790
12 NR7372385247
13 NR9458191001
14 NS1441985494
15 NN1325927665
16 NR8342898887
17 NM7454917614
18 NR8588897299
19 NS1645882230
20 NM7940210389
21 NR5876908403
22 NN2305107363
23 NS0065894950
24 NN1884612711
25 NM8570329872
26 NM7388417013
27 NR9070457741
28 NN0961609212
29 NR6517448809
30 NR6803039493
31 NM8052104242
32 NN2750103024
33 NS0013780703
34 NM8837326504
35 NR7934836137
36 NR6582207532

11 Fort William, Glencoe & Glen Etive

1 NN1790868491
2 NN1801968230
3 NN1043959537
4 NN1878262256
5 NN4396388274
6 NN2124551573
7 NN2424932043
8 NN3289690745
9 NN2801881693
10 NN3397828964
11 NN4829687256
12 NN2981485320
13 NN1225473022
14 NN1271270137
15 NN1673272243
16 NN1656755464

17 (column)

17 NN1253259421
18 NN2067854985
19 NN2287633014
20 NN2566242482
21 NN1276056691
22 NN2976239585
23 NN3563766386
24 NN3297130374
25 NN1013373843
26 NN2826173659
27 NN2709341354
28 NN1195457340
29 NN3563766386
30 NN3713967062

12 Morar, Moidart & Ardnamurchan

1 NM6646191712
2 NM6139383699
3 NM6429676170
4 NM6140469149
5 NM4170267340
6 NM6566590351
7 NM4418169632
8 NM5596661764
9 NM6975293123
10 NM9062180575
11 NM6473077261
12 NM7121580503
13 NM6699083962
14 NM6622172245
15 NM8272463291
16 NM8988280947
17 NM6769796898
18 NM8428852270
19 NM7676582366
20 NM4531066427
21 NM6514789812
22 NM6759396993
23 NM4705862962
24 NM5856462405
25 NM6692373256

13 Applecross, Kintail & Lochalsh

1 NG7715214706
2 NG8497509270
3 NG6835048787
4 NG7007138904
5 NH0183425675
6 NH0389020291
7 NH0264820478
8 NG8446143061
9 NH0729719829
10 NH0125321455
11 NG7741042355
12 NG7964941778
13 NG8814925858
14 NG8498109270
15 NG8377540007
16 NG8375042262
17 NG7104144484
18 NG9503306606
19 NG8133619311
20 NG7104144484
21 NG7659200212
22 NG7224135023

23 NG8829117240
24 NH0533918338
25 NH0793320245

14 Torridon & Gairloch

1 NC0560224931
2 NC0388027168
3 NC1078409614
4 NC0164735243
5 NH0921097479
6 NC2804527739
7 NC1120517846
8 NH2020377994
9 NC2395523637
10 NC0519424772
11 NC2680517001
12 NC2748220606
13 NH2012585300
14 NC1074310631
15 NC1533718376
16 NC2270433839
17 NH1261793827
18 NC2301333770
19 NC0941322816
20 NC2350632967
21 NC0923622200
22 NC1498721114
23 NC2839233699
24 NC0411227435
25 NC0552124712
26 NC0036832965
27 NC0246408479

15 Ullapool & Assynt

1 NG9526189960
2 NG8185055392
3 NG9931357636
4 NG7336067495
5 NG8039975362
6 NG8922395906
7 NG8808774995
8 NG8493953799
9 NG8092671328
10 NG8741480909
11 NG8123255838
12 NG9373161005
13 NH0665859353
14 NG7968559826
15 NG8610955165
16 NG9967164989
17 NG8624881852
18 NG8970506506
19 NG7978059922
20 NG8541990631
21 NG7821273707
22 NH0263761813
23 NG7599678538
24 NH0288961910
25 NH0659580989
26 NH0645491768
27 NG8834254390
28 NG9039155834

16 Cape Wrath & North West Sutherland

1 NC2008658477
2 NC2169165217
3 NC2906472881
4 NC1506344694
5 NC6104060364

6 NC1634541523
7 NC4427865689
8 NC4075867815
9 NC3920168748
10 NC4189067145
11 NC5807556759
12 NC4571545011
13 NC4465459755
14 NC1377948279
15 NC3902471230
16 NC2594274770
17 NC3060273193
18 NC5806158454
19 NC1639648880
20 NC4215067089
21 NC5997359232
22 NC3935067984
23 NC2488755216
24 NC1541544700
25 NC4034667709
26 NC4062867764
27 NC4146059125
28 NC1644542031

17 Caithness & East Sutherland

1 NC8382066027
2 ND3449655659
3 NC8877364980
4 NC8352701363
5 NH6528990483
6 ND1082771509
7 ND4059873357
8 ND3979971989
9 ND0052928382
10 ND3214240252
11 ND0887420095
12 ND3783254925
13 ND2610144103
14 ND3132641124
15 NH4390089710
16 ND2024676684
17 NC8908142501
18 NC5809406789
19 ND3208940253
20 ND0271915385
21 ND3798573298
22 ND0272515396
23 ND3800673186
24 NC8954557694
25 NH3688383937
26 ND2196070435

18 Easter Ross & The Black Isle

1 NH7447459469
2 NH7778763624
3 NH7999565373
4 NH9144484320
5 NH8073195686
6 NH9469587552
7 NH4363366728
8 NH8016297274
9 NH7486555681
10 NH7684376141
11 NH7493781268
12 NH5882166615
13 NH4454058447
14 NH7312957952
15 NH6119652616

16 NH5991063568
17 NH8654978473
18 NH6461853180
19 NH7862467642
20 NH7269256606
21 NH7273056661
22 NH7875267527
23 NH7459460257
24 NH7354356257
25 NH6119952694
26 NH5539254323
27 NH3981455789
28 NH6449255491

19 Loch Ness & Glen Affric

1 NH4978520328
2 NH2881128339
3 NH4210916448
4 NH2798823814
5 NH2002723086
6 NH3677008833
7 NH2360925193
8 NH4285609711
9 NH6382928049
10 NH4758247332
11 NH2944128245
12 NH5945935238
13 NH5509228472
14 NH6400045268
15 NH5170329585
16 NH5588342494
17 NH7159839752
18 NH3903910772
19 NH3296514804
20 NH7036636716
21 NH2003223476
22 NH5009119938
23 NH4985620470
24 NH3827809276
25 NH4005639987
26 NH4040840686
27 NH5983034802
28 NH3404331545
29 NH3032433837
30 NH4179214020
31 NH3778309484
32 NH5129229221

20 Nairn & Morayshire

1 NJ5290068163
2 NJ4927868797
3 NJ1592570201
4 NH9999049548
5 NH9320541456
6 NH6808515332
7 NJ2558835424
8 NJ4799264260
9 NJ5417167213
10 NH7448363638
11 NJ1893567244
12 NJ0046152354
13 NJ1044365697
14 NH9862561800
15 NJ2814159720
16 NJ0400564453
17 NJ0500663605
18 NJ0067650645
19 NJ0393864399
20 NJ5121267125

21 NJ5002267274
22 NJ5112167416
23 NJ4626267890
24 NJ0442258596
25 NH9919748476
26 NJ0498463695

21 Aberdeenshire

1 NK1100938099
2 NK0096025204
3 NJ8245467236
4 NK0769059845
5 NK0496764305
6 NJ8889164685
7 NK0219964848
8 NJ9790318180
9 NJ8374966094
10 NO7452763700
11 NJ6842062656
12 NO6155786487
13 NJ6822022400
14 NO6314686039
15 NO6787893948
16 NJ4864603483
17 NO8802383866
18 NJ4844429282
19 NJ8388666205
20 NJ6122828150
21 NK1019736115
22 NO8760486383
23 NO6959095683
24 NJ7998664853
25 NJ5893965937
26 NJ8461765468
27 NJ8077165584
28 NO6633898658
29 NJ9219865769
30 NJ9061634477

22 Northern Cairngorms

1 NJ0103202157
2 NJ0004310578
3 NH8984308310
4 NH8997309542
5 NH9664417344
6 NH8380502193
7 NH8515004339
8 NJ0018801587
9 NH8405402186
10 NN8501795399
11 NH9918803827
12 NN9744198848
13 NH8760107346
14 NH9020410951
15 NH8956612639
16 NH8945911795
17 NH9012113704
18 NN9810695802
19 NJ0061611510
20 NN8469592779
21 NJ0420103151
22 NJ0167520372
23 NH8724807255

23 Southern Cairngorms

1 NO1775284352
2 NO1175591134
3 NO2997584195

4 NO2442982388
5 NN5663890279
6 NO4396999758
7 NO2462185591
8 NO4802696555
9 NO2085484292
10 NO1609091868
11 NO4250099612
12 NO2595993428
13 NN5820192944
14 NO0621089630
15 NO1517691441
16 NO3698695851
17 NO4059797980
18 NO2672693849
19 NO1780884407
20 NO2571589981
21 NO0426493049
22 NO1552791056
23 NJ4337803986

24 Angus

1 NO6911951614
2 NO6649941393
3 NO7280958980
4 NO7150853957
5 NO3358475051
6 NO4310680131
7 NO3866780228
8 NO5944471868
9 NO5888572675
10 NO2592453680
11 NO2533275380
12 NO4732579552
13 NO5476866083
14 NO7304961308
15 NO3226041727
16 NO7333956728
17 NO3941860210
18 NO2594075647
19 NO5290240177
20 NO2783576215
21 NO3272973082
22 NO6001569013
23 NO6007468823
24 NO6431740632
25 NO5084478908
26 NO3272973082
27 NO3277265912
28 NO4942779553
29 NO4976644276
30 NO3743266095
31 NO2152860507

25 Perthshire

1 NN8190066372
2 NN9159162556
3 NN8556148573
4 NO0088741769

5 NN7571143161
6 NN9957341088
7 NN9099195955
8 NN7629619999
9 NN8807068429
10 NN5765746751
11 NN8953130581
12 NN9796734423
13 NN7417847027
14 NO0232642582
15 NO0327542148
16 NN8787751361
17 NO1616938509
18 NN5987137553
19 NO0424343596
20 NO1373401783
21 NN7652121775
22 NT0166499471
23 NN5772846860
24 NN8565549093
25 NN8718265179
26 NO0265942641
27 NO0453223713
28 NO0686235297
29 NN8031623091
30 NN8075007721
31 NN6152735827
32 NN9002263878

26 Loch Lomond & Trossachs

1 NG6453208440
2 NG6374110860
3 NN5715532453
4 NN5827633496
5 NN3373208415
6 NN5872011781
7 NN5628706159
8 NN4287004336
9 NN4815801650
10 NN3950509486
11 NN5885300236
12 NS4357885939
13 NN5622832941
14 NS4288292125
15 NN4112890329
16 NS5012308242
17 NN3318610008
18 NN4043310232
19 NN4549702280
20 NS3606992948
21 NN3181918430
22 NN5719832429
23 NN3456209174
24 NS3591999283
25 NN4748319722
26 NN5872111814
27 NS3801995771
28 NN4800909309

Converting decimal degrees to minutes and seconds. The whole number of degrees will remain the same (i.e. 50.1355° still starts with 50°). Then multiply the whole decimal by 60 (i.e. 0.1355 x 60 = 8.13). The whole first number becomes the minutes (8'). Take the remaining decimal digits and multiply by 60 again. (i.e. .13 x 60 = 7.8). The resulting number becomes the seconds (7.8").

**Wild Guide
Scotland**

Words:
Kimberley Grant, David
Cooper & Richard Gaston

Photos:
Kimberley Grant, David
Cooper & Richard Gaston

Editing:
Candida Frith-Macdonald

Proofreading:
Anna Kruger

Design:
Daniel Start
Tania Pascoe

Distribution:
Central Books Ltd
1 Heath Park Industrial
Estate, Freshwater Road,
Dagenham, RM8 1RX
Tel +44 (0)208 8525 8800
orders@centralbooks.com

Published by:
First edition published in
the United Kingdom 2017 by
Wild Things Publishing Ltd.
Freshford, Bath, Somerset
BA2 7WG, UK
ISBN 9781910636121

WILD guide

the award-winning, best-
selling adventure travel
series, also available as
iPhone and Android apps:

- South West England
- South East England
- Lakes and Dales
- Wales and Marches
- Central England
- Scandinavia
- Portugal

hello@wildthingspublishing.com

Author acknowledgements:
Kim would like to thank her grandparents, parents and close friends for their continuous support,
patience and encouragement. David would like to thank his parents for everything they did to help him
through the Shetland and Orkney chapters. Richard would like to thank his parents for their
continuous support throughout the duration of the book and all through his photography career. A
further thanks to his close friends, Paul and Steve. Together we would like to thank Tania and Daniel
for the opportunity to work on such a wonderful project, and for all of their ongoing support. We
would also like to thank Candida for her great work editing and those who joined us on Wild Guide
trips; Roos, Harry, Grace & Simie.

Health, Safety and Responsibility:
Like any water-based activity, wild swimming has risks and can be dangerous. The locations featured
in this book are prone to flood, drought and other changes. The locations may be on private land and
permission may need to be sought. While the author and publisher have gone to great lengths to
ensure the accuracy of the information herein they will not be held legally or financially responsible
for any accident, injury, loss or inconvenience sustained as a result of the information or advice
contained in this book. Swimming, jumping, diving or any other activities, such as hill-walking or
climbing at any of these locations is entirely at your own risk.